UNITED STATES TANKS OF WORLD WAR II IN ACTION

UNITED STATES TANKS OF WORLD WAR II IN ACTION

GEORGE FORTY

Line illustrations by John Batchelor

BLANDFORD PRESS
POOLE • NEW YORK • SYDNEY

First published in the U.K. 1983 by Blandford Press,
Link House, West Street, Poole, Dorset, BH15 1LL.

Copyright, © 1983 Lt Col. George Forty (Ret'd)

Reprinted in paperback 1986

Distributed in the United States by
Sterling Publishing Co., Inc.,
2 Park Avenue, New York, N.Y. 10016.

Distributed in Australia by
Capricorn Link (Australia) Pty Ltd,
PO Box 665, Lane Cove, NSW 2066

British Library Cataloguing in Publication Data

Forty, George
   United States tanks of World War II in action.
   1. World War, 1939-1945—Tank Warfare
   2. Tanks (Military science)—United States—History
   I. Title
   940.54'12'73   D769.305

ISBN 0-7137-1214-7
ISBN 0-7137-1818-8 Pbk

Printed by Arcata Graphics
Kingsport, TN.

Typeset by Polyglot Pte Ltd, Singapore
Printed by BAS Printers Ltd. Hampshire in Great Britain

Contents

GIs advance into a Belgian town under cover of a Sherman

Frontispiece
M2A4s on parade in Washington, D.C.

This book is dedicated by a British tanker to his American counterparts in armor, and in particular to the memory of those who fought and died in the cause of freedom in World War Two.

"So let us do real fighting.
boring in and gouging, biting,

Let's take a chance now that we have the ball.

Let's forget those fine firm bases
in the dreary shell-raked places,

Let's shoot the works and win!

Yes win it all!"

George S Patton, Jnr.

Gen. Dwight D Eisenhower, Supreme Allied Commander in Europe watches US tankers training in England before D-Day. Keenly interested in his soldiers. Ike was truly a 'soldier's soldier', always exuding a calm, friendly spirit of confidence. His ability to keep peace and harmony among the Allies was undoubtedly his greatest asset. Smoking a pipe, is his deputy, Air Chief Marshal Arthur Tedder.

Acknowledgements

I would like to thank the following for their invaluable assistance in the preparation of this book: Association of the United States Army; Chief of Military History and Center of Military History US Army; GSA National Archives and Record Service of the USA; US Army Tank Automotive Material Readiness Command; History and Museums Division HQ US Marine Corps; Marine Corps Tankers Association; US Army Staff, US Embassy, London; British Army Staff, British Embassy, Washington; MoD Whitehall Library; Texas State Library; University of London Library; The Museum of Army Flying; The Tank Museum; The Patton Museum; The Airborne Forces Museum; *Armor Magazine*; *Marine Corps Gazette*.

I would also like to thank the following individuals for their kind assistance, all of whom are US Army (Retired) except where shown: Maj Frederick L Adams (USMC Ret); Lt-Col. Jack Badenhoop; Capt Edward R Bolland (USMC Ret); Raymond S Buch; Col. Edward L Bale Jnr (USMC Ret); Lt Ralph R Balestrieri; W S Beasley Secretary 1st Armd Div Assoc; Col. Andrew Barr; MSG John W Cornelius (USMC Ret); Paul W Corrigan Secretary 3rd Armd Div Assoc; Jack Claven; Gen Bruce C Clarke; Capt John Cross Army Air Corps, British Army; Brig.-Gen. Robert L Denig (USMC Ret); Doyle N Davis; Nile N Darling (USMC Ret); Lt-Col. Haynes W Dugan; D Dodge; Bill Dammann; Ralph Dio Guardi; George O Funke; Maj.-Gen. Robert W Grow; Col. Henry E Gardiner; Kenneth H Grice; Prof George F Hofmann; Louis J Holz; Maj. J Frederick Hayley (USMC Ret); Mrs Clifford Howard; Maj. Herbert F Hillenmeyer; Edward J Herterich (USMC Ret); Prof William G Haemmel; Richard P Hunnicutt; Tracy B Harrington; Bernard J Kneer; Forrest Knox; Col. James H Leach; Joseph L Lee late 7th Hussars; Hobart F Lutz; Col. William B Lovelady; Lt-Gen. Louis Metzger (USMC Ret); Col. Arthur F Mitchell; Maj. Conrad M Mueller; MSG Howard A McNeill; Col. Crosby P Miller; Roy Millard; George G Moss Executive Secretary 12th Armd Div Assoc; Nick Mashlonik; James Ovendine; Irving Osias Director 7th Armd Div Assoc; Brig.-Gen. Hal C Pattison; Lester R Pollmann; A J Palfrey; Col. Henry B Rothenburg Exec Director 8th Armd Div Assoc; James V Revell; Roger Radbaugh (USMC Ret); Maj.-Gen. G P B Roberts late Royal Tank Regiment; John J Richter; Edward Rapp Secretary 4th Armd Div Assoc; Malcolm A Reynolds; Edward R Read Secretary 6th Armd Div Assoc; Lt-Col. R K Schmidt (USMC Ret); Mrs George Steinheimer; David E Scobie; Michael J Stepien; George A Stimpson late Royal Tank Regiment; Dr Curtis W Tarr; Lt-Col. William T Unger (USMC Ret); E P Viveiros (USMC Ret); James G Wilson; Frank Woolner; Mrs Claire E Watrous Secretary 5th Armd Div Assoc; Richard B Wolf.

All **photographs** are from the John Batchelor Collection unless otherwise credited.

Introduction

First Action

The first American tank units to enter combat did so towards the end of Word War I, when, on 12 September 1918, the 304th Tank Brigade, under the command of Lt-Col. George S Patton, Jr, supported the United States IV Corps operations in France against the St Mihiel Salient. Assigned to the 1st and 42nd Divisions, the tanks were to support the infantry in attacking the southern edge of the salient. The Brigade comprised two battalions, the 344th and the 345th; both were equipped with French Renault light tanks, and had been trained in their use by their energetic and forceful young commander.

It was misty and drizzling when, at 0500 hours, the attack went in, with Patton at its head. The 345th followed the 42nd Division until it had passed the Tranches d'Houblons and then took over the lead. Despite thick mud and heavy shell fire, the tanks overcame several machine-gun positions, destroyed a battalion of German artillery and captured

The Renault FT-17 light tank was the very first tank used by the US Army, and was subsequently modified and built in the United States as the 6-Ton Tank M1917. It had a crew of two men, and was armed with a machine gun (the French version had an 8 mm Hotchkiss, but the US version had a Marlin machine gun initially, then a Browning). One version of the 4 mph light tank mounted a 37 mm gun.

One of the very first American-built tanks was this Holt Gas-Electric experimental tank, built in 1917 — the first true tank *ever* built in the USA. It weighed 25 tons and was designed to carry a 75 mm pack howitzer low in front (and masked by the GI in this picture), plus machine guns in side sponsons.

30 prisoners. The 344th were operating with 1st Division and they succeeded in cutting through the enemy wire and took on a number of machine-guns around Bois de Rate. There was a shortage of fuel on the second day of the attack which curtailed operations, but on the 14th an eight-tank patrol from the 344th, operating without infantry support, attacked and dispersed an enemy battalion near Woel.

This was the final tank action of the operation and afterwards Patton received a dressing down for putting himself personally at risk — not that he allowed it to deter him! During the four-day battle, the Brigade lost only two tanks from enemy action. However, 22 tanks were ditched and fourteen had broken down. Of the fourteen personnel casualties, only two were sustained inside a tank. The Brigade saw plenty more action during the Meuse-Argonne offensive which began shortly afterwards, on 26 September, and was the largest American operation of the war.

The first tank battalion to be equipped with heavy tanks, British Mark Vs and V★s, was the 301st Heavy Tank Battalion, and they saw action initially during the Battle of Le Catelet-Bony, while attached to the British 2nd Tank Brigade, when they took part in an attack on the Hindenburg Line in late September 1918. They were supporting the American II Corps and an Australian Corps; however, as the operational report of the 2nd Brigade concluded: 'Due to the fact that the 27th Division had never had an actual operation with tanks, the infantry commanders did not seem to grasp the idea of tanks co-operating with infantry.'[1] Later this state of affairs was rectified and the Battalion went on to earn a great deal of praise for the success of the advance.

Origins of the Tank Corps

When the United States entered the war in April 1917, the tank was still virtually an unknown and untried weapon. Indeed, their showing on the Somme in 1916, where they

The Mark VIII (Liberty) International heavy tank was designed to make the fullest use of British experience and American production. Initially 300 and later 1200 of these were going to be built to 'win the war in 1919', but, of course, were overtaken by events. Weighing between 37 and 44 tons, they were powered by a V-12 Liberty aircraft engine and mounted two 6-pdrs in side sponsons, plus up to seven Browning machine guns in armored mounts. They entered service with the US Army in 1920 but never saw active service. Surplus vehicles (like these laid up at Fort George C Meade) were sold to Canada in 1940 for training!

were used in small numbers on impossible terrain, had done little to recommend them to the American Military Mission in Paris, who concluded that they were useless. Thus, no tank arm was organised until after the arrival of the AEF Commander-in-Chief, Gen. John L Pershing, who then detailed a special board to look into the use of tanks. The board's report stated that 'The tank is considered a factor which is destined to become an important element of this war', thus contradicting the Military Mission's findings. They also recommended the organization of a separate tank service, to be equipped initially with

This skeleton tank of 1918 resembled the outline of British heavy tanks, but had track frames made of pipes and other bits of plumbing! It weighed 9 tons and had a small cylindrical turret and simulated armament.

Student officers being shown the workings of the Ford 3-ton tank (called a tractor for security reasons) at Le Valdahon in early 1919.

French light tanks — the two-man Renault — and British heavy tanks — the Mark VI.[2] The initial size of the Tank Corps would be five heavy battalions of 375 tanks and twenty light battalions of 1500 light tanks, but these figures proved too ambitious.

Despite this, planning for the future was on an even more massive scale: 4450 Mark VIII heavy tanks were ordered in January 1918, to be built as a joint British and American venture; 4400 American copies of the Renault light tank (known as the 6-ton M1917) were also to be built, together with 15,000 two-man and 1000 three-man tanks, to be manufactured by the Ford Motor Corporation. Delays in the supply of materials caused the production of both the light and heavy tanks to lag far behind schedule and only a small number were actually completed before the Armistice — 64 Renaults, fifteen Ford two-man tanks and just five Mark VIII!

In the disarmament euphoria which followed the ending of the war most of these large tank orders were canceled. However, those contracts remaining were sufficient to produce some 1000 light and heavy tanks over the next two years, and these became the mainstay of the US Army's tank pool for the next twenty years. At the end of the war the Tank Corps had consisted of just over 20,000 officers and enlisted men, but by May 1919 most of these had been demobilised. A few months later, Congress fixed the size of the Tank Corps at 154 officers and 2508 men, while at Camp Meade, Maryland, which was their demobilisation and storage center, a motley collection of AFVs was assembled. Timothy Nenninger gives the figures as: 218 French Renaults, 28 British Mark Vs, 450 American-built Renaults and 100 Mark VIIIs, built at the Rock Island Arsenal.[3] These then were the tanks and men immediately available to Brig.-Gen. S D Rockenbach, the newly appointed Commandant, for his peace-time Tank Corps.

Rôle of the Tank

The Great War had shown the tremendous potential of this revolutionary new weapon. Gen. Ludendorff of the German High Command had heaped lavish praise upon the Allied tanks saying that they had been a principal factor in Germany's defeat. Sadly, the Allies were more blinkered in their approach and less convinced of the potential power of tanks. The main rôle of the tank was seen merely as close support of the still dominant infantry arm, thus requiring tanks to be farmed out in small numbers across the battle area. No matter how strongly Rockenbach and others protested, the War Department's view was that tanks were incapable of independent action and should not therefore have independent status. It was this inflexible attitude which drove such men as Patton and Eisenhower to leave the tank service.

One might also have expected that the American love of mechanical gadgets, their genius for planning and production, combined with the undoubted success shown by the tank in battle, would at least have produced new and original ideas in tank design. But with the exception of one man, whom we will meet later, it was not to be. The purse strings were tightly closed, and the rhyme: 'Tanks is tanks and tanks is dear: There shall be no tanks this year' aptly summed up the situation that pertained for the next seventeen years. Only 35 new tanks were to be built in the USA between 1920 and 1935, some of which were rebuilds and thus not strictly new vehicles, but all were different models.

In 1920, the infant Tank Corps received its bitterest blow, when the National Defense Act abolished the Corps and assigned all existing tank units to the Chief of Infantry. Battalions were broken up into separate companies and allocated on a basis of one to each infantry division, henceforth to be known as 'Infantry (Tanks)'. Two years later a War Department policy statement reiterated that the primary rôle of tanks was to '. . . facilitate the uninterrupted advance of the riflemen in the attack.' It also said that there should be two types of tank, light and medium. The light tank was to be transportable in the back of a truck and was to have a maximum battle weight of not more than 5 tons. The medium was to be not more than 15 tons, so that it could be carried by rail, and use all road bridges and engineer pontoons.

Although an experimental 15-ton tank, the M1924, got as far as mock-up stage, it was soon apparent that it was impossible to meet all the requirements of the War Department and the Infantry in a 15-ton vehicle. So, in 1926, it was reluctantly agreed that a 23-ton tank could be developed. However, the General staff made it clear that they still expected work to continue on the lighter vehicle. The Infantry decided that they would best be served by the truck transportable light tank, despite protests from their tankers that what they really needed was a more heavily armored and better armed armored fighting vehicle. Undoubtedly this preoccupation with light tanks, coupled with the small amount of money made available for tank research and development, led to the absence of any worthwhile American medium tanks at the beginning of World War II.

Among Cavalry officers there were two very different views: the first, the 'old school', clung to the dying hope that the horse would somehow prove itself indispensable to the Army; the other, whilst recognizing the value of the mounted soldier, fought eagerly for a replacement for the horse. This latter group was comprised mainly of younger officers who based their ideas on the fact that World War I had proved already that the modern battlefield was no place for the horse. As Maj.-Gen. Bob Grow explained to the writer: 'This divergence of opinion brought clearly into focus the true meaning of the term "cavalry". Whereas the older, more reactionary group held firmly to the definition (supported by Webster) that cavalry was that branch of service whose soldiers fought on horseback; the younger and more far-sighted faction held that cavalry was that branch of service whose soldiers fought mounted. The latter were concerned only that the mount enabled the soldier to effectively employ his weapons in battle.'[4]

Experimental Formations

Fortunately, not everyone was stultified by either the infantry tank concept or the desire to retain the horse as a weapon of war. In 1927, the Secretary of War, Dwight F Davis, visited England and watched exercises on Salisbury Plain of the British Army's Experimental Armoured Force. He was so impressed by what he saw that he was determined that the American Army should try a similar experiment.

On his return to the USA he ordered the Chief-of-Staff to organise such a force and the following year the Experimental Mechanised Force was assembled at Fort Meade. The press hailed the force enthusiastically as 'the pride of the Army' with 'terrific smashing power'. However, it was little more than a collection of obsolete, worn out equipment.

As this force was the forerunner of the great armored divisions of World War II, it is relevant to note its outline composition: 16th Light Tank Battalion (equipped with World War I Renaults); 17th Heavy Tank Battalion (equipped with Mark 8s); one separate tank platoon of Renaults (2nd Platoon of 4th Tank Company); a battalion of the 34th Infantry Regiment in World War I Liberty trucks; 2nd Battalion of the 6th Field Artillery, less one battery, armed with 75 mm guns carried 'portée' in the backs of Liberty trucks; an Engineer company; a Signal company; a Medical detachment; the 1st Ammunition Train; a Chemical Warfare platoon; an Ordnance Maintenance platoon; and a provisional Motor Repair section.

By 3 July 1928 all were assembled, a force of some 3000 men. Sadly, the performance of

The Medium 1922 was very like the British Medium D, and had the same wooden swiveling track shoes mounted on a cable. It was armed with one 37 mm gun and two .30 machine guns.

what the press nicknamed 'The Gasoline Brigade' was only what could have been expected from the 'rattle-trap trucks and aged tanks' which could just about make a top speed of 4 mph if they were lucky! State officials in Maryland added to their discomfort by not allowing the tanks to use their roads in case they tore up the surfaces. The Force had a life of just two months before being disbanded on 20 September.

All that was really proved was, as the *Washington Post* put it succinctly in an editorial, that 'a motorised force is superior to one that is not. But a force mounted on broken-down equipment cannot prevail against an army mounted in modern, up-to-the-minute machines. It has been demonstrated that the need is imperative for increased appropriations for mechanization. Congress should not refuse any request for such funds.'[5]

Mechanization

Despite this abortive start not even the most dyed in the wool traditionalist could prevent the coming of mechanization, and in November 1930 the Mechanized Force returned once again, thanks to the recommendations of an eleven-man Mechanization Board, of whom Adna R Chaffee was perhaps the main driving force. This remarkable officer, who became known as the 'Father of the US Armored Force' fought hard in the cause of mechanization, especially of his own arm, the Cavalry. The Board recommended the organization of a force of brigade size, very like the earlier one, and comprising an headquarters, a light tank battalion, two mechanized infantry battalions, a field artillery battalion, engineer company and a medical detachment, in total just over 2000 all ranks. The Force was to be commanded by Col. Van Voorhis (CO 12th Cavalry). Bob Grow, S3[6] to Van Voorhis, accompanied his CO to the new post.

Grow writes: 'The Mechanized Force at

An excellent group photograph of T3 mediums, belonging to the US 67th Infantry (Tanks) Regiment. Note that their tracks are in the stowed position — there was a chain drive from the sprocket (at the rear) to the rear road wheel. The Christie suspension was used both by the British and the Russians, the Soviet T-34 with its Christie-type suspension being one of the best tanks of World War II.

Walter J Christie, brilliant but unpredictable, is seen here in front of his M1932 tank. Its high speed (up to 46 mph on roads and 27 mph cross country) was not appreciated by the US Army, who preferred reliability, so Christie went elsewhere.

12

The 'armored might' of the United States Army at the beginning of World War II comprised under 400 tanks, of which 150 are lined up here during 1st Armored Division maneuvers in June 1941. The vast majority are light tanks and combat cars, the only mediums being the M2s and M2A1s of the front row.

Eustis was not Cavalry. Although the commander and S3 were cavalrymen and the Armored Car troop was a cavalry unit, the force was a composite group of all Arms and Services . . . . In the first demonstration given to orient Van Voorhis and me, Brett (the Executive Officer) led the attack on foot, with colored signal flags. From this we made our first basic decisions: that all equipment must be capable of high battlefield, as well as road, mobility and, most important, leaders must learn to think and to command mounted.'

Grow goes on to talk about the lack of funds

and professional jealousy which hindered the would be Armored Force as it traveled about the eastern USA endeavouring to introduce mechanization to the rest of the Army. It took part in ten field exercises and marches during the period 1 January–30 June 1931. It did a good job and when it was considered that its mission was completed it was disbanded by the then Chief-of-Staff, Gen. Douglas MacArthur, who directed all Arms and Services to adopt mechanization and motorisation, 'as far as is practicable and desirable'. They were permitted to conduct research and to carry out experiments as necessary. The infantry, for example, were ordered to give attention to increasing their striking power against strongly held positions, while the cavalry were told to develop combat vehicles to 'enhance its power in rôles of reconnaissance, counter-

reconnaissance, flank action, pursuit and similar operations.'[7]

However, because the 1920 National Defense Act had laid down that only the infantry could have tanks, the Cavalry had to get around this legal restriction by calling its armored fighting vehicles 'Combat Cars'. Thus, the infantry light tank T2 was also used by the Cavalry, but called the Combat Car T1, and it was followed by Combat Cars T2, T3 and T4. None of this subterfuge helped the situation, nor did the 'love-hate' relationship which existed between the War Department and one of the most brilliant, but most difficult to handle, tank designers of all time, J Walter Christie. Ian Hogg describes him as a man 'variously classified as an unrewarded mechanical genius or a dangerous lunatic, depending upon your point of view.' This is no place to go into that argument in detail, but it is worth recording that while the Americans did not make sufficient use of Christie's designs, they were avidly seized upon by the Russians for their BT series — the T34 being undoubtedly one of the finest tanks of its generation — and by the British for their A13 and all subsequent cruisers up to the Comet.

The disbanding of the Armored Force was naturally a sad blow for all like Van Voorhis and Grow who had worked so hard for an independent mechanized force, but as Grow puts it: 'In retrospect we can now say that in spite of equipment that varied from obsolete World War I tanks to passenger cars framed in boiler plate plus commercial trucks, we had been able to develop tactical doctrine which, in a large measure, withstood the test of World War II.'

Clearly, wholehearted support for complete mechanization was now assured, but it would still take the shock of the German *Blitzkrieg* in Poland to add the impetus which would bring about the startlingly rapid transformation of the US Army into the most mechanized force the world had ever seen.

1
Now Thrive the Armorers

'You Always Haff Eleven!'

The building and equipping of the American Army in World War II, which transformed it from a small, outdated and ill-equipped force into one of the mightiest armies the world has ever seen, was rightly described by Sir Winston Churchill as being a 'prodigy of organisation'. Among the individual items produced tanks must rate as a prime example of the way American industry tackled the job. In total 88,410 tanks were built, and in 1943, when wartime production was at its peak, an incredible 29,497 tanks were manufactured in one year alone! Sheer numbers of course are not the only criterion and the light tanks delivered in 1940 and 1941 were really not up to the standards required for the modern battlefield; however, once the emphasis shifted to the production of medium tanks, the situation improved.

It was a pity that the production of heavy tanks in any volume was not achieved until 1945, too late to be used to much effect. One may well comment that Allied tanks were generally out-classed by the superiority of such enemy tanks as the Tiger and Panther. However, as Frank Woolner, who was a recon tank destroyer sergeant and later a combat correspondent for 3rd Armored Division, put it to the writer, most of the German tankers they captured seemed to have a stock joke: '"Von off our tanks iss better than ten off yours," the captured German would say. Then, just about when you had decided to punch the guy on the whiskers, he would shrug, grin and say: "But you always haff eleven!"'

Early Plans

'Production of guns and ammunition rested on a solid foundation of more than a century of development and use, but production of tanks in World War II was based upon twenty years of neglect.' That is how the writers of *The Ordnance Department: Procurement and Supply*, one of the excellent volumes about the United States Army in World War II produced by the Office of the Chief of Military History, begin the chapter on the building of tanks. It continues: 'A few American tanks had been built in 1918 but none saw action in World War I. The Mark VIIIs assembled at Rock Island Arsenal after the war were crude specimens with a top speed of only five miles an hour. All through the next two decades there was no real production, only the building of hand tooled test models, some described as capable of "bursts of speed up to 18 miles an hour". From 1920 to 1935 no more than 35 tanks were built, every one a different model. The essence of mass production — acceptance of design and its exact reproduction in volume — was altogether lacking. Not until 1935–36, when sixteen medium tanks were made at Rock Island Arsenal, was more than one tank of any specific model produced.'

A Drop in the Ordnance Bucket

This sorry state of affairs stemmed from the fact that, as we have already seen, a Tank Corps as such did not exist and control of tanks was vested in the infantry who had stated their preference for light tanks, armed only with machine-guns and made of armor plate under one inch thick. Until 1941, the Ordnance unit responsible for fighting vehicles was merely a very small *ad hoc* addition to the Artillery Division, while the test facilities at Rock Island were almost non-existent. Tank procurement before 1940 has been rightly described as being merely 'a drop in the Ordnance bucket'. The high cost of tanks (estimated even then at between 25,000 and 50,000 dollars each) did not help matters, so no major programmes to educate industry about the complexities of building tanks were ever considered. Only two small orders were placed, one with the Van Dorn Iron Works for light tank hulls, the other with the Baldwin Locomotive Works for ten light tanks (M2A4). Even then, design changes and slow deliveries of machine tools and armor plate, delayed the start of production at the Baldwin plant until after Pearl Harbor.

Design Difficulties

Of course, the complexity of a fighting vehicle, even a light tank, did not make the job any easier. Take as an example the tank order placed in early October 1939 for the building of 329 light tanks (M2A4). This order was the first placed with industry for twenty years and was awarded to the American Car and Foundry Company (ACF), whose engineers immediately set to work checking over some 2000 blueprints and then placing orders for the parts and materials they needed. The little 12-ton M2A4 required more than 2800 different parts, totaling over 14,000 individual items — not counting engines or accessories. When ACF found that the steel mills could not supply the correct type of armor plate needed, the company installed its own heat-treating furnaces to make its own face-hardened plate. To its eternal credit ACF delivered the first tank to Ordnance in April 1940, well ahead of schedule, and the order was completed by March 1941.

Changes in design was another continual problem which affected production. Early in the war it was realised that thicker protective

United States Tank Production 1939–45							
Type	1939 – 40	1941	1942	1943	1944	1945	Total
light	325	2,591	10,947	8,212	4,043	2,801	28,919
medium	6	1,461	14,049	21,250	13,468	6,793	57,027
heavy	0	0	1	35	54	2,374	2,464
Total	331	4,052	24,997	29,497	17,565	11,968	88,410

A good view of three main assembly lines for early M3 medium tanks in a US tank arsenal, photographed in September 1942.

armor was needed and this meant added weight, thus requiring a stronger suspension. In the light tank field this led to the emergence in July 1940 of the much improved General Stuart and orders were placed for its production with ACF. During the next year the riveted seven-sided turret took on a rounded shape; welding took the place of riveting; a power traverse was added for the turret; a gyrostabiliser was installed to allow the 37 mm gun to be fired on the move . . . . 'ACF received a steady stream of engineering change orders during 1940 and 1941, and, as the contract was of the fixed-price type, nearly every change required a change of contract price.'[1]

In August 1941 a new model (the M3A1) was adopted and ACF was directed to switch over its production as soon as possible. The following year the M3A3 appeared, with an

M3s on the assembly line at Chrysler's enormous tank arsenal in Detroit.

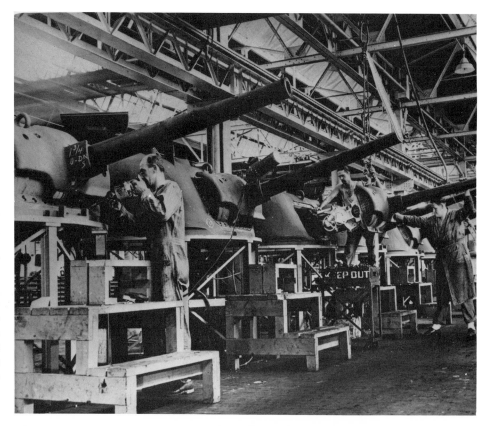

all-welded hull, sloping frontal armor and an improved radio compartment, but again this was soon to be replaced by the M5. This model had two Cadillac engines and two automatic transmissions, requiring countless revisions to be made to all existing drawings and specifications. While all these design improvements were necessary in order to save tankers lives and to make their tanks more efficient, one can well imagine how they complicated the procurement task and of course made the supply of spare parts for field maintenance extremely complex and difficult. It is a tribute to American industry that they were able to meet such problems and overcome them.

Speaking of the men who 'translated drawings into tanks', the military chief of the development section of the Detroit Ordnance District once said: 'All engaged to make something they had never seen. They were frustrated and exasperated by late drawings

Good view of a busy Sherman assembly line in this mid-West tank arsenal.

Putting finishing touches to a line of M36 tank destroyers, which mounted a very effective 90 mm gun capable of knocking out both Tiger and Panther at reasonable battle ranges. They destroyed many enemy tanks during the Allied drive through northern France in the summer and autumn of 1944.

and changes of design, shortages of everything they needed, late deliveries and engineering bugs, yet we never heard a bitter word from them. For such men I have, as a soldier and a citizen, the highest respect.'[2]

The Mediums are Coming

While most effort at the start of the war was directed towards the production of light tanks, the manufacture of mediums had begun slowly at Rock Island Arsenal. Eighteen M2s were built during 1939, while they also began work on an order for 126 improved mediums, the M2A1. The following year much larger orders were under consideration. However, Ordnance rightly opposed them, urging instead that a more powerful tank with a 75 mm gun and better armor should be

A freshly painted Sherman is completely dried in under four minutes by the use of this tunnel of powerful infra-red lights. Normally it would take all day to dry, but this innovation helped to speed up production.

adopted. Although this policy led to a worrying state of affairs in that, when the Germans invaded Poland, the United States had only twenty-eight new tanks (eight mediums and ten lights) in service, it was clearly essential. The medium tank production program really took off in 1942 and in the end far more

Newly completed M10 tank destroyers outside a Ford tank factory in the mid-West.

mediums were produced than all other types put together, especially the Sherman M4 series with the 75 mm gun, of which an incredible 33,671 were built.

The Armored Force

One of the most significant events was, of course, the annoucement on 10 July 1940, that a separate Armored Force was to be created, thus ending the Infantry's stranglehold on armor and heralding the upsurge of the tank to its place as undisputed 'Queen of the Battlefield'. As one US Army historian has put it: 'Armor as the ground arm of mobility, emerged from World War II with a lion's share of the credit for the Allied victory. Indeed, armor enthusiasts at that time regarded the tank as being the main weapon of the land army.'[3] With the adoption of the Munitions Program on 30 June 1940, the War Department began to plan in earnest for the mass production of all types of weapons, including thousands of tanks. While in 1940 the initial orders for tanks were modest and production gained momentum only gradually, the events of the following year were destined to shatter this calm forever.

It was President Roosevelt who dropped the 'bombshell' in September 1941, as the Ordnance history recalls: 'At a White House conference, where Generals Charles Harris and Burton Lewis represented Ordnance, the President reviewed current military production plans. When he came to the schedule calling for production of 1000 medium tanks and 400 light tanks per month, the President paused, placed a cigarette in his famous long holder, lit it and then calmly issued this cryptic directive: "Double it!" Monthly production was to be 2800 — or 33,600 per year. The cost would be close to a billion dollars for one year's production.'[4] And even this was not enough.

After the USA had entered the war Roosevelt again raised the tank building requirement, calling for annual production rates of 45,000 tanks in 1942 and 75,000 by 1943. It could well have been, as some biographers have concluded, that he was merely ordering such target figures as a means of capturing the imagination of the American people by giving them an even greater challenge. 'When Harry Hopkins questioned the President on the figures, Roosevelt shrugged, "Oh . . . the production people can do it if they really try"'.[5]

Of course, the production figures called for by the President were far more than were actually needed, enough in fact to equip over 300 armored divisions, with 100 percent replacements, whereas the number of armored divisions actually activated during World War II was a mere sixteen. To be fair, this only accounted for part of the nation's armored strength, as there were, for example, a large number of non-divisional tank battalions, the Tank Destroyer Force and US Marine Corps armor. Nevertheless, the speed at which industry was geared up to produce large numbers of tanks, was undoubtedly due in no small measure to the stimulation that Roosevelt provided.

A completed M3 is loaded onto a flat car by a powerful crane at the Detroit Tank Arsenal, ready for shipment to the US Army, March 1942.

Tank Production

Reduced to its simplest terms, wartime tank production followed the already established pattern for the building of motor cars. Major components, produced in widely dispersed factories, were brought together and assembled at an assembly plant. Although some manufacturers made more components than others, none of the tank contractors were able to make everything. For example, armor plate and castings came from the steel mills and foundries of Chicago and Pittsburg in a semi-finished state; guns were supplied by the Ordnance arsenals or commercial producers; rubber bushed tracks came from one of the major rubber companies in Ohio; internal components, engines, transmissions, radios, periscopes, ammunition racks and the hundreds of other components needed, were produced all over the USA and then brought together at the assembly plants. These plants required heavy cranes to handle the tank parts, a great variety of huge machine tools to cut and shape the materials and ingenious fixtures to hold parts in position while they were being worked on.

The Ordnance history gives details of one such operation at the Schenectady-based American Locomotive Company plant, as reported in a wartime magazine called *Fortune*, and it is worth repeating here as it must have been very typical: 'Its tank assembly line — adjacent to continuing locomotive areas — was a series of seven stations at each of which a major component was added. Starting with the lower hull, or chassis, the gas tanks and the mount for the big gun were first put in place. At the next station the giant transmission was added. At the third stop an overhead crane lowered the engine into place and the drive shaft was connected with the transmission. As the hull moved slowly from station to station it gradually took on the appearance of a fighting tank, finally rolling on to its tracks and receiving its big gun and turret.'

In his book *Tanks are Mighty Fine Things*, Wesley W Stout recounts the story of the production of tanks and other weapons by the Chrysler Corporation, who had never made tanks before in their history, indeed most of their engineers had never even seen one! The Detroit Tank Arsenal which they built from scratch, eventually produced 25 percent of all the tanks built in the USA between 1940 and

1945. It was a complete contrast to the locomotive plants as it was designed with the sole purpose of building tanks and not merely adapted.

The speed at which the Arsenal was built and put into production was staggering. On 7 June 1940, K T Keller, the President of Chrysler, was told of the task by William S Knudsen, General Motors President, who had been called in by Washington earlier that year as industrial production expert to the National Defense Advisory Committee. He immediately put his planners to work. They visited the Rock Island Arsenal and collected 186 lbs weight of blueprints. By 17 July construction plans were ready and it was decided that their first tank was to be the yet undesignated derivative of the M2 medium, which would be armed with the 75 mm gun. At the same time as the plant was being designed and constructed, the design of this new tank (the M3 Grant/Lee) began.

In fact a contract was signed by Chrysler to

produce the new tank *before* either the prototype tank or the plant was completed! Chrysler sent an engineer to the Aberdeen Proving Ground, where the M3 was being designed. 'He mailed the blueprints to Detroit, telephoned other information, and made suggestions to Ordnance designers on engineering changes that would mean cheaper and faster production.'[6] By the end of the year the skeleton of the new arsenal had been erected, and in mid-April 1941 the first tank rolled off the assembly lines. Three months later they were gearing up to a production rate of 100 tanks a month, while the following year the Arsenal was enlarged to increase production to 700 tanks a month.

Everything about the Detroit Arsenal made it the nation's most spectacular war plant, its best production show, and the first place that every distinguished visitor asked to be taken. 'From it', wrote Wesley Stout, 'came 25,059 medium and heavy tanks of twelve different types, including tanks which first turned

Still lacking their armament, standard production M3 light tanks on a test run from the American Car & Foundry factory in summer 1941.

How to impress the customers! An early M3 — in fact this one was the first Chrysler production pilot (serial number 2) which was completed in April 1941 at the Detroit Arsenal — shows off its tree smashing ability to the press and the workers just outside the arsenal.

the tide in North Africa for the British. Of these 22,234 were new and 2825 were rebuilt .... The size of the tanks built there grew from 23 tons to 65 tons .... The Chrysler tank contract approached the two billion dollar mark at its peak .... The Corporation returned to the Government in voluntary cash refunds and price reductions more than 50 million dollars .... For planning and directing the building and equipment of the arsenal, Chrysler was paid a fee of just four dollars .... The original arsenal was expanded more than half again in 1942 to 1,248,321 square feet, yet the contract overflowed into twelve other Chrysler plants and at its peak came to employ close to 25,000 Chrysler workers and 3200 feet of Chrysler space, this exclusive of the thousands of sub-

contractors scattered over the nation .... Arsenal test track drivers, driving 24 hours a day in all weathers throughout the war, logged a mileage of more than 50 times around the earth.' The list of such superlatives goes on and on, but that should suffice to get the message across.

Thus, within the space of two years, American industry had got to grips with the problem of producing tanks and still more tanks, so successfully that they were able to supply not only the needs of their own armed forces, but also those of the majority of other Allied nations as well. Once they had satisfied the initial requirements for quantity, then they were able to turn their attention to standardization, improvements and efficiency generally, but this did not necessarily simplify matters, for example, at the end of 1942 there were no less than five different models of the Sherman tank in production in the USA. 'We are beginning to run into the motor car dealer's problem', commented Col.

Christmas (Head of the Ordnance Tank and Combat Vehicle Division) in May 1942. 'Our customers, the fighting men, want only the latest models.'

Perhaps the best way of making a quantitative assessment of American tank production during World War II is to compare it with German and British tank production. As the table below shows American production was nearly four times as great as that of either Germany or Great Britain.

Year	German	British	American
1940	1,459	1,399	331
1941	3,256	4,841	4,052
1942	4,098	8,611	24,997
1943	6,083	7,476	29,497
1944	8,083	2,476	17,565
		(6 mths only)	
1945	988	—	11,968
	(1st qtr only)		
Totals	23,967	24,803	88,410

2

Basic Tank Unit Organizations

Prior to World War II the American Army had little experience in the organising of large armored formations. In World War I the Tank Corps followed the British pattern, with tank brigades containing two light and one heavy tank battalions. However, only four tank brigades were actually formed and were originally designated 1st, 2nd, 3rd and 4th Provisional Tank Brigades, but in late 1918 they were renumbered as the 304th, 305th, 306th and 307th. At the same time, tank battalions were numbered also in the 300 series, 301 through 346, although those from 309 through 325 were not actually organised. During 1918, above brigade level, the Tank Corps, AEF, and the Tank Corps, National Army, were separately organised in three areas — the United States, England and France. To make matters more complicated, there was no direct command relationship between the Tank Corps in the USA and the Tank Cops, AEF. By June 1918, despite great efforts to organise and equip as many units as possible, there were only 700 men in the AEF Tank Corps and about 5000 in the continental US organisation. Only three battalions of light tanks and one of heavies actually saw active service.

After World War I the Tank Corps was disbanded in 1920 and tanks became an integral part of the infantry, with single companies allocated to infantry divisions. The various abortive attempts to form an experimental armored force have already been recounted, as has the beginning of the mechanization, of the cavalry. It was not until 10 July 1940 that an entirely separate 'Armored Force' was created, with Brig.-Gen. Adna Chaffee as its commander. Seven days later, I Armored Corps was formed, consisting of the 1st and 2nd Armored Divisions, both of which were activated on 15 July. The only other armored units in the Armored Force at that time were one non-divisional tank battalion, the 70th, stationed at Fort Meade; the Armored Force Board; and an Armored Force School and Replacement Training Centre. In fact, I Armored Corps was the first 'marrying up' of

the tank and mechanized cavalry elements of the Army. 1st Armored Division was organised from the Provisional Tank Brigade, which had comprised elements of infantry tank battalions. Although we are dealing here primarily with the details of organisation, it is worth noting that to equip the Armored Force at that time there were less than 1000 mostly obsolete tanks and other vehicles, while just one fully equipped armored division required over three times that number.

As the US Army grew in size so the numbers of armored corps and divisions increased; II Armored Corps was organised in February 1942. This was in line with the then current doctrine that armored divisions should only be employed in special corps, composed of two armored and one motorised divisions. One can see how far the pendulum had swung away from the pre-war 'armor in penny packets' concept, to one of using armor only *en masse*. Experience in battle inevitably showed that neither of these extremes was the correct solution and by 1943 the 'private army' approach had disappeared and armor was no longer treated as a special force which should only operate on its own, but rather as a vital component of a battle winning all-arms team. In 1943, the Armored Force was redesignated as the Armored Command and in February 1944 became known as the Armored Center, the new names accurately describing its changing functions as the war progressed. By early 1944, all armored units had been assigned to other Corps while the three Armored Corps had been redesignated as ordinary Corps.

The Armored Division

During World War II, the armored division had no less than six different organizations evolving logically as battle experience was gained, AFVs altered, and changes in the conduct of the war dictated changes in tactics and organisation. The initial armored division (*see* Fig. 1) comprised an armored brigade of

three tank regiments, two equipped with light tanks and one with mediums; a field artillery regiment of two battalions; an infantry regiment of two battalions; an armored reconnaissance battalion; an air observation squadron (also for reconnaissance); another field artillery battalion; an engineer battalion; signal company; maintenance company; QM truck battalion and a medical battalion. The basis of this organisation was the need to build a force that was self-sufficient, composed of all arms and contained the five essential ingredients of command, reconnaissance, strike, support and service, and was powerful enough to be used for rapid offensive action against vital enemy rear area installations. These objectives would be reached by penetrating enemy weak points or going around open flanks, rather than by attacking the enemy main position. In other words, it was a direct copy of the German *Blitzkrieg* force, relying upon high mobility, firepower and armored protection, the three basic characteristics of armor, to produce shock action wherever and whenever it was needed, to disrupt and demoralise the enemy. Although this principle worked on occasions, and the US Third Army's unforgettable 'Gallop across France' under the great Gen. George S Patton, Jr, is a prime example, this type of formation was unsuited to the long, hard fought slogging matches which became the 'norm' once the German Army had been forced on to the defensive.

Of the five reorganisations which took place during the war, only two were really of any great significance. The first took effect on 1 March 1942 and the second on 15 September 1943. The 1942 reorganisation resulted in what were known as **Heavy Armored Divisions.** Although the number of armored regiments was reduced from three to two, each containing three tank battalions as before, two battalions were now equipped with medium tanks and one with light. The armored brigade organisation disappeared and in its place there were two self-contained headquarters, known as Combat Commands (CCA and

The All-Arms team. American tanks and infantry advance together during maneuvers. Once contact was made, the infantry would dismount from the tanks and spread out — riding on tanks was fine during an approach march, but invited casualties among the infantry, and prevented the tanks from using their guns properly.

CCB). Either was capable of taking under command whatever divisional units the divisional commander allocated to them for a particular operation. This greatly increased the flexibility of the division. The artillery was reorganised into three identical battalions under a divisional artillery commander. In actual tank strength the division gained only a few more tanks, its total strength now being 390. However, as the proportion of medium to lights had been reversed, the new Heavy Armored Division was considerably more powerful than its predecessor (*see* fig. 2).

The second major reorganisation produced what was called the **Light Armored Division**. It reduced the divisional tank strength by replacing the two regiments (i.e. six tank battalions) by three separate tank battalions. In fact the tank strength was only reduced by about one third to 263 instead of being halved as one might have expected, because, at the same time, the number of companies within tank battalions was increased from three to four (three with mediums and one with lights). This reorganization meant that the regimental organization was abolished in all armored divisions, with the exception of the 2nd and 3rd which remained on the old organization. The tanks, infantry and artillery each now had three matching battalions. Another Combat Command headquarters was introduced to control the divisional reserves, and was known as CCR (or sometimes CCC). The armored reconnaissance battalion changed to a cavalry reconnaissance squadron and the total division strength fell by nearly 4000. The 1943 reorganization took time to take effect, for example, 1st Armored Division, in Italy, did not change until July 1944.

Summarising the trends which these reor-

ganizations followed: the first was the marked increase of mechanized infantry making the division a more balanced force; secondly, the elimination of unnecessary levels of command, although the addition of CCR showed that this had been initially too drastic; thirdly, the slimming down of the service support elements, which of course made the division less able to operate for long periods on its own; finally, the increase in numbers of medium tanks at the expense of the lights, giving the armored division far more effective 'teeth'. By 1945 yet another type of division had been proposed, based largely upon the latter wartime experience of armored commanders. This time the trend was towards 'Heavy' armored division, with a capability to perform missions outside the capabilities of the then 'Light' armored division. Although the date of this is shown in the tables below as 16 June 1945, it did not become fully effective until 1948, therefore I have not shown its detailed organization.

Fig. 1: Armored Division 1940

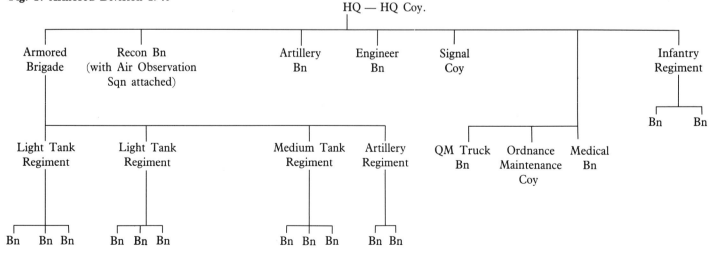

Fig. 2: 'Heavy' Armored Division 1942

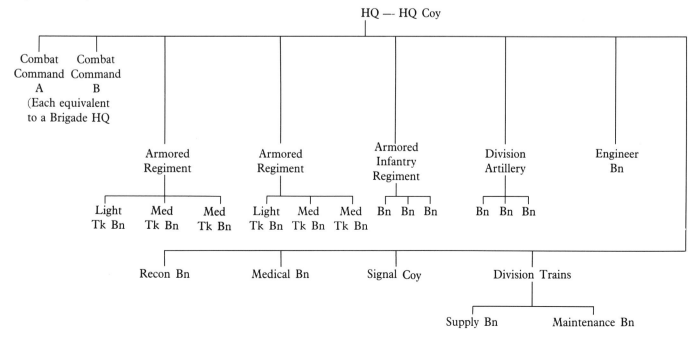

HQ — HQ Coy

Combat Command A Combat Command B
(Each equivalent to a Brigade HQ

Armored Regiment

Light Tk Bn   Med Tk Bn   Med Tk Bn

Armored Regiment

Light Tk Bn   Med Tk Bn   Med Tk Bn

Armored Infantry Regiment

Bn Bn Bn

Division Artillery

Bn Bn Bn

Engineer Bn

Recon Bn   Medical Bn   Signal Coy   Division Trains

Supply Bn   Maintenance Bn

Fig. 3: 'Light' Armored Division 1943

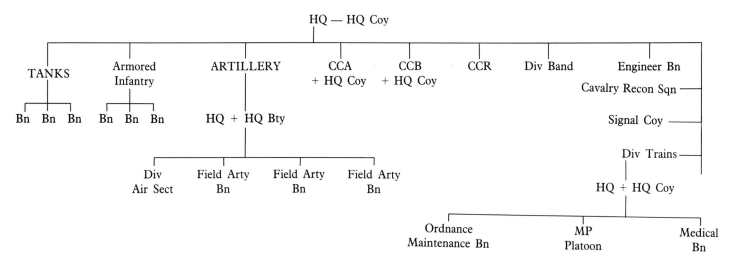

Fig. 4: A Comparison of the Organization of the Armored Division 1942–43–45

Armored Division, TO 17 of March 1942		Armored Division, TO 17 of 14 Sept 1943		Armored Division, TO 17 of 16 June 1945	
Entire Div	14,620	*Entire Div*	10,937	*Entire Div*	10,670
Div HQ	307	Div HQ	164	Div HQ	174
HQ Coy	111	Tank Bns (3)	729	Tank Bns (3)	700
Service Coy	160	Inf Bns (3)	1,001	Inf Bns (3)	995
Armd Sig Coy	256	CC HQ & HQ Coy (2)	184	Recce Sqn	894
Armd Recce Bn	872	Div Trains HQ & HQ Coy	103	Field Arty	1,625
Armd Regts (2)	2,424	CCR HQ	8	*Auxiliary Units:*	
Armd Field Arty Bns (3)	709	Field Arty	1,623	CC HQ & HQ Coy (2)	178
Armd Inf Regt	2,389	*Auxiliary Units:*		Engr Bn	660
Armd Engr Bn	1,174	Cav Recce Sqn (Mechanised)	935	Div Trains HQ & HQ Coy	99
Div Trains	1,948	Engr Bn	693	Med Bn	400
Attached Medical	414	Med Bn	417	Ord Bn	732
Attached Chaplain	14	Ord Bn	762	Sig Coy.	293
Principal Armament		Sig Coy	302	MP Plat	87
Rifles .30-cal.	1,628	MP Plat	91	Div HQ Coy	115
Carbines .30-cal.	6,042	Div HQ Coy	138	CCR HQ	8
Pistols .45-cal..	3,850	Band	58	Band	58
LMGs .30-cal.	237	Attached Medical	261	Attached Medical	254
LMGs (ground) .30-cal.	54	Attached Chaplain	8	Attached Chaplain	8
MGs HB .50-cal.	103	*Principal Armament*		*Principal Armament*	
SMGs (inc on ord vehicles)	1,654	Rifles .30-cal.	2,063	Rifles .30-cal.	1,980
SMGs (on ¼ ton trucks)	506	Carbines .30-cal.	5,286	Carbines .30-cal.	4,998
Mortars 60 mm	57	MGs .30-cal.	465	Auto Rifles .30-cal.	81
Mortars 81 mm	27	MGs .50-cal.	404	MGs .30-cal.	433
ATk Guns SP	126	Mortars 60 mm	63	MGs .50-cal.	385
ATk Guns Towed	68	Mortars 81 mm	30	Mortars 60 mm	27
Hows 105 mm SP	54	ATk Rocket Launchers	607	Mortars 81 mm	12
Assault Guns SP	42	Hows 57 mm	30	ATk Rocket Launchers	609
Lt Tanks (w/armament)	158	Hows 75 mm	17	ATk Guns 57 mm	30
Med Tanks (w/armament)	232	Hows 105 mm	54	Lt Tanks	77
Armd Cars Recce (w/armament)	79	Med Tanks	186	Med Tanks	168
M2 Halftracks (w/armament)	691	Lt Tanks	77	Med Tanks (105 mm how)	27
M3 Halftracks (w/o/armament)	42	Armd Cars	54	Armd Cars	50
Scout Car (w/armament)	40	Halftracks Carriers	455	Halftracks	452
Other Vehicles (inc trailers)	2,146	Halftracks 81 mm Mortar Carriers	18	Motor Carriages 75 mm	8
		Vehicles All Types (expect boats & a/c)	2,650	Motor Carriages 105 mm	54
		Less Combat Types	1,761	Halftracks Mortar Carriers	18
				Vehicles All Types (except boats & a/c)	1,869

Basic Components of an Armored Division

The number of active armored divisions grew rapidly from two in early 1941 to fourteen by late 1942. By the end of the war a total of sixteen had been activated (1st to 14th, 16th and 20th) and all saw combat service. Figs 5 and 6 show, first, details of the nicknames and battle honours of the divisions and secondly their organic components.

Non-Divisional Tank Battalions

The armored divisions contained a total of fifty-four tank battalions, but these represented only a part of the armored strength of the US Army. There were in addition a large number of separate non division tank battalions. By the end of 1944, for example, there were sixty-five of these, plus a further twenty-nine in course of formation. There were also seventeen amphibian tractor battalions which certainly deserve to be classified as tanks. As the majority of these separate battalions were there to provide close support to infantry divisions, their initial organization was very similar to that of the infantry tank battalions of pre-war days. However, they were later put on to exactly the same organization as the tank battalions in armored divisions, so that all were completely interchangeable. As one can imagine, this considerably simplified training, supply and reinforcement. A tank group Headquarters was initially put in control of up to five non-division battalions, but this proved to be too many for them to handle and later the number was reduced to three. The system did not work all that well as battalions were never sure exactly under whose command they should be, the infantry division HQ or tank group HQ. Some groups included armored infantry battalions, becoming armored groups.

Fig. 5: Active Armored Divisons Of World War II

Div	Date and where activated	Nickname	Campaigns*
1st	15 Jul 40, at Fort Knox, Kentucky	Old Ironsides	North Africa (Tunisia), Italy.
2nd	15 Jul 40, at Fort Benning, Georgia	Hell on Wheels	North Africa (Algeria, French Morocco), Sicily, North-West Europe 1, 2, 3, 4, 5.
3rd	15 Apr 41, at Camp Beauregard, Louisiana	Spearhead	North-West Europe 1, 2, 3, 4, 5.
4th	15 Apr 41, at Pine Camp, New York	None, but occasionally called Breakthrough	as for 3rd
5th	1 Oct 41, at Fort Knox, Kentucky	Victory	as for 3rd
6th	15 Feb 42, at Fort Knox, Kentucky	Super Sixth	as for 3rd
7th	1 Mar 42, at Camp Polk, Louisiana	Lucky Seventh	as for 3rd
8th	1 Apr 42, at Fort Knox, Kentucky as a training cadre: became a combat division in Feb 43	Originally Iron Snake, then Thundering Herd, and finally Tornado	North-West Europe 2, 3, 4, 5.
9th	15 Jul 42, at Fort Riley, Kansas	Phantom	as for 8th
10th	15 Jul 42, at Fort Benning, Georgia	Tiger	as for 8th
11th	15 Aug 42, at Camp Polk, Louisiana	Thunderbolt	North-West Europe 3, 4, 5.
12th	15 Sep 42, at Camp Campbell, Kentucky	Hellcat	as for 11th
13th	15 Oct 42, at Camp Beale, California	Black Cat	as for 11th
14th	15 Nov 42, at Camp Chaffee, Arkansas	Liberator	as for 11th
16th	15 Jul 43, at Camp Chaffee, Arkansas	None	North-West Europe 3, 5.
20th	15 Mar 43, at Camp Campbell, Kentucky	None	as for 16th

* The North-West European Campaign was divided officially into five separate campaigns viz: 1. Normandy 2. Northern France 3. Rhineland 4. Ardennes-Alsace 5. Central Europe.

It was, of course, vital to be able to get US built tanks to all the theaters of war for the use of their own armored formations and for those of their Allies. Here, M18 *Hellcat* tank destroyers are unloaded at a British port in July 1944.

Fig. 6: Organic Components of the Active Armored Divisions of World War II

Div	Armd Inf Bns			Tk Bns			Div Arty	Armd Arty	Fd Bns	Cav Recce Sqn	Armd Engr Bn	Armd Med Bn	Armd Ord Bn	Armd Sig Coy	Combat Commands
1	6	11	14	1	4	13	27	68	91	81	16	47	123	141	A — B — R
2	41*	63*	67*	—	—	—	14	78	92	82	17	48	2	142	A — B — R
3	32*	33*	36*	—	—	—	54	67	391	83	23	45	3	143	A — B — R
4	10	51	53	8	35	37	22	66	94	25	24	4	126	144	A — B — R
5	15	46	47	10	34	81	47	71	95	85	22	75	127	145	A — B — R
6	9	44	50	15	68	69	128	212	231	86	25	76	128	146	A — B — R
7	23	38	48	17	31	40	434	440	489	87	33	77	129	147	A — B — R
8	7	49	58	18	36	80	398	399	405	88	53	78	130	148	A — B — R
9	27	52	60	2	14	19	3	16	73	89	9	2	131	149	A — B — R
10	20	54	61	3	11	21	419	420	423	90	55	80	132	150	A — B — R
11	21	55	63	22	41	42	490	491	492	41	56	81	133	151	A — B — R
12	17	56	66	23	43	714	493	494	495	92	119	82	134	152	A — B — R
13	16	59	67	24	45	46	496	497	498	93	124	83	135	153	A — B — R
14	19	62	68	25	47	43	499	500	501	94	125	84	136	154	A — B — R
16	18	64	69	5	16	26	393	396	397	23	216	216	137	156	A — B — R
20	8	65	70	9	20	27	412	413	414	30	220	220	138	160	A — B — R

*These units were armored regiments during World War II.

Fig. 7: Cavalry Reconnaissance Squadron (Armored Division Organization)

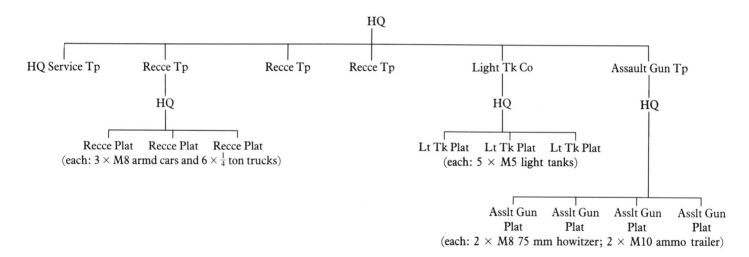

Cavalry

Apart from the two cavalry divisions which remained active for part of the war, all the rest of the cavalry was eventually mechanized and served with distinction as reconnaissance units with both armored and infantry divisions. The two cavalry divisions never actually served with horses as it was decided that to ship horses abroad would have taken up too much precious tonnage and presented too many problems in an otherwise fully mecha-

nized army. Consequently, when the 2nd Cavalry Division went to North Africa in early 1944, it was rapidly inactivated and broken up in May 1944, its personnel being transferred to service units. The 1st Cavalry Division went to the South West Pacific, where it fought with distinction as dismounted infantry.

A typical cavalry reconnaissance squadron with an armored division in the middle of the war was equipped with both armored cars and light tanks as well as other AFVs including

assault guns. Its light tank company comprised a Coy HQ of two M5 light tanks and three platoons, each of five M5s.

Behind the battle lines there had to be workshops where damaged vehicles could be properly repaired, such as this Ordnance Base Workshop in France. Although the job of these fitters was not so immediate as those in workshops much nearer the front line, they still had a vital job to play in the repair and recovery chain which kept the whole army functioning. US Army Service Forces even set up munitions factories and vehicle assembly plants in Normandy within a few weeks of the Allied landings.

Fig. 8: USMC Tank Battalion Organization (D, E, F and G Series)

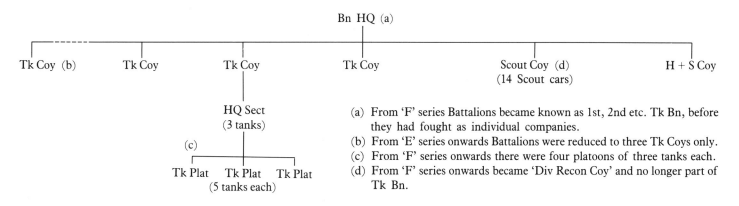

Bn HQ (a)

Tk Coy (b) — Tk Coy — Tk Coy — Tk Coy — Scout Coy (d) (14 Scout cars) — H + S Coy

HQ Sect (3 tanks)

(c)

Tk Plat   Tk Plat   Tk Plat
(5 tanks each)

(a) From 'F' series Battalions became known as 1st, 2nd etc. Tk Bn, before they had fought as individual companies.
(b) From 'E' series onwards Battalions were reduced to three Tk Coys only.
(c) From 'F' series onwards there were four platoons of three tanks each.
(d) From 'F' series onwards became 'Div Recon Coy' and no longer part of Tk Bn.

Fig. 8A: USMC Tank Totals

Type	D	E	F	G
Light Tank M3	72	54	—	—
Medium Tank (M4A2 or M4A3)	—	—	46	46
Medium Tank with flame throwers	—	—	—	9
Light recovery Tank	—	3	—	—
Medium recovery Tank	—	—	3	14
Total	72	57	49	69

USMC Tank Units

In the 1920s there were a few light tank companies in the US Marine Corps, equipped with the 6-ton tank, the copy of the Renault which was known as the 6-ton M1917. Some work was done experimenting with both armored cars and light tanks, but very little was achieved between the wars, until the Landing Vehicle Tracked (LVT) came into existence in the early 1941 (*see* Chapter 12). A series of the LVTs was developed and saw much service with both the USMC and the US Army in the Pacific theater. Soon after the outbreak of World War II, the 1st Marine Division came into existence and it contained a light tank battalion within its basic organization. This battalion was on what was known as a 'D Series' organization. It comprised four tanks companies, a scout company, and an HQ and Service company, and was equipped with 72 light tanks. The Scout company initially had scout cars but these were left in the USA and replaced with jeeps.

'Old Tanker never die, they only fade away!' Typical of the continuing spirit of comradeship and esprit de corps is this group of old tanker buddies and their wives, from 37th Tank Battalion, 4th Armored Division, taken at their annual convention, July 1981. Lt Col. J H Leach

When the tank battalion was first employed (at Tarawa in November 1943) the scout company actually went ashore in rubber boats. Tank battalions formed a standard part of every marine division as it was activated, and as the war progressed, the medium tanks (Shermans) began replacing the lights.

Initially tank battalions were not organized to operate as a unit, each infantry regiment of the division getting one tank company attached during combat. The fourth tank company was divisional reserve. Each company had eighteen tanks, divided into three platoons of five. Later this organisation was changed when it was discovered that, at close quarters, three tanks operated better together under one officer. For what was known as the 'F Series' and 'G Series' each company had four platoons of three tanks, and three in HQ (one of which was a dozer). There were now only three companies in a battalion and only forty-six medium tanks and three medium recovery tanks in a battalion. However, in the G series these were supplemented with nine mediums armed with flame-throwers and the scale of recovery vehicles went up from three to fourteen. After Okinawa it was recommended that platoons should have five tanks, but the war ended before this could be effected.

Operational Requirements

Like all organizational tables, these can only be taken as a guide, because they were frequently altered to suit a particular operational requirement. For example, Lt-Col. R K Schmidt, who commanded the 4th Tank Battalion from its inception, writes: 'Both the 1st and 2nd Tank Battalions initially had Scout Companies equipped with the old White scout car. Before Tarawa the cars were replaced with Jeeps. About six months after war started, the I Corps medium tank battalion was formed, however, before it saw combat it was disbanded with a company going to the 1st, 2nd and 4th Tank Battalions. The company coming to the 4th came without tanks and became my flame-thrower company for Saipan-Tinian. For the Marshalls my battalion's organisation was two light tank companies each with eighteen M5A1 light tanks, one company with eighteen M4A2 medium tanks (Diesel GM), plus a Scout Company with Jeeps, which, after this operation became the Division Recon Coy. Thus the organization was:

For Saipan Three medium tank companies, each with eighteen M4A2 plus one Vehicle Tank Recovery (VTR), each platoon of five tanks had a dozer blade. One light tank Coy with Ronson flame-throwers (M3A1 or M2A4 and 6 M5A1 command vehicles). Battalion HQ — 1 medium tank M4A2 and 1 VTR.

For Tinian As for Saipan, except that B Coy was re-equipped with M4A3 Mediums with Ford engines.

For Iwo Jima Three medium tank Coys with fifteen M4A3 tanks each and three POA (Pacific Ocean Area) CWS (Chemical Warfare Service) Main Armament flame-throwers on M4A3 tanks. Each Coy had a retriever and each platoon a dozer blade. Battalion HQ — one medium tank and one retriever.'

Basic Tank Living

A few reminiscences on what it was like to live in a tank in combat are appropriate in this chapter on organization. Although George Moss of Springfield, Illinois, served on medium tanks in 12th Armored Division, much of what he says applies to all tankers and should stir up a few memories.

'Living conditions! A medium tank in World War II was the hottest in the summer, the coldest in the winter, the dustiest anywhere on earth. It was a miserable "thing" to live in. Everything about it was harder than all flesh and bone. For a warrior to win a battle it has to be the most gratifying, the most fulfilling for any combat anywhere, anytime.

'When the tanks were moving we always had hot coffee, simply by having the driver place two canteens on the transmission, which was at the front end of the tank, between the driver and the assistant driver. We would

Tank/infantry co-operation. In Belgium on 3 January 1945 machine gunners of the 10th Armored Infantry Regiment, 4th Armored Division, cover tanks crossing snow covered fields in the Bastogne Corridor. US Army

have the loader warm the rations (against regulations) on the little Coleman heater, the size of a roll of duck tape.

'In cold weather we would be very miserable as the frost from our breath would hold on to the inside of the turret roof and freeze. I allowed the men in our platoon to sew one blanket into their sleeping bags, cut holes for their feet and arms, and "wear" the damned sleeping bag. This started in November 1944, when the miserable French rains began turning to snow in the eastern hilly sections of the Ardennes to the north and the Vosges to the south.

'This "clothing" system helped quite a lot where these young men were asked to sleep sitting or standing. One at a time could lay on the turret floor and then he had to be shorter than five feet nine inches. As I was over six feet I simply used the tank commander's 8-inch diameter seat to sit on to sleep. The gunner stayed in his seat, with its back rest. It was impossible to stretch out. One could take a chance when we stopped, to get out and move about. A far cry from the regimental calisthenics of stateside duty.

'My tank crew obtained a 20 lb coffee can,

Tanks and infantry of 6th Armored Division co-operate in the tricky business of street fighting in Oberdoila, Germany, on 4 April 1945. US Army

Sergeant Bob Grady's tank crew (*Berlin Bound*) of Coy. B, 37th Tank Battalion, 4th Armoured Division, while at Devizes, Wiltshire, in May 1944, wearing full tankers rig. On the sleeves of their windcheaters can be seen the three-coloured triangular patch with the symbols of armor superimposed, which was the 'symbol of armor' in the US Army. The colours are blue for infantry, red for artillery and yellow for cavalry—the three basic components of armor. In 1940 three superimposed figures were added — the tank track for mobility, the gun for fire power and lightning bolt representing the shock effect of armor. The original three-coloured patch was designed in January 1918, when the Tank Corps of the US Army was created; while the other symbols came from the 7th Cavalry Brigade (Mechanized). When the Armored Force was formed in 1940 the two symbols were combined to give the present-day patch. 'It is a union of separate arms which yet preserves the integrity of those units in an organisation with a high degree of esprit de corps traditional to the mounted soldier'.

one with a round lid on the top, a lid that would seal tight. We used this to defecate and emptied it when the opportunity offered. To urinate we simply used the helmet. The assistant driver would dispose of the gunner's, the loader's and his own, through the turret hatch. For the three years plus that I was in a tank, that was the system.

'The tank came equipped with an axe, a shovel, a tow cable, a pick, a wrench to tighten the tracks, and a tarpaulin. We were issued with the "squirt-gun" — the .45 caliber sub-machine gun, all metal and held thirty rounds. Tank commanders were issued with the .30 caliber carbine, but most of these were given to the armored infantry for their better use.'

The Company B Project

The veterans of Company B, 37th Tank Battalion, 4th Armoured Division, have recently carried out an interesting exercise, namely trying to remember exactly how they were organized on the day they went over to Normandy, which was 11 July 1944. One of them, Col. Jimmie Leach of Arlington, Virginia, very kindly sent the writer details of this project, which gives a good basic impression of the make-up of the unit in which most tankers found themselves, namely the company. One of their starting points was to write to the Military History Center of the US Army, asking to be sent the relevant 'TO & E' (Tables of Organisation and Equipment)[1] No. 17–27 of 18 November 1944 which in-

cluded changes from 23 September 1943 up to that date. The details are given opposite.

Having got that information to work on they began to sort out names of vehicles and to put in crews. The tables opposite show the situation they had reached in April 1981. (The abbreviations used are: TC: tank commander; G: gunner; L: loader; D: driver; B: bow gunner; KIA: killed in action.)

The following had to be located within platoons:

1:—Brown; Clark; Devanport; Hale; Irish, Nelson; Reynolds; Tyler.
2:—Bradley (KIA); Gellman; Gregor; Grieb; Kaczmarek; McVicker (KIA); Miller; Rhoades; Ross; Simcik.
3:—Hodges (left in UK—who took his place?); Gregor.

Company B were due to have their next reunion in the summer of 1981, so I hope they were able to find answers to their queries. They would then have a 'point of reference' by which they could remember 'those who left before and those who came afterwards.'

'To & E' No 17–27, 18 November 1944

Vehicles: 16 Tanks (there should have been 17, one but was given to Bn HQ); 1 Tank equipped with a 105 mm Howitzer — the Assault Gun;[2] 1 Half-track; 2 Peeps[3]; 1 Kitchen truck; 1 Vehicle Tank Recovery (VTR).

Personnel: The official TO was for 5 officers and 112 men (four of which had gone with the tank to Bn HQ), so that the actual TO was 5 and 108 of one, the Coy clerk, was in rear echelon, so did not ride in a TO vehicle.

Thus, the 'Crossing TO' was:

Vehicles	Officers	Men
Command tank	1	4
15 tanks (3 platoons of 5)	3	72
Assault gun tank (105 mm)		5
1 truck and trailer (Kitchen/Supply)		7
1 VTR		5
1 Half-track (maintenance)		7
2 Peeps		
No 1, Motor Officer		2
No 2, First Sergeant		4
Extra man from tank sent to Bn HQ, his place taken by the S3[4]	—	1
Totals	**5**	**107**

Headquarters Platoon

Company Command

Buccaneer (M4)
TC — Teigs
G — Williams
L — Zynn
D — Blume (KIA)
B — Connelly (KIA)

Target-for-Tonight (M4)
TC — Bautz, S3, Bn, HQ.
G — Slifka
L — Darling
D — Brindle
B — Johnson

Back Breaker (M4 with 105 mm Assault Gun)
TC — Grimm
G — Hayward
L — Boyer
D — Bieniek
B — Holland

Beulah (Peep, 1st Sgt/ADMIN)
D — Powell
— Guffey, 1st Sgt
— Kaplin, Supply (KIA)
— Saxon

Communications — Supply-Mess/Maintenance

Back-N-Forth (Jeep)
D — Kilanowski
— Mixon
— Jefferis

Biscuit Buggy (6 × 6 Truck)
D — Quinlan   — Crigger
— Ramey   — Aulicino
— Garrison   — Colasanti
— Scates   — Strulowitz
Co Clerk — Luthye

Maintenance
VTR — *Black Panther*
Cmdr — Cortese
D — Debevc
B — Roberti

Half-Track
Cmdr — Mullen   — Mollo
D — Mercer   — Brooks
— Digangi   — Salvaggio
— Gross
Displaced TC from Bn tank.

The Three Tank Platoons

1st Platoon

Blockbuster
TC — Leach
G — Coffee
L — ?
D — Boggs (KIA)
B — Popovich (KIA)

Berlin Bound
TC — Grady
G — Litherland
L — ?
D — Caisey
B — ?

Betty Boop
TC — Fitzpatrick
G — Creviston
L — ?
D — Baay
B — ?

Beer Barrel
TC — Nobela
G — Weitzman
L — Simo (KIA)
D — Levins
B — ?

Bulldozer
TC — Morphew
G — Sandrock
L — ?
D — Kelly (KIA)
B — ?

2nd Platoon

Boilermaker
TC — Bohn
C — Peskar
L — ?
D — Porter
B — ?

Budweiser
TC — Lewis
G — Checki
L — ?
D — Machen
B — ?

Bock Beer
TC — Langmeier
G — Hauptman
L — ?
D — Moe
B — ?

Blue Ribbon
TC — Sowers
G — Wenrich (KIA)
L — ?
D — Drew
B — Cunningham F

Ballantine
TC — Del Vecchio
G — O'Hearn
L — ?
D — Wright
B — ?

3rd Platoon

Brother Toby
TC — Marston
G — Custo
L — Daly
D — Chelmecki
B — Troxell

Blondie
TC — Heintz
G — Ginoli (KIA)
L — Niski
D — ?
B — Graham

Brooklyn Boy
TC — Farese (KIA)
G — Bordner
L — Martin
D — Parks (KIA)
B — Ritland

Beaufighter
TC — Krassner (KIA)
G — ?
L — Cariello
D — Peck (KIA)
B — Gagliardi.

Blenheim
TC — Whiteside (KIA)
G — Chernick
L — Maguire
D — Paulus
B — Ayotte

3
Early Light Tanks and Combat Cars

At the beginning of World War II, the United States had four basic types of light armored fighting vehicle all of which were closely related. The Infantry had Light Tanks M2A2 and M2A3, while the Cavalry had Combat Cars M1 and M2. The simplest way of telling them apart was that the light tanks had twin turrets, earning themselves the nickname of 'Mae Wests' (for obvious anatomical reasons)! Both turrets had limited traverse (270 degrees), the commander's on the left mounting a .50-cal. machine-gun, while there was a .30-cal. MG in the right hand turret. The Combat Cars had single turrets with a .50-cal. and a .30-cal. machine-gun mounted co-axially. All had a second .30-cal. in the hull, and a third for AA defence, the first recorded instance of this provision on any AFV. All were totally inadequate for operating on the modern battlefield, except in a scouting rôle, but fortunately they never had to prove themselves in battle.

Forrest Knox of Janesville, Wisconsin, drove one of these small machines and he told the writer: 'Those 10-ton Mae Wests were fun to drive. At 1800 rpm the road speed was supposed to be 32 mph — convoy speed. I had a Mae West up to 3600 rpm once myself. They drove like a sports car at that speed, easy to handle — hummed right along. Problem was there were never any brakes on the tank. You came down the gears to slow down, the final 5 mph being handled by the steering clutches. Then they put a governor on the engine and now you couldn't get top speed, worse still in heavy going you could not overspeed the engine enough to work the gearshift. If you tried it would hammer and overheat like crazy. A radial engine has got to turn to get enough cooling air around its cylinders. Then they increased the weight, tied the engine down so it hammered and overheated — and blamed the drivers for engine failure! We never held an engine at a howling speed for long, but you simply had to overrun to get the momentum up high enough to shift [gear].'

In his book *To The Regiment*, Col. Ford E

Top
Goodbye to boots and saddles! Evocative of photograph as an M2A4 light tank the 7th Cavalry Brigade (Mechanized) overtakes a squadron of horse mounted cavalry during US Army exercises summer 1940.

Above
A Combat Car M1, belonging to the 1st Cavalry Regiment, 7th Cavalry Brigade, moving at speed during maneuvers in 1939.

Young recalled his mixed emotions when he took part in his 'last ride as a cavalryman' on 2 June 1940, a 'cross country ride with many jumps and slides'. The following month he reported to Fort Knox, Kentucky, to command E Troop of the 1st Cavalry Regiment, who, with 13th Cavalry Regiment, were part of the 7th Cavalry Brigade Mechanized, under Gen. Adna Chaffee, and were the first US cavalry to be turned into tank units. Later, of course, they became the 1st Armored Division. Young arrived, wearing breeches, boots and spurs, for his first experience of being in a tank on Battalion Tank Drill. He had to rely on the troop First Sergeant, who was in the tank with him, to tell him which flag to wave and how to wave it for each maneuver, as the Battalion Commander gave his flag orders from the head of the column — radios were yet to become a standard fitment. Later, on field exercises, E Troop possessed just one crystal-type radio and the soldiers would take it in turns 'grinding the hand pedals to keep the radio operative', while the Sergeant Radio Operator remained 'alert and attentive', waiting for the all important message — 'return to the Motor Park' (the British equivalent is 'Exercise Ends')! The training at Fort Knox in those early days of the Armored Force was strenuous and Young gives a graphic impression of crews coming off field exercises every day 'with a quarter of an inch of dust on our faces, except only around our eyes when we took off our goggles'. He also explains how the early tanks maneuvered: 'To speed up, the tank commander (whose head and shoulders would be out of the turret), would tap the driver with his foot, successively, on the driver's back about a foot below the neck. To go to the right, the tank commander would tap the driver's right shoulder with his foot. For a turn to the left, a tap on the left shoulder. To slow down, a light push in the driver's back; and to stop, a hard push by the tank commander's foot into the driver's back.'

All four AFVs were developed from the T2 tank series which had been first designed in 1933. The T2 carried a crew of four, was armed with a .50-cal. machine-gun and two .30-cal. It weighted $7\frac{1}{2}$ tons, was of riveted construction, and was powered by an air-cooled, seven cylinder radial aircraft engine,

Right
This M1A1 Combat Car was used by Maj. Gen. George S Patton, while he was commanding 2nd Armored Division, during the Third Army maneuvers in Louisiana in 1940. The bands around the bottom of the turret were red, white, blue and yellow from top to bottom, while the 2nd Armored Division crest was on a red/yellow flag and the two silver stars on an all red one.

Below right
M2A2 and M2A3 light tanks ready to move out from Camp Beauregard, Louisiana, for the Third Army maneuvers of 1941 (note that no weapons are fitted).

Below
An excellent close-up of Combat Cars M1, belonging to 1st Cavalry Regiment, with the commanders manning the pintle-mounted machine guns.

Opposite top
M2A2 light tanks surmounting obstacles during exercises at Fort Benning, Georgia, in early 1940.

Opposite bottom
A flight of light twin-engined bombers fly over some of the 200 light tanks and combat cars which took part in the 1940 maneuvers on a 97,000 acre reservation near Fort Benning, Georgia.

Left
The Combat Car M2 was the first to be fitted with the distinctive trailing idler. In 1940, it was redesignated as the Light Tank M1A1 (Diesel).

Below
An interesting convertible was this 11-ton Combat Car T7 with three bogie wheels.

the quartet, the Light Tank M2A3, was an improved version of the M2A2, with better transmission, slightly thicker frontal armor, better engine cooling and improved engine access.

Forrest Knox again: 'our first issue of a light tank was highly regarded, three guns — one .50-cal., two .30-cal. plus a roadspeed of 32 mph. I thought the ball-joint or bow gun through the front deck was kind of silly — no sights. It [the M2A2] had a seven-cylinder radial aircraft engine and a straight tooth sliding gear transmission. Going to first gear with the tank stopped was easy, after that the shift had to be precise. If the gear tooth speed did not match it was near impossible to get into gear. Now the bad part — there were no brakes. The stop was made by down shifting in gears and the engine made the stop. The tank helped, but mainly it was a feel for road speed and engine speed. It was the reason I had enlisted to drive this 10-ton toy. Later on the transmission was made synchromesh, but the early model still needed my touch, so I was happy with my early years in the service.'

Light Tank M2A4

The last model of the M2 Light Tank series was perhaps the most important and best of them all — the M2A4. For the first time it mounted a larger gun than a machine-gun, namely the 37 mm M5 tank gun which had an armor-piercing capability. A total of 103 rounds of ammunition were carried on board for the 37 mm gun. The gun was similar to the one carried in the T1 light tank series and while it was an improvement on the .50-cal. machine-gun it certainly did not have much hitting power even though it was just coming into service as the US Army's standard anti-tank gun.

Light tank T2E2, built in 1934, which weighed 8 tons and had twin 'Mae West' turrets mounting .50 cal. and .30 cal. machine guns.

located in the rear of the hull, which gave it a top speed of about 35 mph. One model (the T2E1) had a single turret, another (the T2E2) twin turrets. It was the first American AFV to use the twin wheeled suspension unit with vertical volute springs and a return roller on top of the unit, which became so familiar on later American tanks. It also had a double toothed sprocket, its teeth engaged in recesses in the flat double pin track plates. The T2E1 was standardised as the Light Tank M2A1; the T2E2 as the Light Tank M2A2 which was still in service in 1939/40.

At the same time as they produced the T2 tank for the Infantry, the Rock Island Arsenal built a similar vehicle for the Cavalry, which was called the Combat Car. Developed as the T5E2 and then designated as the M1 Combat Car, the AFV entered service in 1937. It was powered with the same engine as the T2 tank.

An improved version, the M2, had a trailing idler to give more ground contact and, by keeping the nose down thus, a more comfortable ride. It had a rectangular turret and an air-cooled seven-cylinder Guiberson T1020 diesel engine with more pulling power. Once the Armored Force came into being in July 1940, the Cavalry subterfuge of calling its light tanks 'Combat cars' was no longer necessary, so they became Light Tanks M1A1 and M1A2 respectively. The fourth member of

Specifications	CAVALRY		INFANTRY	
	Combat Car M1 (Light Tank M1A1)	Combat Car M2 (Light Tank M1A2)	Light Tank M2A2	Light Tank M2A3
Crew	All had a crew of four, commander, driver, co-driver and gunner			
Combat Weight	19,644 lbs	19,644 lbs	19,100 lbs	20,050 lbs
Length	13 ft 7 in	13 ft 7 in	13 ft 7 in	14 ft 6½ in
Height	7 ft 9 in	7 ft 9 in	7 ft 9 in	7 ft 9 in
Width	7 ft 10 in	7 ft 10 in	7 ft 10 in	8 ft 2 in
Armament *and*	All had one .50-cal. MG and three .30-cal. MG			
Mountings	Single turret with all round traverse		Double turrets with limited traverse	
	All had one .30 MG in hull and one for AA defence			
Armor thickness max./min.	15 min/6.25 mm	15 mm/6.25 mm	15 mm/6.25 mm	17.5 mm/6.25 mm
Max. speed	45 mph	45 mph	30 mph	40 mph
Radius of action	140 ml	140 ml	130 ml	130 ml

The M2A3, built in 1938, was essentially just a refinement of the T2E2 (also called the M2A2) but had better transmission and thicker armor.

Forrest Knox again: 'The 37 mm cannon round was totally useless. If you could get an enemy vehicle to turn sideways to you it would go right in, but face on, all it left was a streak on the armor where it glanced off. We had Ordnance make up our own shells by using the projectiles out of old World War I ammo. It was designed for the close support of infantry in a World War I field piece and the tenth of a second delay was perfect for our use. ... The 37 mm was the same gun as the one designed as an anti-tank weapon with the recoil shortened up to eight inches so it would not hit the back side of the turret. It was a hodge-podge design that should have been junked. Trouble was they didn't have anything else. ... The sponson guns were fired by the driver who had folding triggers on the steering clutches. This set-up was also completely useless. Driver could aim his tank, but if there were other targets available everyone else was too busy to load the fixed guns where they were put. And the empty brass — that was the real curse. It jammed the driver's clutch rod and put the tank out of action until it was cleared. Very distracting when in action. The British and Aussies removed the sponson guns — a smart move.'

The pilot model of the M2A4 was completed at the Rock Island Arsenal in early 1939, the 37 mm gun being mounted in a single riveted turret with all round manual traverse — the single turret of the Combat Cars having been found to be much superior to the twin turrets of the light tanks. The front of the hull and hull sides had been up armored to 25 mm which increased the tank's all up weight to 12 tons and reduced the top

All round views of the M2A4 first production model. Mounting a 37 mm gun it was certainly the best of the early light tanks and led directly on to the M3.

Above
M2A4s on parade. With both the driver's and co-driver's vision hatches open it is possible not only to see both of them, but also the gunner who was presumably squatting on top of the transmission housing between them.

Above right
A small number of M2A4s were delivered to Britain in 1941 where they were used for training. *Al Capone* belonged to an armored regiment based in the UK.

Right
An M2A4 belonging to the US Marine Corps moves into the jungle on Guadalcanal in the Solomons, September 1942.

Below right
British Home Guard are taken for a ride in an M2A4 'somewhere in England' in summer 1942.

speed accordingly. There were no less than four .30-cal. MGs, one co-axially mounted in the turret, one 'bow' gun in the hull and two more in fixed-firing mounts one in each side sponson. There was also a pintle AA mount for a fifth MG to be fitted at the rear of the turret.

The firepower of the M2A4 was thus considerable although Forrest Knox pointed out to the writer that only two of the machine-guns were really valuable: '. . . the coax in the turret with the 37 mm and the bow gun fired through a ball joint in the front deck. No sight, strictly guesswork, loose firing. It worked to perfection. Of course, they put a limit on firing three short bursts only but in action each burst was the length of the belt — 100–250 rounds as the case may be. . . . A good bow gunner could shoot his way across a minefield, moving about 20 ft a time. The gunner would have to hose two tracks for the driver to run in, the rest then stayed in the exact same tracks to cross. Official reaction was absolutely not! First it was a terrible waste of ammo, second it was against recommended procedure — regulations you know! ... The S4 Supply Officer whined like a bitch dog with the worms — about the 10,000 rounds used a day, but we didn't lose any more tanks to mines either!' (Knox is referring here to the M3, because he did not 'fight' in an M2A4.)

The contract for building the M2A4 was won by the American Car & Foundry Co. of Berwick, Pennyslvania, despite the fact that they had no previous experience of building tanks or of mass production. Like so many American firms in those early days, they found out the theory of how to do it and then dealt with the problems as they went along, but kept on building tanks! It was the first American tank order placed with industry for twenty years. The total order was for 375, the vast majority being built in 1939–40. The last ten were in fact produced by the Baldwin Locomotive Works in 1942. The M2A4 was the very first tank to be mass-produced in the USA in World War II. Although its success has been greatly overshadowed by its successor, the M3 (the start of the famous General Stuart series which the British called 'The Honey'), it did form the backbone of the Armored Force in the early days of the war and also saw active service in the difficult early campaigns in the Pacific theater.

A few M2A4s were delivered to Britain — the first of the Lend-Lease tanks — and were used for training in the UK and the Middle East. This was also, of course, their main rôle in the US Army. Knox took part in this early training and his memories of the Army maneuvers held in Louisiana must be typical of the many frustrations of the tankers who were part of the Armored Force in those early days and fought umpired 'battles' in Tennessee, Louisiana and Carolina in 1941, with senior officers who knew little or nothing about the right way to deploy tanks:

'... Army maneuvers in Louisiana July and August 1941. The one thing I had learned at Tank Commanders School, was to always flank attack an anti-tank gun. Well, I was in charge of two tanks, mine and one more of the platoon of five. When we located the first anti-tank gun position I got off the road to flank it but we got trapped in a ravine and hung one tank between the trees — had to chop them down to get it out. Then the other tank lost a track climbing out of a gully. We had to back the track on, but first had to cut another tree down so we could get a cable on to help.

Finally we were out of the woods and started up the road. We were soon flagged down by an infantryman who asked if we were out of action. I said "No, just trapped in the

An M2 medium tank being ferried across a river during exercises in the USA in June 1941. The ability to move armor across water obstacles, etc, was always considered very important, consequently, weight, reliability, and mobility were given preference over protection (i.e. thick armor). This worked well on the great armored 'swans' accomplished by the Third US Army, but when it came to slogging it out with German tanks and anti-tank guns, the more lightly armed and armored American tanks were at a decided disadvantage.

woods." He said "Fine" and explained that they had an anti-tank gun to knock out — he pointed out where it was, top of a rise by a schoolhouse. "Good," I told my other tank. "You go left and I'll go right about 100 yards, then straight on until you think you are level with the school, then come for the road as fast as you can. The gun crew can only lay one way or the other, so one of us will get him." Then the "General" issued his attack order — charge the gun straight up the road, I was taken by surprise so I asked "Up the road?" He got uppity and said again "Up the road, sergeant." So I told Bob, my other tank commander, "OK, up the road." 150 yards and a referee flagged us down — both knocked out. We reported to the holding pen and found the entire battalion parked there. That stupid "General" had been doing the same thing from first light and hadn't learned a

damn thing — threw away the entire battalion in one day.'

M2A4 Specifications

Battle weight	23,000 lbs
Length	14 ft 6 in
Height	8 ft 1¼ in
Width	8 ft 1¼ in

Armament

(a) one 37 mm and one .30-cal. MG (coaxially mounted) in all round hand traversing turret.
(b) three hull-mounted .30-cal. MGs, two in side sponsons and one in the hull front.

Armor thickness,
  max/min   25 mm/6 mm

Engine:

As for M2A3, but slightly uprated. A few late production vehicles were fitted with the Guiberson T-1020 Series 4 Diesel in place of the Continental petrol engine.

4

The M3: A 'Honey of A Tank'

The M2A4 was really more a prototype vehicle for the next light tank series, rather than being just the last of a particular line. Many of its features, such as the 37 mm gun in its single fully rotating turret, were carried forward to the M3 light tank. Battle experience in Europe had already shown that thicker armor was essential, so that when the M3 was designed in spring 1940 the main requirement was for more protection. On the frontal area of the AFV this was increased to 38 mm (51 mm on the nose), while the minimum thickness was raised from 6 mm to 10 mm. Other safety factors included removing the vision ports in the sides of the turret, and thickening up the armor on the engine decks. However, this could not be done without increasing the weight by some 4400 lbs, which meant that a stronger suspension was needed. Consequently, a large trailing idler was fitted, thus increasing track ground contact and giving a better distribution of weight.

The M3 was approved and standardised in July 1940 and went into production at the American Car and Foundry Company who had already built the M2A4. During the next two years of production, up to August 1942, 5811 M3 light tanks were built. Numerous mechanical and technical changes were made to the design of the M3, or General Stuart as it was now unofficially called, for example: the seven-sided riveted turret took on a rounded shape; welding took the place of riveting (to conserve weight and protect the crew lest the rivet heads broke off when the tank was hit by enemy fire and flew around inside the turret);

Above
The standard production M3 light tank. Note the all-riveted construction, the six-sided cupola on top of the turret which was identical in shape to the M2A4, but had improved vision slots. The Honey, as the British called the M3, had thicker armor and a better suspension — note the trailing idler.

Right
The next major development was to replace the riveted turret with a welded one, made of face hardened armor. This one was part of the order delivered to Britain, so it was known as the Stuart 1. Note the extra stowage boxes, sandshields, track links, and the double barreled smoke grenade discharger on the side of the turret.

a powered traverse was added; armor thickness was increased; and a gyrostabiliser was installed to steady the 37 mm gun while the tank was moving. 'ACF received a steady stream of engineering change orders during 1940–41, [and] when the new model (M3A1) was adopted in August 1941, ACF was directed to switch over its production as soon as possible. In 1942, the M3A3 appeared with an all-welded hull, sloping fronted armor and an improved radio compartment, but this was soon replaced by the M5.'[1]

The powerplant of the M3 was either the original Continental W670–9A petrol driven radial engine or the T1020–4 Guiberson radial diesel engine. The diesel was only used because it was felt that demands by the aircraft industry for the Continental engine would produce a shortage. The M3 and M3 (Diesel) were produced concurrently and the only external difference was a slightly larger exhaust pipe on the diesel version. Most M3 (Diesel)s were kept in the USA for training.

Conrad Mueller of Delray Beach, Florida,

had this to say about the Guiberson diesel: '... when I was an enlisted man in the newly activated 6th Armored Division at Camp Chaffee, Ark, we had the old organisation — one light battalion and three medium battalions. I was then a sergeant tank commander and our light battalion was an experimental unit testing the radial Guiberson diesel engine, manufactured in Texas. This company was attempting to sell their engine rather than a gasoline powered unit. It was a good engine and had some advantages, such as not being as explosive as gasoline when hit by enemy fire. The main disadvantage, we found, was it had no self-starting devices. Being radial in design, the engine had to be turned over twelve times by hand to drain the oil from the cylinders, otherwise on starting up the engine with the "Breeze" Cartridge shell, the cylinders were prone to damage. ... the Louisiana–Texas war games of 1943 proved this as some units were put out of action in their bivouac areas due to the time taken to start up their vehicles.'

Apart from US forces, the M3 series light tanks were used by the British in Burma, North-West Europe (from 1944) and Italy, as well as in North Africa, and the United Kingdom (for training), while several other countries including Russia, France and China received deliveries of M3s. The M3 was declared obsolete by the US Army in 1943 but stayed in service with its other users throughout the war and beyond. Indeed, some M3s are still in service in various parts of the world.

The British were the first to use the M3 in action and, as a result of their experience in the Western Desert, other modifications were made. These included the removal of the two sponson machine guns which could only be fired remotely and were of limited value;

In early 1941 the turret was again changed, this time a welded / cast turret of homogenous armor of 'horseshoe' shape replaced the multi-faced one. From mid-1941 a gyrostabilizer was fitted for the main gun and twin 25 gallon jettisonable fuel tanks (clearly visible) were fitted to increase the range.

increased fuel capacity, initially by means of two jettisonable twenty-five gallon fuel tanks (on the M3A3 the all welded hull was enlarged, giving room for extra internal fuel tanks and more ammunition storage).

First Combat

The M3 light tank has the distinction of being the first American-built tank to see action and this was with the British Eighth Army in the Western Desert. Soon after the outbreak of war Britain had turned to the United States to buy weapons and ships. However, by the end of 1940 she had run out of dollars. President Roosevelt then came up with a novel scheme of 'destroyers for bases', which was extended in March 1941 to the Lend-Lease Act. The Act allowed Britain credit to obtain war material and left the payment until later (the total Lend-Lease bill came to over 4300 million dollars by the end of the war).

Much of the early M3 light tank production was thus earmarked for Britain, and was used in the great tank battles in North Africa. The first shipment of eighty-four M3s arrived there in July 1941 and were used to re-equip the 8th King's Royal Irish Hussars, subsequent shipments going to the 3rd and 5th Royal Tank Regiments of 4th Armoured Brigade. Despite drawbacks, such as the fact that the tank's main armament was even less effective than the British two-pounder, the Stuart quickly became a firm favourite with British tank crews, thanks to its mechanical reliability and ease of handling. They nicknamed it the 'Honey'. 'They were great little tanks', wrote one of the tank crewmen in 5 RTR, '... fast and reliable, but the gun was just 37 mm' 4th Armoured Brigade first used its new tanks, on 18 November 1941 at Gabr Saleh, during the opening battles of the 'Crusader' offensive.

In Burma

Joe Lee of the 7th Queen's Own Hussars crewed a Stuart Mk 1 (the British nomenclature for the basic M3) during the retreat out of

Top
American-built M3s wind along a road at the Southern Russian front. A total of 3200 tanks was shipped from the US to the USSR between October 1941 and January 1943, under Lend-Lease, along with many aircraft and trucks.

Above
Hidden by a smoke screen, a 4-ton US Army Ordnance Battalion 'Wrecker' tows a General Stuart back to a field repair base during an exercise 'Somewhere in England'. Note that the tank is an M3A1 with both an all welded hull and turret.

Left
An M3A3 belonging to the Free French on an exercise in England.

Right
A trainload of M3 lights and M3 mediums at an Egyptian railhead, ready to be transported 'Up the Blue' to 7th Armoured Division. Note the British extras such as sandshields, smoke dischargers, etc, and the 'Desert Rat' symbol on the front mudguards, which was the divisional sign of this famous division.

Bottom
Crews of the 8th King's Royal Irish Hussars try out their new M3s before taking them into action.

Below
An 8th Hussar squadron commander uses flag signals to pass orders to his other tanks during training in the desert. Note that he and the other member of his crew are wearing the American leather 'doughnut' crash-helmet.

Below right
This Honey was one belonging to 2nd Royal Tank Regiment, which as part of 7th Armoured Brigade, covered the retreat out of Burma. Maj. N T Plough

Burma in February 1942. 7th Armoured Brigade had come to the Far East from the Western Desert where they had already earned a tremendous reputation as part of the famous 7th Armoured Division. They acted as covering troops to Burcorps throughout the retreat and gained further glory.

Lee writes: 'We didn't have any American tanks in the desert but drew them up in Egypt prior to the move to Burma — although no-one knew exactly where we were likely to end up — Singapore, Java (as some did), but I don't think Burma was ever mooted. It was all rather a rush job if I can put it that way. We had a couple of American Top Sergeants with us to give us all the gen. Of course, there were many amusing incidents. The Yanks had a type of headgear which they had to wear in tanks, something like jockeys' wear, but we never wore them.

'The tanks were simple, and good workhorses, no sophisticated equipment. The turrets were all manual control and the driving sprockets were at the front of the tank. So, to move around in the tank, the crew had to step over the prop shaft — as you will appreciate there were many harsh words said at times, as this ran right through the turret at knee height. The petrol switch was in a very awkward place inside the turret at the back. So to start up one had to try to reach it from the driver's seat. I'm sure my right arm finished up a foot longer than the left! The gears were simple and steering easy enough.

'The tanks had radial engines and ran on high octane, so it was possible to catch fire when starting up, especially when the engine was cold after lying still all night. Being radials one had to turn them over by a big hand crank which looked like a big starting handle, to move the oil that would have collected in the bottom pistons. This amused the Burmese, who really thought we were winding the tanks up, like clockwork, which I

Fitters from 2nd Tanks, get to work on an engine out of a Honey. The engine looks so new that it is probable that they have just taken it out of its storage container and are checking it before installing it into a tank. Maj. N T Plough

suppose could be a logical deduction!

'To get at the engine, there were two doors at the back of the tank, held together by bolts. I think there were about four, but we very soon saved time by just using one. They were very accessible and one could service them even under fire without being too exposed, as opposed to a British tank where the engine openings were all on the back decking of the tank.

'The driver's hatch was quite big and one could almost jump in, but the front of the hatch hinged from the top was crude and simple ... the Commander's hatch was literally a top of a lid, it opened completely or shut — not halfways. The tank was a simple steel box with no trimmings. Firepower was on a par with English tanks and they were really reliable. For my part, from landing in Rangoon until leaving the tank at the Chindwin River (some hundreds of miles north through impossible going with no proper roads through the jungle), I never had any trouble and I certainly covered some miles "to and fro".

'As regards tank versus tank actions, well, there was one flap when the whole brigade expected a mass confrontation with Jap armour (you must appreciate, our intelligence was really hit and miss), however, nothing much materialised. I think that there was only one tank action when the 7th Hussars met three Japanese tanks and immediately disposed of them and the Japanese never ventured to use them against us again. Mind you, to force any tank action, the terrain would

have to have been carefully chosen. In some places it would have been useless. The Japanese was good with his big mortars, accurate, and of course the ground before the monsoon was rock hard so that they were like 'daisy cutters' when they landed, spreading out all over before the shrapnel could dig into the ground. One other item of interest, there were no anti-tank mines on the retreat, no barbed wire or fortified positions as such.

'The biggest hazard on the Stuarts was, I think, fire. One place we came through we had Molotov Cocktails thrown at the tank, which, having high octane petrol, made us all wary. And from then on we went into villages and smashed all the bottles we found — that was an order. One drawback was of course just having a 37 mm gun, which only fired solid shot. Even in the short time available Ordnance tried to find a means to make a sort of 'grapeshot' but to no avail. So most of the solid shot was wasted, although where there were houses built of teak then the solid shot was about the only thing that would move anyone out. At least in a Stuart you could get about in double quick time, and in the circumstances, speed was often of the essence.'

First American action against the Japanese

The M3 Lights were also the first American tanks to see action against the Japanese. They were used by 192nd and 194th Tank Battalions which had been shipped to Luzon, in the Philippines, shortly before the Japanese invasion and formed a Provisional Tank Group under Brig.-Gen. James Weaver.

Forrest Knox was a member of this force. He told the writer: 'I joined the National Guard in 1938. We were inducted into regular

army service in November 1940 and sent to Fort Knox, 1st Armored Division training base. At the time of induction our unit, 192nd Tank Battalion, had four letter companies (Coy A was made up from Wisconsin National Guardsmen, Coy B from Illinois, Coy C from Ohio, and Coy D from Kentucky), each letter company had just two M2A2 tanks, making a total of eight. We then drew enough tanks from Post Ordnance to make up our battalion to a training strength of twenty-four, drawing sixteen 'discards' from 1st Armored Division. Our maintenance got trained first — they had to rebuild them! Our battalion received 350 draftees, but we never did get up to full strength, so when we went into action we had three man crews instead of four. ... Our battalion was a bastard unit, the only one in the Army with four letter companies and draftees. Later the 194th had one letter company split off and sent to Alaska, so when we went to the Philippines Coy D was attached to the 194th.

'At Camp Polk we turned in our twenty-four M2A2 tanks and drew fifty-four M3s, stripped the armored division stationed there and made up the rest by a special shipment direct from the manufacturer. I got a brand new tank — five miles on the speedometer. ... after drawing the tanks I had to go to the armored div that gave up their M3s and collect the machine-guns. First the Supply Sergeant would drag out all their old guns — I had to find something wrong with every one. Then they brought out the new guns which I signed for.

'After three days around the clock I was dead on my feet. So I got stuck with one bad gun out of 350 — and got chewed out by the Lieutenant. Well that's normal. I didn't have the time left to draw fifty-four spare parts tool boxes — that was my fault too. I began to wonder if I was the only man in the 192nd! Loaded everything aboard a train — five days to 'Frisco', five days to Angel Island while the stevedores loaded ship, then twenty-eight days to PI.

'We landed on Thanksgiving Day, eighteen days before the war started. After they unloaded the transport we were trucked to Manila and drew our tanks. The convoy back to Fort Stosenburg was the first time most of us had ever ridden in an M3. We still had ten days to war.

'The morning the war started our guns were still in cosmoline. Because I had been to gunnery school I was told to clean the cannons. That's when I found out Ord at Polk hadn't given us any rammer staffs or brushes. It is a 'no-no' to clean a gun with gasoline. It's a worse 'no-no' to fire a cannon with grease in the barrel. So I cut bamboo shoots, tore up a

A very aggressive-looking commander, stands guard over his early model M3A1, with his Thompson sub-machine gun at the ready. Note that the sponson machine guns are still fitted; they were eliminated on later M3A1s, having proved of limited value as they could not be properly aimed and wasted a lot of precious ammunition. The tank and crew fought in the battle of Tenaru River in the Solomons.

gunny sack, drew a bucket of gasoline and cleaned the barrels. I told every tank crew they had to oil their guns and walked away.

'I had got to the point when everything could not be my fault. No-one could find the ammo belt loaders — so we loaded 5000 rounds by hand — everyone had blisters on their thumbs by noon. By one o'clock I had fired most of it away. Don't guess I hit anything. That was another thing they never told us — how much do you lead on an airplane. I didn't know there was such a thing as an aircraft sight 'til we stripped guns from a B-17 shot up on the field. Talk about on the job training! Learning to fire a cannon when a Jap tank is coming towards you is the ultimate in stupidity.

'We became 1st Tank Group Philippine Islands. About 800 men in all I guess. We took fifty-four tanks I think, so 194th should

have had seventeen per Coy, two HQ, thirty-six total, makes about ninety sent to PI. That number is debatable but close. We lost about half in the ten day withdrawal to Bataan . . . . Like any other operation at the start of a war it was totally screwed up. The Philippine Engineers were blowing the bridges before we could get to them, so we had to have our recon units behind us, guarding our bridges until we got across. Lost one complete company of tanks at one river. Some were knocked out by cannon fire, most simply lost a track and had to be abandoned before a rescue wrecker could get there ... some drivers were just plain untrained. You had to hold the throttle down on a turn, if you tried to slow down the slack in the track went to the rear and off came the track at the idler. Our half-tracks did the same thing. We lost several like this. Supposedly you could put it into front wheel drive and limp home. I got a 75 mm SP home this way one night. Later my tank was given to D Coy to replace one left at a blown bridge. They tried to give the SP to me, said I was a cannon man and could handle it. I asked why they didn't give it back to the artillery — they needed it . . . .

'We had some men with claustrophobia — couldn't stand it locked up inside. I never minded, felt safe, even with the rivet prob-lem — a hit might not penetrate, but it was reputed that it would blow the heads off the rivets which would then fly around inside like shrapnel.

'In action we used to shut off the engine to conserve the gas. That was our shortage, not ammo. Then, without the cooling fan on the engine running, the inside quickly got like an oven. The transmission was the size of a barrel and at about 140 degrees, and the guns so hot they would cook off by themselves. It was a rather warm job. The empty brass (cartridge cases) burnt a lot of men, so you had to wrap a towel around your neck and keep your collar buttoned tight to avoid burns. All pockets were cut off — caught brass and held it against you. You had a choice, burn your fingers getting it out or burn your ass if you left it in. The empty brass catcher on the turret gun was just plain silly. You had to unzip the bag after every belt, open the turret signal port and dig the brass out with your bare hand because the bag was too small to use an asbestos mitten. Some cut

47

M4A3 STUART (1943)

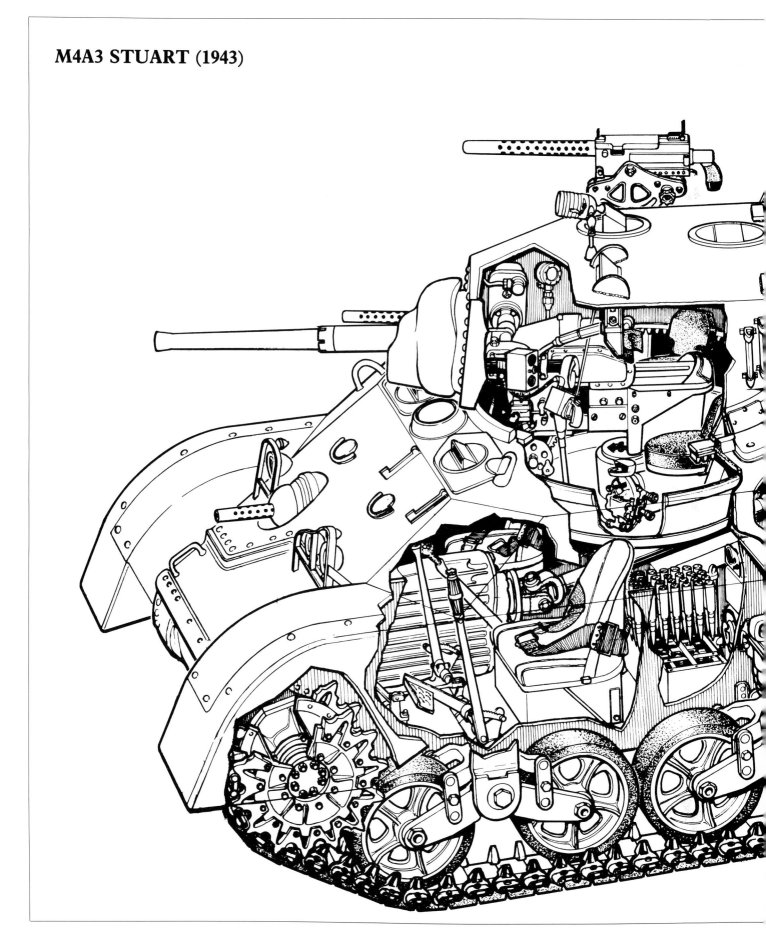

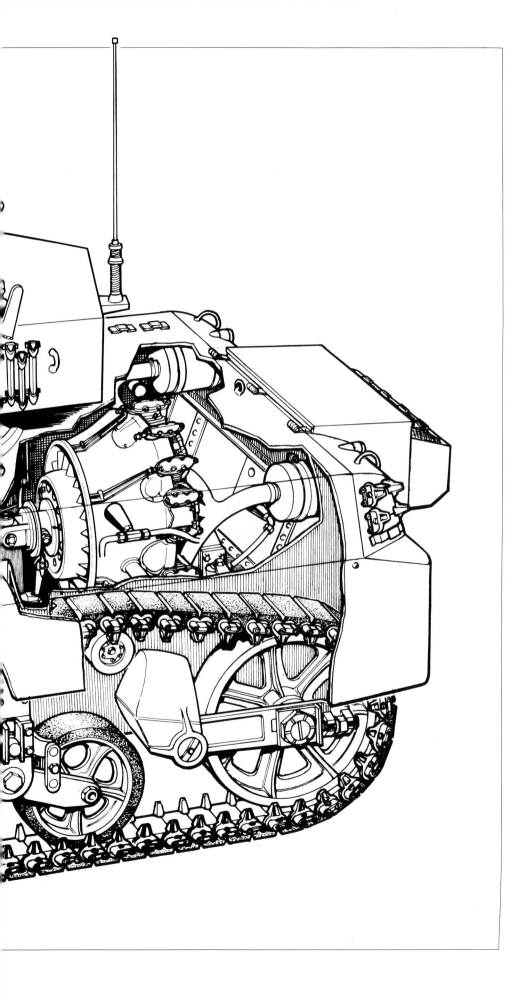

the bag off, others just unzipped it all the way around and let the brass run out. The driver and assistant driver [bow gunner] had a constant rain of hot brass. One other little problem — the empty brass jammed the clutch linkeage so you couldn't move. First thing you thought of was "we lost a track" when she wouldn't move. Then you had to double up and dig empty brass and stuff it into an empty ammo locker until you could free the clutch linkeage so that the tank would move. Very upsetting.

'You always lost men when you tried to leave a tank in action. We were fighting at close quarters and had to shoot the Japs off each others tanks. They would be up on top trying to kick the gas caps off so they could put a hand grenade in the tank. When we fueled up we dogged the caps on with a 3-pound hammer. My buddy caught one Jap in his sights. He ran down the front deck and off down the trail — a 37 mm at that short range was unbelievable. Hit him in the middle of the back and his arms and legs just flew off — kind of like shooting a gallon plastic jug full of water with an army rifle.

'The system we used to fight in the jungle — as we went in there would be three or four scouts walking right up with us, under the bustle. The tanks would try to line up abreast, sometimes only a yard apart. With all guns firing the brush was laid down like with a big wind. Then, as the fire slackened off it would straighten back up. As the tanks crept forward the Philippines would shoot anything they saw in the spider-holes, [Japanese trenches]. Each night as we pulled back out the Japs would move back into the area. Turned out to be a real killing ground — by the end of the month we had killed many Japs and had an area about the size of a football field blown clear of trees and brush. Our losses were one tank crew killed — track off and crew were burned during the night by Molotov cocktails. Two more from maintenance were killed retrieving a tank. One man from A Coy was killed by a sniper, he was on the firing line watching the action — curiosity killed the cat. We lost two tanks on Trail Eight, one to an anti-tank gun, other had the belly blown up. It must have been a limpet mine stuck on to it as it crossed a spider hole. . . . . A tank is blind at the best of times and when you get all wrapped up in jungle vines it is next to impossible to maneuver, but battle conditions are never ideal.

'Well, we lasted about four months until the surrender on Bataan. As totally screwed as everything was, I didn't think we did that bad. Pentagon War Dept plans said we would be done in 6 weeks. One last twist. The night

pines in early 1945 so they were thus both the first and the last M3s to see action in the Pacific area.

M3 Layout

Before dealing with the variants of the M3 Light Tank family, it is useful to describe the basic layout of the M3 Light Tank. There were three main components mounted on the chassis and running gear: the engine compartment which was at the rear; the fighting compartment containing the main armament and two of the crew (commander and gunner); at the front, the driving compartment with the driver and co-driver. Like the M2A4, the M3 had no turret basket which meant that the turret crew had no seats and had to move round with the turret as it traversed. This was not easy because the propeller shaft, which took the drive from the engine to the transmission, passed through the fighting compartment and impeded their movement. A turret basket was added to the M3A1 and later Marks, but in solving one problem this created another, as the basket obstructed the vital escape route between the driving and fighting compartments, making it impossible to get casualties through.

In his excellent little book on the Stuart Light Tank, Bryan Perrett (an ex-Captain, RAC) explains how, in Burma, the 7th Light Cavalry, who were equipped with M3A1, did not believe that the convenience of having the turret basket outweighed the risks involved, so they stripped them out, despite the fact that this meant that the turret crew had to stand, and, if necessary, perch on the propeller shaft housing to look out of their hatches. The M3 fighting compartment had only one exit — through the hatch on the top of the commander's cupola, another safety hazard if the tank 'brewed up' (caught fire). The M3A1 had no cupola and was fitted with hatches for both the commander and gunner.

The Commander As in any two-man turret, the commander not only had to command, but also load the guns and work the turret radio when fitted (M3A3 only), so he had plenty to do. On the M3 he had an *ad hoc* cupola on the left of the turret roof, so he stood to the left of the gun right behind the gunner, while in the M3A1 and M3A3 he was on the right of the 37 mm with a proper seat in the turret basket.

The Gunner The gunner was on the left of the combination gun mount (which of course mounted the 37 mm and .30 cal. Browning machine-gun), His main controls were relatively simple, *viz*: elevation and traverse.

On the gunner's right was an elevating

Top
An M3A3, showing clearly the larger, welded hull, which gave more stowage room for additional fuel tanks and ammunition stowage. This model was known by the British as the Stuart V.

Above
M3 fitted with a Maxson turret, mounting four .50-cal. Brownings. It was tested in 1942, but eventually rejected in favor of the same mounting on a half-track.

before we surrendered, 1st Tank Group was on the road just short of the airfield. The Japs held the northern edge. Our mission — cross the airfield and disrupt the Japs advance as much as we could. The very mission we had trained so long for. But

they canceled the attack, said it was too late. We went back to bivouac and burned our tanks. Silly note to end a war on. Right?'

As Knox relates, some tanks had to be abandoned at blown bridges or through breakdowns, and were then taken into Japanese service to be used for garrison duty. The remainder all had to be destroyed on the general surrender of the US forces in the Philippines and their crews then took part in the notorious 'Death March'. The captured Stuarts were used against the Americans by the Japanese during the fighting in the Philip-

Right
Field Marshal Smuts takes the salute as M3A1s (British Stuart IIIs) belonging to the South African Tank Corps march past in Johannesburg, June 1944, during a large 'Unite for Victory' rally, described as 'the greatest military spectacle in South Africa's history'.

Below
Pilot model of the M3A1, easily recognizable because of the absence of a commander's cupola. Later vehicles had all-welded hulls in addition to the cast/welded homogenous armor turret. The M3A1 eventually replaced the M3 on the production line.

wheel (+20 degrees elevation to −10 degrees depression) which incorporated a firing button in the centre for the 37 mm; an alternative method of elevation was by means of a-shoulder-piece; the elevating mechanism of the 37 mm and .30-cal. could be by the hand/shoulder or controlled by a gyrostabiliser, the aim of the latter being to maintain the position of both guns so as to assist the gunner in aiming and firing accurately while on the move. It controlled the guns in the vertical plane *only*. Crews did not like it as the gunner was, by virtue of his shoulder-piece, forced to conform to its movements, while the commander found difficulty reloading or dealing with stoppages, as the breeches of the guns were constantly moving up and down.

On the gunner's left there was a second handwheel for the general traversing of the turret, with another small traverse control wheel for final, fine laying. This latter control could move the gun only 10 degrees left or right and incorporated a firing plunger for the coax machine-gun. When powered traverse was introduced with the M3A1 the gunner had a spade grip incorporating a safety trigger, mounted to his left, on top of which were two electrical firing triggers for the 37 mm (left button) and coax machine-gun (right button). There was also a foot firing pedal for the 37 mm. Thus, to fire the gun normally (*i.e.* electrically) the gunner squeezed the safety trigger with his fingers and at the same time pressed down with his thumb on the left hand firing trigger. To fire manually he squeezed the safety trigger as before and, with his right thumb, pressed the hand firing button in the centre of the elevating wheel.

Sighting equipment varied slightly, being either a telescope and/or a periscope. On the M3A1 and M3A3 there was a periscope M4, also used for observation, and a telescope M40. On M3A1 and M3A3 there was a periscope M6, solely for observation, and on the M3A3 *only*, there was a telescope M54 for direct laying. Generally the gunner's telescope had a magnification of 1.44, a field of view of 9 degrees and was graduated from 600–3000 yds (graduated for AP shot M51, fired with a muzzle velocity of 2900 ft per sec,

Specifications	M3	M3A1	M3A3
Battle weight	27,4000 lbs	28,500 lbs	31,752 lbs
Length	14 ft 10¾ in	14 ft 10¾ in	14 ft 10¾ in
Height	8 ft 3 in	7 ft 6½ in	7 ft 6½ in
Width	7 ft 4 in	7 ft 4 in	8 ft 3 in
Armament main	One 37 mm M5 or M6 gun		
secondary	One coaxial .30-cal. Browing machine-gun		
	Two .30-cal. in sponsons		
Armor thickness, max/min	51 mm/10 mm	51 mm/10 mm	51 mm/10 mm
Engine	*Either* Continental W670, Petrol, 7-cylinder		
	or Guiberson T1020 diesel radial, 9-cylinder		
Max speed	36 mph	36 mph	36 mph
Road Radius	70 miles	70 miles	70 miles

which, in fact, stood little chance of penetrating any German tank even at its minimum range).

The driver The driver sat in the left bow of the tank, to the left of the transmission. On the M3 and M3A1 there were two panels of instruments, one in front of him and one between him and the co-driver. However, on the M3A3 the complete instrument panel was clustered in front of the driver, but could still be seen by his assistant. They included a speedometer, tachometer, engine oil pressure and temperature gauges, oil pressure warning light, voltmeter, ammeter, magneto and starting switches. His driving controls comprised: a foot accelerator pedal (on right of the clutch pedal) and a hand throttle; a clutch pedal operated by left foot; two steering levers one each side and in front of the driver's seat, which were also used for braking — pulling back simultaneously on both steering levers slowed or stopped the tank depending upon the effort applied. To keep the brakes on the driver had to turn knobs on the tops of the steering levers through 90 degrees, there were no other brakes provided; finally, a gearshift lever to the right of the driver (five forward, neutral and reverse gears).

Later Combat

M3 Light tanks went into action again in North Africa with the American 1st Armored Division as part of the 'Center Task Force' of Operation *Torch*, landing in the Oran area on 7–8 November 1942. Both armored regiments (1st and 13th) had one battalion of light tanks (the 1st Battalion in each case) and two battalions of mediums.

George F Howe wrote of the landings: 'Combat Command B had persuaded the Center Task Force that it could put its light tanks and some other armored vehicles including the self-propelled 105 howitzers of Battalion C, 27th Armored Field Artillery Battalion, on to the beaches in an unusual way. The medium tanks (M3 General Grants) had to be swung out from the transporters on to piers, presumably in a captured port like Arzew, but the light tanks were to roll out of the bows of modified, shallow-draft oil tankers on to pontoon treadway bridging, the method tested by the Division in Northern Ireland.'[2]

The Vichy authorities met the landing with heavy fire in some places, but Red Task Force, led by the Reconnaissance Company of 13th Armored Regiment (the first unit

to leave the beach), seized the airfield at Tafaraoui, thus denying it to the Vichy French air force. On the following day, Green Task Force took La Senia airfield, as the 1st Armored Division history relates: 'Col. Todd's force consisted of his own 1st Battalion, 13th Armored Regiment (less Companies A and B and a detachment from HQ Coy); two platoons of Coy B 6th Armored Infantry; one platoon of Coy C, 701st Tank Destroyer Battalion; and one platoon of Coy A, 16th Armored Engineers. In all, after leaving the infantry at road blocks in the Lourmel area, he had twenty light tanks and a smaller number of halftracks. Radio communication was very poor. Todd pushed east slowly during the afternoon, out of touch with Robinett's Command post even though it moved inland from the beachhead. The flying column broke through road blocks defended by French armored cars with 37 mm guns at Bou Tlelis and by 75 mm guns at Bredeah, and lost vehicles to various causes along the way. The force made a short night bivouac south of Misserghin. . . . Col. Todd's column

US tanks (Honeys) support British troops as they advance to new positions, somewhere in Tunisia, during their drive against the Axis forces.

moved out of bivouac at dawn and pushed along the northern edge of the Grand Sebkra to La Senia airfield. With seven Light Tanks and three or four tank destroyers, he quickly gained possession of La Senia and was ordered to destroy all French planes.'

Marine Tankers

In the South Pacific 1st Marine Division spearheaded the American counter offensive with its landing on Guadalcanal on 7 August 1942. 'The Old Breed' like all Marine Divisions now had its own Tank Battalion (1st Tank Battalion).

A history of the 1st Tank Battalion describes the landings thus: 'On the morning of 7 August 1942, units of the 1st Marine Division, reinforced, went ashore on the north side of Guadalcanal and the Islands of Tulagi, Florida, Gavutu and Tanambogo. Company A, 1st Tank Battalion was attached to Combat Group A (5th Marines, reinforced). The first wave of Combat Group A landed on Beach Red, Guadalcanal at 0910 [hours], meeting no

Stripped to the waist because of the heat, these USMC tankers clean out and 'bomb up' (fill up with ammo) their M3A1s on Bougainville in the Northern Solomons.

opposition on the beach. By 1130 the beachhead line on Beach Red was reported secured by Combat Group A, and shortly thereafter Combat Group B passed through and advanced toward the southwest, while Combat Group A moved forward toward the Tenaru River. The M3 light tanks of Companies A and B, 1st Tank Battalion were landed with the Combat Groups and moved to cover near the east boundary of the beachhead. They were not committed to action until the next day.

'At 0930, 8 August, Company A, 1st Tank Battalion supported the 1st Battalion, 5th Marines in an unopposed crossing of the Tenaru River. At 1330 these units reached the airfield (later designated as Henderson Field), and found it undefended by the Japanese. During the early morning of 21 August 1942, enemy forces estimated between 800 and 1000, well-equipped and well-armed, attempted to break through our lines at the mouth of the Ilu River, held by the 2nd Battalion, 1st Marines, and B Battery, 1st Special Weapons Battalion. 1st Battalion, 1st Marines crossed the river on the right flank and enveloped the enemy forces from the

rear. The fighting continued until about 1400. Five tanks from Company B, 1st Tank Battalion, crossed the sand spit at the mouth of the river and assisted in mopping up, using canister and machine-gun fire on enemy positions. Two tanks were disabled, one by an anti-tank mine, but the crews were rescued by the close supporting action of other tanks. Following the tank action, troops of the 1st Marines closed on the enemy position and mopped up the remaining resistance. The entire enemy force was destroyed except for a rear guard of about 100 men, which later was found to have stayed near Koli Point.'[3]

A Marine tanker with wide experience of the light tanks which took part in these initial operations is ex-Sergeant Major 'Vi' Viveiros of Oceanside, California who recalled his tanking days thus: 'My association and assignment with tanks began on requested transfer as a 'buck sergeant' from an infantry unit of 1st Marine Division in October 1941. . . . This was the beginning of the formation of the 1st Tank Battalion as an intrinsic infantry supporting arm of the division. During earlier years tanks were present within the Marine Regiments and at Brigade at Quantico, Va, and on maneuvers in the Caribbean. These light tanks were mainly experimental, manned for testing and evaluation by personnel of a company sized unit — by name: Separate Tank Company. Hardly if ever, did this unit participate in any tactical maneuvers with the Brigade components.

'Our training began immediately on M2A4/M3 light tanks . . . Generally speaking everything operated manually — from the selection and shifting of gears to the 360 degrees traverse of the turret and the elevation of the gun; plus, with no radio intercom system, touch signal had to be used between the tank commander to direct the driver in movement. Communication between tanks was possible with aircraft type radios. However, to limit air traffic, hand and flag signals were employed.

'This is the tank we used in the Guadalcanal operation (7 August to 9 December 1942). Little offensive action was seen initially by either of the two tank companies present. They were used mainly in a defensive role and located between the airfield and beach area of the division perimeter. From here it was possible to move quickly to deal with any counter-attack from the sea or paratroop landing on the airfield. All the tanks, at 25-yard intervals, were in a circular displacement, 'dug-in', with only the turrets above the ground surface, with our CP location in a coconut grove. The forward ends of these pits were graded to allow quick exit or entry. The purpose of this was mainly for maximum protection against aerial bombing or naval shelling that was constant during the early months of the campaign. All our digging — by pick and shovel — paid off, as neither company lost a tank although there were many close misses. ... being strictly a defensive perimeter, action was mainly in the form of extensive patrolling, but the tank crews spent much of their time in ground firing positions, supplementing the infantry machine-guns.

'There were two limited offensive actions. One involved a platoon of five tanks without any co-ordinated support, advancing from a sector of the perimeter across a large open area of thick grass. Three of the tanks were quickly knocked out by an anti-tank gun concealed on the far side where the heavy jungle continued. Of the two tanks that re-

Famous Stuart Recce AFV (on a Stuart 1 chassis), which belonged to the Indian 7th Light Cavalry in Burma. It was the command vehicle and its strange name had been given to it by the Regiment's CO — it means the nine of diamonds in card games. The original Stuart 1 tank had belonged to the 7th Hussars, being the *only* tank to reach India during the Retreat, having been towed across the Chindwin on a raft by a ferry boat captain.

turned, one, the platoon leader's, had taken a 37 mm hit dead center on the side of the turret that decapitated him. Nine of the crews of the other three tanks were killed and three escaped to safety. Of the second action, again only one platoon was involved in mopping up the remnants of a force of 700–800 Japs who had attempted to break through our lines in the east sector one night. By 1500–1600 hours, the foe had been annihilated, except for 15 POW, 13 of whom were wounded. Having boxed them up in a coconut grove just in from the beach, the tanks at random, ran up and down the grove between the trees. More enemy were crushed and mangled than shot, as evidenced by the remains of flesh entwined in the tank suspension. Two of the tanks were disabled in the action (blown track) but no personnel were lost.'

The next major action in which tanks of the 1st Tank Battalion took part was the Battle of Bloody Ridge, 13–14 September 1942. Although the enemy's main effort was along the ridge, he launched attacks against the Marine lines on the eastern and western flanks. At 2215, 13 September, a Japanese force attacked positions east of the airfield which were held by the 3rd Battalion, 1st

Marines, concentrating their efforts against K Company. This company, supported by mortars, artillery and tanks of the 1st Tank Battalion, repulsed the assault. The following morning, the CO of the 3rd Battalion ordered six tanks to sweep the grassy field in front of Company K's position, in order to prevent any attempt by the enemy to hide in the tall grass. The tanks moved up to the area at about 0945 hours, over the track from the airfield, and searched the tall grass thoroughly without incident.

At 1100 hours the tanks were again moved up and ordered to destroy enemy machineguns located in a native hut on the eastern side of the grassy plain. Meanwhile, the Japanese had moved German made 37 mm anti-tank guns into position along the wood's edge at the eastern side of the field. When the tanks were within fifty yards of the hut the anti-tank guns opened fire with armor-piercing and high explosive shells, knocking out three tanks. The crews of two were rescued, but one tank had toppled over into a stream, imprisoning the crew and thus making escape impossible. This tank was later salvaged, but the others were too badly smashed by armor piercing shells to be recommissioned.

The history of the 1st Tank Battalion,

A mine exploder T1 fitted onto an M3 (left side roller is missing).

already quoted, records: 'Shortly after the Battle of Bloody Ridge, the 1st Tank Battalion, then in Division reserve, was directed to "conduct intensive route and employment reconnaissance of areas in and adjacent to the position which lend themselves to tank action." On 18 September the 7th Marines, reinforced, arrived at Kukum to rejoin the 1st Marine Division, having been detached from the 3rd Marine Brigade, at Samoa, on 26 August 1942. Company C, 1st Tank Battalion rejoined its parent unit upon landing at Guadalcanal.'[4] 1st Tank Battalion went on to participate in the campaigns in New Guinea, New Britain, Peleliu and Okinawa.

Variants

Among numerous variants the following were the most important:

M3 Command tank This was normally a local modification which entailed removing the turret and substituting a welded box-like superstructure (very like the one on the M5 light tank which is mentioned later). Arma-

ment was a .50-cal. Browning machine-gun on a flexible mounting.

M3 or M3A1 flame thrower About twenty M3s were converted and used by the USMC in the Pacific, the 37 mm gun being replaced by a Satan flame gun, described shortly. Another type had a flame gun fitted in the ball mounting in place of the hull machine-gun.

Stuart Kangaroo This was the British conversion of the M3 into an APC by removing the turret and adding seats. Similar conversions produced both a recce and a command vehicle.

The main problem with all variants of the M3 series was the fact that the basic tank was too light and unstable for adaptation to special purpose uses like those devised for medium tanks. Thus, although there were versions of an AA tank, a mine exploder, a 75 mm Howitzer, a 3 in Gun, and others, none were successful and all these projects were eventually abandoned.

M3 and M3A1 with the Satan Flame Gun

In late January 1944, twenty Ronson Canadian vehicle flame-throwers were taken to the Central Pacific area by the US Fifth Amphi-

bious Corps. The Ronson flame-thrower had been designed to be mounted on the Universal Carrier. It weighed 1350 lbs complete with 72 gallons of fuel. The driving force for fuel ejection was derived from carbon dioxide and the fuel was ignited by an electric spark. After various trials it was decided to mount them in medium tanks but few mediums were available, and, as the M3 light tanks were being replaced by the new M5 light, it was decided to use them instead. The 37 mm gun was removed and replaced by the Ronson flame gun which was protected by a howitzer-like shroud and had a traverse of 180 degrees and elevation of −15 to +18 degrees. Four specially built fuel tanks were added which had a total capacity of 175 gals approximately two minutes of sustained fire.

After training all volunteer crews, twelve of these flame-throwers were issued to both the 2nd and 4th Marine Divisions and were landed in Saipan on 17 June 1944 (D + 2). They were employed there continuously until 13 July, and on 24 July were taken to Tinian by these divisions and employed with the assault wave. Tactically, twelve flame tanks and three light tanks formed a company. Four flame tanks and one light (lead) tank formed a platoon. Normally, a platoon was attached to

An M3A1 armed with the Satan flame gun in place of the 37 mm (facing), and two M5A1s belonging to D Coy, 4th Tank Battalion USMC. The Satan was produced in Hawaii, using the Canadian Ronson flame-throwing 20 M3s and M3A1s were converted to this role. Lt Col. R K Schmidt

a medium tank company which was in turn attached to a marine regiment.

During operations the light tanks remained in the rear ready to be called forward when it became necessary to neutralize a strong point, the mediums usually covering the flame tanks while they moved into firing positions. Initially, of course, COs were unfamiliar with the capabilities of the flame guns and so on the first day they were only used for mopping up. On the second day, however, they were used in the assault and thereafter remained in the front line being used more and more often. They fired on dugouts, canefields, buildings and caves. For example, when it was thought that a canefield hid snipers or machine-guns,

it was fired by the armored flame-thrower. On one occasion a flame tank attacked a building. A Japanese soldier with a light machine-gun started firing at the tank and the flame gunner gave one un-ignited burst which was aimed so accurately that it knocked the machine-gunner down. The next burst ignited and the building went up in flames. One operator claimed to have killed more than 130 Japanese with his flame thrower during the two operations. Another, having been ordered to destroy an enemy bomber located in a house, approached under covering fire from medium tanks and with his own machine-gun blazing. He fired the house, and shot and killed two enemy who ran out. Inside the bunker were ten others who were all apparently killed instantly, since they still occupied their firing positions. Another tank commander reported that when his flame tank was employed against a large cave, 250 Japanese surrendered; while in another area

150 yards square, 300–400 Japanese were flushed by a lone tank flame thrower.

During the landing on Tinian on 24 July 1944, the first wave to hit the beach were medium tanks, followed immediately by flame tanks. When resistance was met, the mediums opened fire, followed immediately by the flame tanks which reduced the positions. After the landing 400 burned bodies were found on the beach. A concrete pillbox which had held up the advance for a day was fired — un-ignited fuel was first fired into the position, then it was ignited, causing an intensely hot fire. No further resistance was met from that particular pillbox! At another point, the flame-thrower flushed out 200 Japanese.

Undoubtedly, the Satan flame guns proved their worth. However, since light tanks were so vulnerable to artillery and anti-tank weapons, it was decided that the flame thrower should be mounted in medium tanks for future operations.

56

5

The M5: The End of A Line

In mid-1941, the Ordnance Department began to get very concerned about a possible shortage of the Continental radial engines which powered the M3 light tank series. This was because they were competing with a similar demand from the mushrooming aircraft industry as the US Air Forces also rapidly expanded. This underlined the need to include various different types of power-plants in the tank programme, as well as bringing in additional manufacturers, which led to the introduction of the Guiberson diesel radial engine. It also led to a proposal by the Cadillac Division of General Motors, to build a new prototype light tank, which would be powered by twin Cadillac V-8 petrol automobile engines, and fitted with automatic transmission, the latter being a recent new development in the car industry.

At first the Ordnance Department were reluctant to change from radial air-cooled engines, but the need for more tank engines was acute, besides which tests soon proved that the Cadillac-powered model was superior to all the others. It was easier to start (remember what Joe Lee said about starting the M3), performed better when idling and the hydromatic transmission made driving much easier and far less tiring.

In October 1941, a Cadillac-powered light tank proved its reliability by driving the 500 miles from Detroit to the Aberdeen Proving Grounds (APG), without a hitch. Subsequent exhaustive testing at APG showed the new engine gave more power, was quieter, ran smoother and was available in large numbers.

In the course of installing their engine into the M3 light tank, Cadillac had made so many design changes that, when the design was officially accepted, the tank was given a new model number — M4. Later, this was changed to M5 in order to avoid confusion with the M4 Sherman medium tank. Another major advantage of the new M5 was the fact that the automatic transmission occupied less space than the synchromesh system, so it did not project into the fighting compartment

quite so far, thus allowing space for a much better designed turret basket assembly to be fitted.

At the same time as these engine and transmission developments were taking place, a revolution in tank armor was under way. In the 1930s tanks had been made of face-hardened plate, fixed together with thousands of rivets and inevitably producing box-like structures which were easily penetrated by enemy tank and artillery fire. Ordnance had therefore to develop a radically new type of homogeneous armor which could be much thicker and permitted welding of joints rather than rivets — greatly speeding up production as well as producing better armored protection on the battlefield.

As the Ordnance history puts it: 'Flat, angular surfaces gradually disappeared as cast hulls and turrets with rounded contours — less vulnerable to enemy fire — came into

The M3E3, which was a converted M3 light tank and was the prototype for the M5 light tank series, so called to prevent confusion with the Medium Tank M4, the Sherman, which was then in full production.

production. . . . The armor on 1945 tanks was as different from that on 1939 models as the 90 mm gun was from the 37 mm on pre-war tanks. More than any other factor, it accounted for the doubling and tripling of tank weights, for armor accounted for more than half of the weight of World War II tanks.'

In the light tank series, the new model with a fully welded homogeneous armor hull was designated the M3A1E1. Clearly it was non-sensical to continue these two projects in isolation and in November 1941, they were merged under the M5 designation.

The M5 was put into production and the first combat bound tank came off the Cadillac assembly line in Detroit at the end of March

1942. In July the same year, the Cadillac plant at Southgate, California, produced its first M5 tank, while the Massey-Harris Company, farm implement makers, were also brought into light tank production. They took over the former Nash-Kelvinator plant at Racine, Wisconsin, and with Cadillac's aid, quickly began producing the M5. In October 1943, American Car and Foundry (ACF) also switched to M5 production, stopping building the M3.

The changeover from building cars to building tanks had been speedily accomplished at the Cadillac plant, but even there they had their problems: 'Makeshifts were the order of the day, for new equipment specially designed for tank production was virtually unobtainable. Because jigs and fixtures, so essential to mass production take a long time to make, Cadillac did without them at the start, building its first tanks almost by hand.'[1]

In September 1942, the M5A1 was standardized in order to bring up the M5 to the same standard as the much improved M3A3. A number of the new features were in common with the M3A3 and included: a new turret which incorporated space for the radio installation in a rear 'bulge'; larger hatches for both the driver and co-driver; an improved mount for the main gun; improved all round vision devices; an escape hatch in the hull floor; dual traverse controls for the turret which enabled the commander to traverse on to a target; detachable sand shields; a shield on the turret to protect the AA machine-gun mounting, a very late modification. The M5A1 replaced the M5 on the production lines from early 1943, by which time some 2074 M5s had been produced.

A relatively small number of M5s and M5A1s were in British service during 1943–44 and were used in North-West Europe only. The British gave both AFVs the same designation, 'Stuart VI'.

General Description

Both the M5 and M5A1 had four man crews and were equipped with dual driving controls. They were powered by two eight cylinder, 90 degree, V-type liquid-cooled engines, located in the rear of the hull. The flywheel end of each engine was connected to a hydramatic transmission. The propeller shaft from each power plant went forward through the fighting compartment, to a transfer unit lo-

Above
Nice shot of an M5 pilot model with fixed bow machine gun negotiating rough country at speed.

Left
An M5 negotiates thick mud while on training. Note the five-pointed star and white stripe around the turret which was one of six different National Identification Symbols used on US military vehicles.

Above left
An M5, belonging to an American cavalry recce unit stationed in the United Kingdom, breasts a crest during training in spring 1943.

Above right
Excellent view of an M5A1 during pre-D Day training. The commander is presumably throwing a grenade into a suspicious looking enemy position. Note the short windcheater jacket worn by tank crews (and highly prized by other arms!).

Left
Rear view of the M5A1, note the larger turret 'bulge' at the rear to accommodate the radio set (cf: the M3A3), and the larger access hatches.

cated at the right of the driver's seat. The transmission, plus the two-speed transfer unit, provided six forward and one reverse gears. They were wired for radio installation and for an intraphone system within the tank.

The basic hull armor plate was a completely welded structure, except for portions of the front, top and rear, which were removeable for servicing. Armor on the front was $1\frac{1}{8}$ inches thick (apart from the nose casting which was $1\frac{1}{2}$ ins), and the sides of the fighting compartment were also $1\frac{1}{8}$ inches thick, while the sides and rear of the engine compartment, and hull roof were 1 inch thick.

There were two driver's hatches located in

59

Specifications	M5	M5A1
Combat weight (with rubber tracks)	33,138 lbs	33,484 lbs
		34,684 lbs (with steel tracks)
Overall width	7 ft $4\frac{1}{2}$ in	7 ft $4\frac{1}{4}$ in
Overall height	7 ft $6\frac{1}{2}$ in	7 ft $6\frac{1}{2}$ in
Overall length	14 ft $6\frac{3}{4}$ in	14 ft $6\frac{3}{4}$ in
Engine horse power at 3,400 rpm	110	110
Armament	One 37 mm gun and one .30-cal. machine-gun M1919A5 fixed, in combination gun mount M23, in the turret; one .30-cal. machine-gun, M1919A4 flexible in ball mount in bow; one .30-cal. machine-gun, M1919A4 flexible AA, on turret roof; 123 rounds of 37 mm ammunition were carried (39 HE, 65 AP and 19 cannister).	
Radio	SCR 508 (SCR 506 in command vehicles).	
Fuel capacity	89 gal	86 gal
Max speed	40 mph	40 mph
Road Range (at 25 mph)	180 miles	172 miles
Cross Country (at 10 mph)	135 miles	86–129 miles
Max vertical obstacle	2 ft	2 ft
Max fording depth	3 ft	2 ft 6 in
Max ditch crossing	5 ft 5 in	5 ft 5 in

the fighting compartment roof and two turret hatches in the turret roof. Access to the engine compartment was via two hinged double doors in the rear of the hull. There was also an escape door in the hull floor behind the assistant driver (M5A1 only).

The M5 in Combat

The M5 first went into action with units of the 2nd Armored Division, during Operation Torch, in the Casablanca area of the North African coast. Task Force 'Goal-post' was to seize and hold the airport at Lyautey and Sale and cover the northern flank of the operation. It was the smallest of the three task forces, was commanded by Brig.-Gen. Lucian Truscott, and consisted of the 60th Regimental Combat Team of 9th Infantry Division and 1st Battalion Combat Team of 66th Armored Regiment, 2nd Armored Division.

The planners estimated that the French would be defending the Port Lyautey area with a regiment of infantry, twelve anti-tank guns, artillery and engineers. Reinforcements would be available from the Spanish Moroccan border towns of Meknes and Rabat and included two more infantry regiments, a tank battalion (forty-five tanks) and some 1200 mechanized cavalry. All were able to reach Lyautey by D + 4, so it was essential for the Task Force to get their tanks and anti-tank guns ashore as early as possible.

Two plans had been drawn up, the first was for a single landing south of the airport and then for a move as a complete unit. The advantage of this plan was that it was very simple indeed. However, the problems were that the likely enemy opposition would be about the same strength and that it would take most of the day, even in good weather, to land all the troops. In the alternative plan, the Americans would land at several places and advance on the airport from numerous directions. The advantages of the speed and surprise of this second plan had to be balanced against its added complexity and the fact that the enemy could be in superior numbers at any of the landing points.

Truscott went for the second and more daring plan. The armor landing team was to land inside the breakwater at Port Lyautey, on orders, about 0750 hours, on 8 November

1942. Their mission was to protect the southern flank against enemy approaching from that direction. Also, as the reserve force, they had to be ready to assist in the attacks to secure the airports at Port Lyautey, Rabat-Sale and Sibi-Yahia, and the radio station at Rabat-Sale. The armored battalion would have one reinforced infantry company in direct support. The 1st Armored Landing Team personnel were on the *John Penn*, the light tanks on the *Electra*. The Armored Battalion was to land as quickly as possible after dawn, directly after the infantry assault battalions.

It was the surf rather than the French which hampered the landing. Three of the landing craft bringing the tanks and other AFVs ashore were swamped and a light tank, a scout car and a half-track were lost. The light tanks had been sealed for the amphibious operation with compounds which contained fish oils, and one theory was that the crew were asphyxiated by the smell because the tank motored in a big semi-circle on leaving the landing craft, re-entering the breakers and going on into deep water, where it disappeared with the complete crew still aboard. Landing progress was slow thereafter and only six or seven tanks had reached the shore by nightfall.

The armored commander, Lt-Col. Harry Semmes, was ordered to the southern flank to take command of infantry and anti-tank units there and the following morning fought his initial action, the first in which 2nd Armored Division took part in World War II. Semmes had his tanks in good positions and about 0430 hours, fourteen French tanks (old Renaults) were seen moving north along the Rabat-Port Lyautey road. Pulling back into defilade positions behind a low ridge, the American tankers opened fire when the opposition came in range and forced them to retreat to a eucalyptus grove which the Navy then shelled. But Semmes had his problems. The M5s had been issued with new radios just before leaving the States but had not had a chance to calibrate them or maintain them properly because wireless silence had been

imposed for the entire voyage over. In addition, the tank guns had not been bore-sighted (this is the alignment of the telescopic sight with the axis of the bore of the gun so that one is certain to hit the target aimed at with the sights) and crews had to use trial and error methods of aiming.

After repulsing this first enemy tank attack there was a lull for about an hour before the enemy attacked again, this time with infantry on their own at about 0600 hours. The small force once again repulsed the enemy and then, for a second time, beat off a French tank attack. Four enemy tanks were knocked out, Semmes himself accounting for two of them. The French tank gunnery was of a high standard as was evidenced by two shells actually embedded in the front slope armor of Semme's M5!

The infantry too did their fair share of fighting and their history recounts one story that shows just what can be done in an emergency and features Lt Dushane and Corporal Czar of the 2nd Infantry Battalion. Their unit was being driven out of its positions by enemy tanks and the Americans had no anti-tank guns or artillery ... not even a grenade! As the 9th Division history relates: 'Standing near the intrepid pair was a captured anti-tank gun. Its breech had been removed partly before being abandoned by the French, but that deficiency did not stop the two "Go-Devils". Although the weapon was in full view of the approaching enemy Dushane and Czar manned it; Czar aimed the piece at the advancing armor, while Lt Dushane set off the shells by firing at the base of each projectile with his Tommy gun. Continuing to fire they destroyed one tank and halted the attack. Cpl Czar miraculously escaped without injury, but Lt Dushane died while operating the gun.'

The tempo of the action continued to increase and at about 0815 hours some ten tanks from C Company 70th Tank Battalion, arrived just in time to help deal with a determined attack by thirty-two French tanks which were attempting to break through to the beachhead area. The American tanks held them, then counter-attacked, driving them back some three miles and forcing them to abandon twenty-four of their tanks. All in all it was a most successful action albeit against a poorly equipped enemy force with out of date

Top
A late model M5A1 (note the AA machine gun shield), belonging to 43rd Tank Battalion of 12th Armored Division, in Neustadt soon after the town had surrendered.

Left
Engineers camouflaging an M5 with whitewash so that it will blend into the snowy background in France, January 1945.

armor. 2nd Armored did not experience such heavy fighting in North Africa as did 1st Armored Division which rapidly showed just how useless light tanks were against the German mediums and heavies. This led to a considerable reduction of light tanks strength in armored divisions and their replacement by mediums. However, light tanks were still used to provide fire support for set piece attacks by mechanized infantry, and were, of course, ideal for the type of work carried out by reconnaissance units of the mechanized cavalry, where their mobility and speed came to the fore.

Conrad Mueller of Company D, 37th Tank Battalion, 4th Armored Division told the writer that his M5s were used ' . . . mainly as point for the Combat Command in conjunction with the Recon, which consisted of Peeps and armored half-tracks with .50-cal. MGs as their main armament. We were also used as flank protection when medium tanks were engaged; and to escort battalion supply

Above left
An M5 command vehicle. This had the turret removed and a boxlike superstructure put in its place, complete with a .50 cal. on a flexible mount. It was then used as a runabout' for senior officers. This one belonged to Brig. Gen. George Read, Asst Division Commander of 6th Armored Division. On the back of his AFV are two German POWs. The location was Zweibrucken, Germany in March 1945.

Far left
A good shot of a Culin hedgerow cutter, which was used in Normandy to cut through the bocage hedges and undergrowth, June 1944. Here a Belgian family greet American tankers in Rongy on the Franco-Belgian border. The tank belongs to 113th Cavalry Recon Unit.

Left
Training for the invasion. Two Howitzer Motor Carriage M8, which was armed with a 75 mm howitzer, on exercise in England in May 1944. The M8 was used for close support and was ideally suited to this role.

Above
One and a half miles from the Dutch border, M8s belonging to a cavalry recon unit prepare to engage enemy near Heure-le-Roman, Belgium in October 1944.

columns and Div. Trains. Another frequent duty was road blocks at exits of towns the Combat Command had neutralised. However, in tank versus tank battles their little 37 mm shell would bounce off the Tiger, Panther, and the Panzer IV, even at point blank range — 'like peas off a tin pot' is the way one frustrated 37 mm gunner explained it to the writer.

In the Pacific it was quite another story. In many places they were the only tanks available. The 4th Tank Battalion of 4th Division USMC, for example, were equipped with M5A1s when they took part in the battles of Kwajalein (1–2 February 1944), Saipan (15 June–9 July 1944) and Tinian (24 July–1 August 1944). The M5A1 was quite capable of dealing with the Japanese light and medium tanks, and provided valuable support both in its main role as a gun tank and when fitted with other devices.

Variants
Among the variants which saw service the most successful were:

M5 Command tank Basic M5 with turret removed and a box-like superstructure fitted, with a .50-cal. Browning machine-gun in a flexible mount.

M5 Dozer Basic M5 with turret removed and fitted with a dozer blade at the front end.

T8 recce vehicle M5 with turret removed and a .50-cal. Browning machine-gun, fitted on a ring mounting. Some had extra storage racks plus a rack for carrying land mines.

Howitzer Motor Carriage M8 Basic M5 on which the normal turret was replaced by a larger all-round traversing open-topped turret in which was mounted a 75 mm howitzer. The gun could be elevated from −20 degrees to +40 degrees. Forty-six rounds of 75 mm ammunition were carried. The all-up weight increased to 36,000 lbs. Cadillac built nearly 1800 M8s between September 1942 and January 1944 and they were used to equip the HQ Companies of medium tank battalions, until replaced by the 105 mm-howitzer.

Other M5s had the E7–7 flame gun fitted in place of the main gun; the Culin hedgerow cutter — used to cut through 'bocage' hedgerows and undergrowth; or loudhailer and PA equipment for Psy-warfare.

6

An Airborne Tank: The M22 Locust

A New Dimension to Warfare

On 9 April 1940 the Germans invaded Norway and Denmark. Although the majority of their landings in Norway were by sea — two mountain and five infantry divisions forming the main seaborne striking force — valuable support was provided by German paratroopers, who, for example, captured airfields at Oslo and Stavanger. These operations and later ones in Holland and Belgium, where German paratroopers landed behind Allied lines in gliders on top of Fort Eban Emael, came as a nasty shock to the Allies, despite the fact that the use of airborne forces was by no means unknown, even before the war — witness the Russian use of paratroopers on maneuvers and of airborne tanks in taking over Besserabia. One major disadvantage of such a force of paratroopers was the fact that they could not carry heavy weapons on their bodies — even their machine-guns had to be separately parachuted — while larger caliber weapons had to be flown in later. And they landed with no form of mobility other than their own two feet. Clearly, if these troops could be provided both with transport and armored support, then their fighting potential could be greatly enhanced.

Developments of An Airborne Tank

With this in mind, the Ordnance Department, in February 1941, held a meeting with representatives of the General Staff (G-4), the Armored Force and the US Army Air Corps, to consider the possibility of developing a special lightweight tank together with an aircraft to carry it. Design studies began for a tank of about $7\frac{1}{2}$ tons, which the Air Corps confirmed could be air transported and airlanded by a suitable aircraft. Several designs were considered and the one submitted by the Marmon-Herrington Company was considered the best.

A pilot model, designated the Light Tank T9 (Airborne), was approved in autumn 1941 and was followed in January 1942 by a con-

tract for two additional pilot models. The T9 looked very like a miniature Sherman tank. It had a crew of three and mounted a 37 mm gun with a co-axial .30-cal. machine-gun, plus two more .30-cal. machine-guns in the bow. The hull was welded and the maximum armor thickness was 1 inch. It was quickly found

Top
The second pilot model, designated the T9E1, which incorporated various improvements including an easily removable turret to make air transportation easier.

Above
Close-up of the Locust, looking through the driver's open hatch into the turret. The ground mounting for the .30-cal. machine-gun is strapped on the mudguard.

that the original weight limit could not be achieved and so it was increased to 7.9 tons with the agreement of both the Army Air Corps and the British, who were by now also very interested in the project.[1]

The new pilot model, designated T9E1 was completed in November 1942 and sent to Aberdeen Proving Ground for testing. A second pilot, which was completed shortly afterwards, was sent to England for testing.

Meanwhile, in April 1942, production of the T9E1 had been approved, even before

A total of 830 M22s were built between March 1943 and February 1944 by Marmon-Herrington, but were never used by the US Army in combat principally because they lacked a suitable glider. These three photographs show all round views of the little 7.7-ton airborne tank.

development and standardization was complete, the first production vehicles coming off the line in December 1942. The total order was for 1900 airborne tanks, but only 830 were built before production was cancelled. Extensive testing took place in 1943 and 1944, including flight tests in C-54s and these resulted in several essential modifications being made. In August 1944, after production had ceased, the T9E1 was adopted as a limited standard vehicle and redesignated the M22.

Several hundred of these airborne tanks were shipped overseas to Britain and to US forces. However, the only unit to use them in action was the British 6th Airborne Armored Reconnaissance Regiment (AARR), commanded by Lt-Col. Stewart 13th/18th Hussars and comprising men from many armored regiments. A short article in *Pegasus* (Britain's Airborne Forces magazine) explained that no other unit could boast such an assortment of different cap badges and to make matters more complicated the men wore black tank berets whilst working on their AFVs and red airborne berets at all other times.

Initially the regiment contained a tank squadron of five troops of four Tetrarch tanks each, plus a recce squadron of four troops of Bren carriers and scout cars. They took part in both Operation 'Overlord' and the Battle of the Bulge, after which their establishment was

Above
An interesting photograph showing how the M22 (less its turret) was fixed to the belly of a C-54 cargo aircraft.

Below
Two members of the three man crew of a Locust doubling from the glider (just visible over their left shoulders).

changed to two recce squadrons each of four recce troops and one tank troop. The tanks were now M22 Locusts which, once the follow-up land elements arrived, were supposed to be exchanged for heavier Cromwells. There was also a support squadron of medium machine-guns (MMGs) and 4.2-in mortars.

Operations in the Ardennes and in Holland were ideal for settling down the new establishment and the MMGs, mortars and tanks were given plenty of opportunity to weld themselves into the Divisional fire plan. The next

operation was the Rhine-Crossing in which twelve Locusts, together with the 4.2-in mortars, went in by air.

Here is how C L Collins explained their part in Operation 'Varsity' in his article 'Flying Tanks' also published in *Pegasus*: 'This time only about half of each unit in the Division were taken back to England. This was all in preparation for the crossing of the Rhine. The AARR left behind trucks and other non-airborne equipment. These and the men were to cross the Rhine with other

A production M22 Locust in British service, with its 37 mm fitted with a Littlejohn adaptor.

ground troops whilst those that returned once more to Larkhill found that they had a new type of tank to take on the flight to the Rhine. It was the Locust, an American-built, solid-cast turret affair, mounting a 37 mm and a Browning machine-gun as an equivalent to the two-pounder and Besa machine-gun of the Tetrarch.

'On 24 March 1945, the 6th Airborne Divison landed on the far bank of the River Rhine. It was on this day that the tank, commanded by Sergeant 'Doc' Dawson, with him and his crew inside, fell from the glider as it crossed the river. The glider landed safely with most of its flooring missing. The tank and its crew were found some months later deep in the mud at the edge of the Rhine.

'Shortly after the landings we gave the Locusts away to the Para boys and continued with the Cronwells. Everyone was amazed with the speed and length of the advances of the 6th Airborne Division.'

The twelve Locusts were in fact reduced by 50 percent during landing by enemy fire, but those that remained gave a good account of themselves. One tank, for example, although it was immobilised outside the perimeter, is reputed to have killed over a hundred Germans. An interesting point which emerged from the briefing of DD Sherman tank commanders employed in the amphibious crossing of the Rhine was a special warning by GOC 6th Airborne Division that a small number of Locusts would be operating with

his troops and would the Shermans please not shoot them up by mistake!

Although the Locust could be carried in the C-54A, the tank itself possessed many limitations, for example: the armor was too thin even to keep out .50-inch AP ammunition; its engine developed only very low horsepower (162 hp); its range was limited as only 57 gallons of fuel were carried; its gun, as we have already seen with other light tanks, was far too small in caliber to deal effectively with enemy tanks; it had little space for either cargo or crew; and, probably most damning of all, it had a poor overall mechanical reliability. And of course landing, reassembling (the turret had to be taken off before loading into a C-54), and driving it from the nearest airfield which could handle C-54s, to the scene of combat — anything from one to one hundred miles — took so long that the enemy had plenty of time to bring up more powerful AFVs to deal with it.

Littlejohn Adaptor

One interesting modification made to some of the M22s sent to England, was the installation of the Littlejohn Muzzle Adaptor on the 37 mm M6 gun. Using this device the AP shot was squeezed down by about one third while passing through the adaptor which thus increased the muzzle velocity. A similar device was used successfully on the 2-pounder guns of the Tetrarch, Valentine Mk V and on Daimler armored cars.

Other Models

One of the M22s was rebuilt as the T10 Light Tractor (airborne) designed to carry five men and tow the 105 mm airborne howitzer, but this project was given up in 1943. Another project which did not even get beyond the drawing board was for a T9E2 Light Tank, armed with an 81 mm breech loading howitzer.

M22 Specifications

Crew	3
Combat weight	16,452 lbs
Length	12 ft 11 in
Width	7 ft 4½ in
Height	4 ft 1 in
Engine	Lycoming 0-435T air-cooled 6-cylinder, petrol (162 hp)
Transmission	Marmon Herrington synchromesh 4FIR.
Steering	Controlled differential
Armament	One 37 mm M6 gun and one .30-cal. machine-gun
Armor	Cast turret: 1 in all round; welded hull: 1 in front, ½ in rear and belly
Max speed	40 mph
Radius of action	135 miles.

7

The Pick of The Bunch: The M24 Chaffee

T7/M7

As the war progressed it became clear that the Stuart series of light tanks were neither properly armed nor armored for survival on the modern battlefield, and that there was therefore a need for an up-gunned light tank with increased protection. In fact, the idea of having a more powerful light tank to replace the M2A4 and M3 designs had been considered as early as autumn 1940. A few months later, in January 1941, this need was translated into a definite requirement which stated that the tank should be a 14-tonner, with a low silhouette, armor of 38 mm maximum thickness and mounting a 37 mm gun. Two pilot models were designed at the Rock Island Arsenal. The first, designated the T7, was to have a welded hull, a cast turret and modified vertical volute suspension. The second pilot, the T7E1, would be of riveted construction, with a cast/welded turret and horizontal volute suspension. In fact the T7E1 was never completed because riveted armor went out of favor, but the chassis was still used for transmission and suspension trials, powered by the Continental engine.

Following on from the building of a wooden mock-up of the T7, Rock Island Arsenal were asked to construct three more prototypes, designated the T7E2, T7E3 and T7E4, to test different armor, engine and transmission configurations. Of these, the T7E2 showed the most potential — it had a cast hull, top and turret and a Wright R-975 engine. The design was approved in December 1941, but while the pilot model was being built it was decided to up-gun it to 57 mm. This gun, an adaptation of the British 6-pdr, was to be fitted to the Canadian-built Ram tank, so a Ram turret ring was incorporated and the tank completed in June 1942.

The Armored Force later asked if it could be modified to take a 75 mm gun and this was also agreed, although it meant that the turret had to be re-designed. The other major change during development was an increase in the armor thickness to 63 mm which put up

Top
The wooden mockup of another prototype of the T7 series, designated the T7E2, is seen here beside an M3 — one can see how large the light tank was getting.

Above
Pilot model for the light tank series T7 was the first prototype T7, which was to have a welded hull, cast turret, modified vertical volute suspension and 15½ in wide tracks.

Right
While the T7E2 pilot model was being built it was decided to fit it with a more powerful main armament — the 57 mm T2 gun which was an adaptation of the 6-pdr from the Canadian-built Ram tank.

the tank weight to 25 tons, thus effectively taking it out of the light tank class! It was therefore reclassified as the Medium Tank M7 in August 1942 and standardized, an order for 3000 vehicles being placed with the Inter-

national Harvester Co., production to begin in December 1942. Meanwhile, the pilot model had been further tested at the Armored Force HQ at Fort Knox, who found that it was grossly underpowered. Its combat weight with crew and full battle stowage was now 29 tons, so work on a re-engined model, the M7E1 was begun.

While this saga was taking place, the Sherman M4 medium tank had gone into full production as the standard medium and the Ordnance Board rightly queried with the Armored Force the need for having the M7 as well. The Armored Force saw the wisdom of this and production was halted after only a handful of M7s had been produced. The work on the M7E1 was also stopped and the T7/M7 series declared obsolete. The M7 was thus never used by the US Army.

T24/M24

Despite this fiasco, the need for a better armored light tank with a more powerful gun was still apparent, so the Ordnance Department began work in conjunction with Cadillac, the makers of the M5 series, to design a completely new light tank which would incorporate the best features of all the previous designs, including everything that had been learnt from the T7/M7 program. Cadillac went ahead with a pilot model, designated the T24. This used twin Cadillac liquid-cooled engines and the hydramatic suspension of the M5. It mounted a lightweight M5 75 mm gun which had been developed from a heavy aircraft cannon designed for use in the B-25 Mitchell bomber. It had a concentric recoil system which thus saved space in the turret and was not as heavy as the normal M3 75 mm gun. A weight limit of 18 tons was set as the target weight of the tank, which meant that the maximum armor thickness would have to be no more than 25 mm.

The first pilot model, the T24, was completed in October 1943 and was so successful that Ordnance immediately authorized a production order for 1000 AFVs, which they later raised to 5000. Production started in March 1944 at the Cadillac and Massey-Harris plants, M5 production ceasing at these plants simultaneously. In all they produced 4731 M24s, including variants. First deliveries were made to the US Army in late 1944 and the first M24s, or Chaffees as they were called after the great General Adna Chaffee, 'Father of the Armored Force', saw action in winter 1944 in Europe. Interestingly, it was the British, with their love of nicknames, who first called the M24 the Chaffee, the name then being adopted by the US Army.

M24 Description

The light tank M24 carried a crew of four — commander, gunner, driver and assistant driver, the latter moving up into the turret and serving as loader when the tank was in action. It was, of course, also possible to have a permanent five man crew when manpower allowed. The layout was normal, with a driving compartment in the front, fighting compartment in the centre and engine compartment in the rear. Dual controls were provided, one for the driver, and one for the assistant driver to be used in an emergency.

The tank was driven by two eight-cylinder, 90 degrees V-type liquid-cooled Cadillac engines, through two hydramatic transmissions, a transfer unit with mechanically selected speed ranges — two forward and one reverse — a controlled differential for steering and braking which was located in the front of the hull, two final drives, and connecting propellor shafts. Wide steel block tracks, 16 inches wide, provided the means of traction. Torsion arm suspension was used for the dual track wheels, and included a compensating wheel at the rear of each side to keep track tension constant regardless of obstacles.

The hull was a completely welded structure, except for portions of the front, top and floor, which were removable for servicing. The hull was divided into two compartments: the fighting and driving compartment at the front and the engine compartment at the rear. These compartments were separated by a bulkhead extending from side to side and from the roof down to the bulkhead extensions, which in turn extended forward far enough to cover the transfer unit. The front of the hull sloped downwards at the top and upwards at the bottom to form a 'V'. The sides of the hull sloped inwards at the bottom. Lifting eyes were provided. The fighting compartment comprised a turret of approximately 60 inches inside diameter, mounted on a continuous ball bearing mounting, with 360 degrees traverse by means of either a handwheel or a hydraulic mechanism. The 75 mm gun and a coaxial .30-cal. Browning machine-gun were mounted in the turret, with elevation from −10 to +15 degrees. A second .30-cal. was mounted in the hull on the assistant driver's side and a .50-cal. Anti-Aircraft machine-gun was pintle mounted on top of the turret. The tank could be fitted with a dozer blade as necessary.

The Chaffee in Action

The M24 entered service with the US Army in

M24 Specifications

Battle weight	40,500 lbs
Length	18 ft (16ft 4½ in excluding gun)
Width	9 ft 4 in
Height	7 ft 3 in (4 ft 11 in to hull top)
Armament main	One 75 mm M6 gun, with 48 rounds of ammunition stowed
secondary	Two .30-cal. machine-guns and one .50-cal. AA machine-gun
Armor thickness, max/min	25 mm/9 mm
Engine	Cadillac Twin 44T24 petrol (110 hp each engine)
Max speed	35 mph
Road Radius	100 miles
Fording depth	3 ft 4 in
Vertical obstacle	3 ft 4 in
Trench crossing	8 ft

All-round views of a standard production M24 Chaffee, the best US light tank of the war. With its 75 mm gun (adapted from the heavy aircraft cannon used in the B-25G Mitchell bomber) it came into increasing use in the closing months of the war and remained the standard US light tank for many years afterwards.

winter 1944, during the Battle of the Bulge. One of the first units to get them was 740th Tank Battalion, which took over two M24s quite by chance during the ensuing 'flap'. The 740th was one of four tank battalions of the 9th Armored Group that had been training for the highly secret Canal Defence Light (CDL) role, a project to mount powerful searchlights on M3 medium tanks to illuminate the battle-field and blind the enemy (*see* Chapter 8). The project was abandoned later in 1944 and the CDL tanks put into storage. 740th were due to be converted back to a standard tank battalion, but at the time of the German offensive in the Ardennes had not yet received any Shermans. On 18 December 1944 they were ordered to bolster up a task force in the defence of the main First Army Ordnance Depot at Aywaille, which was under the command of Col. Lynde.

When the CO of the tank battalion reported to him and explained that he had no tanks, Lynde ordered the Ordnance Vehicle Park to issue to the tankers 'anything the men could drive or shoot'. They found about fifteen medium tanks and worked all night making them combat ready. The next morning they also acquired an assortment of tank destroyers, assault guns, light tanks (including the two M24s that had just arrived from the States).

Here is how their battalion history, written by Lt-Col. George K Rubel, recalls the incident under a chapter entitled 'Von Rundstedt's breakthrough battle of the Ardennes'.

'At 1245 hours on the 18th of December we received a telephone call from Lt-Col. Cox, Assistant Armored Officer, First US Army, to the effect that things were bad in the break-through area and were rapidly becoming worse. He said that a good many outfits had been completely overrun and that von Rundstedt was gaining momentum rapidly. It wasn't definitely known how wide the break-through was because communication had been out in a good many places. Part of this communication tangle was caused by the over-running of unit CPs. The rest of it had been caused by German paratroopers who had been dropped in the rear. Col. Cox stated that the General wanted us to send a reinforced company to protect Ordnance installations in the vicinity of Aywaille, Belgium, which was located on the Amblève River 8–10 miles SW of Spa. This company was to move as quickly as possible to Sprimont, Belgium, an Ordnance Vehicle Depot, draw any kind of combat vehicles we thought it could use — then take up stations where it could delay the enemy.

'I had alerted the Battalion the night before on suspicion. I had felt sure that we would be used somewhere and that we would have little time to prepare for a move. Company C was to be the first company to move out, followed by A, B and D. The Service Company was to move out later ... I left at 1400 hours with Lt William S Wright, Liaison Officer and two recon Peeps ... I reported to Col. Lynde, First Army Ordnance Officer, who had been charged with the defense of the Ordnance Depot. An enemy armored task force was advancing west along the Amblève River and was less than 12 miles away, so it was decided that as soon as C Company could be equipped with combat vehicles it would take up a defensive post east of Aywaille in the vicinity of Remouchamps.

'I made a quick reconnaissance of the area we were ordered to defend and then went over to Sprimont to arrange to draw tanks. I was shocked to find that only three Shermans were on the "ready for issue" line, and that these three were short several essential items of equipment. The job of this Ordnance unit had

Below left
Pilot model of a Bulldozer T4, showing the blade partly raised.

Bottom
M24s belonging to the US Ninth Army crossing the River Rhine on 24 March 1945.

Below
M24 with twin .50-cal. AA Machine guns.

M24 CHAFFEE

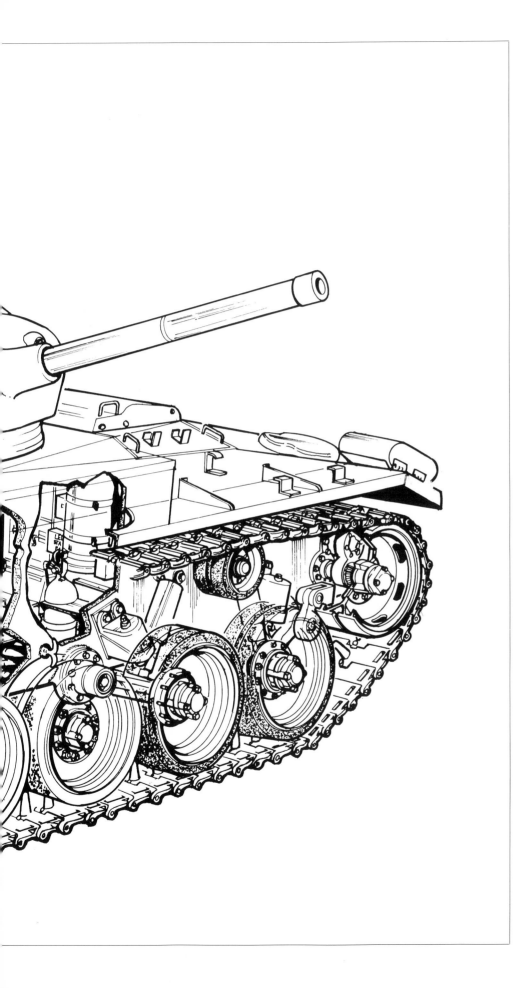

been to repair and recondition tanks that had become unserviceable in combat. Of about twenty-five tanks in the park, only fifteen could be made operable. Even these had been cannibalized to some extent. Generators and starters had been removed from engines, breech parts had been removed from guns, radio transmitters and receivers were absent, not to mention tools, rammer-staffs and other items. None of them had their combat loads of ammo. We had blanket orders from Army to take anything and everything we thought we could use. We picked out fifteen tanks that appeared to be repairable and worked all night and up until noon the next day robbing pieces from other tanks to put the ones we had selected in running condition.

'The tactical situation was going from bad to worse and at about 1800 hours on the 18th I decided to order the balance of the Battalion to move to Sprimont on my own initiative. They moved out at 1020 hours on the 19th. The Service Company took over the ordnance plant at Sprimont and the Battalion CP was established there. The combat vehicle situation looked a pretty hopeless mess. We assigned a tank crew to any vehicle that they thought they could put into operation. For instance, Sgt Loopey and his crew found an M36 tank destroyer and other tank crews took over M10 assault guns. The light tank company found two brand new M24 light tanks that had arrived in First Army area through error, and seven M5 light tanks, but had to fill up the rest of the company with M8 assault guns with 75 mm pack howitzers. The assault gun platoon drew M7 105 mm assault guns. Very few of these vehicles had radios and the platoon leaders found it necessary to use hand signals for control. By noon of the 19th Capt Berry (who commanded C Company), had two 5-tank platoons in position at Remouchamps . . .'

About this time the S-2 of the 119th Infantry Regiment of 30th Division came by, en route for his Regimental CP at Stoumont. He told them that his Regiment was in a desperate situation, with one battalion completely overrun and destroyed. The other two were down to less than half their effective strength and were being pushed back slowly. He pleaded for tank support but of course the CO of 740th was powerless to help. Later in the afternoon he returned with Gen. Hobbs, CG of 30th Infantry Division, who said that he had talked to Gen. Hodges and had got authority for the battalion to be attached to the 30th Infantry Division and that he in turn was attaching them to 119th Infantry. He ordered them to move out immediately with everything they could muster to help the situation out.

RESTRICTED

Col. Rubel's account continues: 'We encountered sniper fire from the ridges paralleling the Amblève River two miles before we reached the Regimental CP. Upon arrival we found that the enemy was less than 500 yards away. As I arrived, a tank company which had been supporting the 119th were withdrawing from the fight, stating that they were low on fuel and ammo. They also stated that at least five Panther tanks were coming this way and were only about 1000 yards down the river. The tankers said that the infantrymen were beginning to move back.

'Capt Berry, leading his tanks in a Peep, arrived at 1530 hours and we outlined the situation. He was ordered to attack at once before the Infantry were overrun completely. Lt Powers was to spearhead the attack with his platoon, and Lt Oglensky with his platoon was to follow. We advised Lt-Col. Hurlong, Battalion Commander of the 1st Battalion of the 119th Infantry that we were coming in to help, — that we would commence our attack at 1600 hours, and asked him to attack abreast of us as we came into his position.

'Lt Powers spearheaded the attack. He had gone scarcely 800 yards when he saw a Panther tank about 150 yards ahead at a curve in the road. His first shot hit the gun-mantlet, ricocheted downward, killed the enemy driver and bow-gunner and set the tank on fire. Powers kept on moving and about 100 yards further on came upon a second tank. He fired one round which hit the Panther's front slope plate and ricocheted off. His gun jammed and he signalled Lt Loopey [then Sgt Loopey] to move in quickly with his TD. Loopey's first round with his 90 mm gun set the tank on fire, but he put in two or three more shots for good measure. By this time Lt Powers had cleared his gun and had resumed his advance. About 150 yards further on he came upon a third Panther. His first shot blew the muzzle brake off the Panther's gun, and two more shots set the tank on fire.

'All during this action, which occurred within 30 minutes after the attack had started, a slow drizzling rain was falling, and a blanket-like fog covered the whole area. It was difficult to see an object 400 yards away. Lt Power's platoon had not only knocked out three tanks that had been raising hell with the Infantry, but his machine-guns had sprayed the roadsides as well as the sides of the hills and quite a number of enemy soldiers were

Top left
Deep water fording kit installed on an M24.

Above left
M24 with grousers fitted (see also the photograph of the M20 swimming device on page 77).

Left
An M24 Chaffee on the back of a 20-ton recovery trailer.

Right
The M20 swimming device fitted to a Chaffee. This comprised fore and aft pontoons to give flotation, plus grousers on the tracks to give better propulsion in the water. It was not used operationally.

Below
T77E1 multiple Gun Motor Carriage was begun in 1943 to mount a quad .50-cal. machine gun turret on the M24 chassis. The project was abandoned at the war's end.

killed. Our success in 30 minutes of combat had greatly heartened the doughboys of the 119th. They not only stopped giving ground but joined in the attack and recovered better than a thousand yards of terrain they had lost during the day. Von Rundstedt's thrust had been definitely stopped and hurled back in these 30 minutes, and it was the first good news that had come out of the entire Battle of the Ardennes up to this time.'

Unfortunately Col. Rubel's account does not specifically say what part the M24s played in this or subsequent actions, but one can be sure that the 'Daredevil Tankers' of the 740th (the name was their battalion code name) made full use of them.

In his book *US Light Tanks in Action* Steve Zaloga tells of another combat action in which M24s took part, in March 1945 near the village of Domagen in Germany. Some Chaffees belonging to F Troop of the 4th Cavalry Recon Squadron, came unexpectedly upon two Tiger tanks. Although they knew that their 75 mm guns could not penetrate the frontal armor of a Tiger, they were much quicker into action, thanks to their powered traverse. While the German gunners were still desperately trying to swing their manually controlled turrets round to engage the M24s, the latter fired several rounds and scored numerous direct hits. Although these did not penetrate, they set off internal stores which 'brewed up' both Tigers.

There were a few Chaffees in British service, supplied by the United States in 1945 and they remained in service for a short while after the war ended. The M24 really proved itself during the opening phases of the Korean war in 1950 when they were the only armor available to the hard-pressed US and South Korean forces. The Chaffee was finally replaced in the US Army by the M41.

Variants

At the same time as the M24 was being developed there was a stated requirement for a family of AFVs, known as the 'Light Combat Team'. This would comprise a series of gun tanks, self-propelled guns, and special purpose tanks, all of which would use the same basic chassis. The advantages of standardization of components for manufacture, and, just as importantly, the simplification of maintenance, spares holdings and repairs, from such a system can be well imagined. This led to a number of variants being made.

M19 GMC Some 285 of these only had been completed at the end of the war, but this AA tank, which mounted twin 40 mm guns in an AA mount, became standard US Army equipment for many years after the war. It had a crew of six, weighed 38,500 lb's and 336 rounds of 40 mm carried.

M41 HMC Known unofficially as the 'Gorilla', it mounted a 155 mm M1 howitzer and, although only sixty were completed before the end of war, it became a standard US Army post-war equipment, like the M19GMC. It had a crew of twelve, eight of whom had to be carried in an accompanying ammunition carrier. It weighed 42,500 lbs, and 22 rounds of 155 mm ammunition were carried on vehicle.

Other less successful variants included the T38 Mortar Motor Carriage, and the T77E1 Multiple Gun Motor Carriage. There was also a swimming device designated the M20, which allowed the standard M24 to swim ashore from a landing craft, and comprised fore and aft pontoons, plus grousers added to the tracks to give better propulsion through the water.

M24 in retrospect

Although no light tank can seriously hope to win the tank *versus* tank battle against a heavier opponent, the Chaffee was undoubtedly a highly successful design, simple, reliable rugged and with satisfactory hitting power for a tank of its size and weight. The way in which it has gone on in service all over the world (nineteen countries still have it in their armies even today) is a glowing tribute to its designers.

8

The Mediums are Coming:
The M3 Generals Lee and Grant

Introduction

In the early 1920s, the Americans built three prototypes in the medium tank range: the Medium A built in 1921, which was also known as the M1921; the Medium A of 1922, also called the M1922; and the T1 of 1925. They all weighed about 20 tons, mounted a 37 mm gun as main armament, together with various machine-guns co-axially, in sponsons, or in AA mounts, etc. The top speed of the T1 was in the region of 20 mph, as compared with 6 mph for the M1921, and 12 mph for the M1922. The three models were never put into production, because, with the demise of the Tank Corps as a separate arm after World War I, there was considered to be little requirement for this class of tank. However, further development continued and in 1930 the next medium, the T2, appeared. It weighed 12.7 tons, had a 47 mm gun, plus both .50 and .30-caliber machine-guns. Its 300 hp engine gave it a good power to weight ratio and thus a very fair cross-country performance. Externally it resembled the British Vickers Medium Mk II to which it owed many of its design features. It was followed by further prototypes, the T3, T3E2 and the T4, all of which were based on designs by J Walter Christie, using his suspension with its large wheels and steel track. The tanks were both fast and reliable, but only lightly armored and never went into production, except for the T4, of which sixteen were built at the Rock Island Arsenal. This was the *very first* quantity production of a medium tank since the end of 1919! These T4s never saw any action, but continued in service until 1940, being used for training and doing much useful work up to the day they were scrapped.

However, as has already been explained, neither Christie nor his new designs found much favor in America, so it was decided that the next medium to be built would follow more conventional lines. It was designated as the T5, and initially was within the set 15 ton weight limit, but not for long. It had a 37 mm gun and, in the interests of standardization,

incorporated many features and components from the M2 light tank. It was powered by the same radial aircraft engine (the 250 hp Continental seven-cylinder), had similar suspension, sprockets, tracks and transmission, which had proved so successful in the light series. The T5 was completed at Rock Island in 1938. It was later re-engined with a larger, more powerful nine-cylinder Wright Continental engine and standardized as the M2A1 medium tank. By now its weight was about 20 tons, although its armor plate was still not even as thick as that of the standard light tank.

If the United States was slow to act between the wars, then she certainly made up for it once World War II had begun. Study of the battlefields showed clearly that, to survive in modern war, a tank needed thick armor and a powerful gun with a dual capability — that is to say, the ability to be able to fire both

The medium tank M2 was the production version of the T5 tank, fifteen of which were built at Rock Island Arsenal in August 1939. With a crew of six (commander, driver and four gunners), its main armament was a 37 mm in a central turret, with eight .30-cal. Brownings as secondary armament, four of which were in the corners of a barbette which supported the turret. Two more machine guns were on flexible mounts on each side of the top of the turret and two fixed guns mounted in the sloping hull front.

armor piercing and high explosive ammunition, the caliber of the AP being sufficient to penetrate the armor of enemy tanks, whilst the HE was vital for dealing with anti-tank gun crews. It was decided to go for the 75 mm which, at that time (1941) seemed to be adequate for the foreseeable future.

As the Ordnance history puts it: 'To meet the crying need for tanks with bigger guns and tougher armor, the Armored Force and the Ordnance colaborated in rushing through plans for a new tank, salvaging what they could from the existing M2A1 model and profiting from British battle experience. For the first time a turret basket, power operation of turret, and a gyro-stabilizer were applied to an American tank. The 75 mm gun was put into the right sponson, where it had limited traverse, because Ordnance had tried out such an arrangement some months earlier with good results, but it was understood that a completely new design with the gun in the turret, giving all-round traverse, would be more desirable.'

As if it was not difficult enough to have to try to design new tanks at such a 'belly to the ground gallop', the USA was, at the same time of course, trying to build the factories where the new tanks would go into quantity production. This was the case with the new medium, and while the design stage was still in progress, contracts were being negotiated with Chrysler to build it, and a new tank arsenal to produce at least one thousand of these new tanks, was being designed simultaneously. All this had to be done at the same time and at breakneck speed. For example, it was early in September 1940 when work began on the site chosen for the new Chrysler tank factory (where the M3 was to be built) on the outskirt of Detroit, yet it produced its first tank in mid-April 1941, and it was in quantity production only three months later, truly an amazing achievement.

The M3

The new medium tank was thus developed from the M2A1 which had been ordered to re-equip the Armored Force, an initial order for 1000 M2A1s having been placed with the Rock Island Arsenal for production at the rate of ten tanks per day. However, before they could be produced, the M3 project had taken their place. In addition to the US Army the British were also anxious to obtain suitable American tanks to make up for their considerable losses in France, most of the British armor having been left there when the BEF was evacuated. A tank purchasing commission arrived from the United Kingdom in June 1940 and one of the designs they chose was the projected medium M3. However, they insisted on certain minor modifications including a larger, but slightly lower, turret, with a rear bustle to provide room for the

The improved version of the M2 was developed in 1940 with increased armor thickness, wider tracks and a supercharger fitted to the engine to increase the horsepower to 400 hp. It was designated as the M2A1 and its chassis was the basis of the M3 and M4.

Below left
Rear three quarter view of the wooden mockup of the medium tank M3, complete with dummy commander.

Below
Pilot model of the M3 under test. Design work was completed in March 1941 and the pilots produced the following month. Full scale production was under way by August 1941. The British called the standard M3 the Lee (after Gen. Robert E Lee), its main armament was a 75 mm gun in the side sponson.

radio, standard American practice at that time being to mount the radio in the hull, while the British preferred theirs in the turret as they could thus save one crew member. The British also did not like the very prominent machine-gun cupola on top of the tank, as it made an already tall AFV even higher. The British version of the M3, incorporating these modifications, came to be called the General Grant, after the famous Union leader of the Civil War, General Ulysses S Grant, while the original version with the machine-gun cupola, earned the nickname General Lee, after his opponent, General Robert E Lee. Thus the crew of the Lee was seven men — commander, 37 mm gunner, 37 mm loader, 75 mm gunner, 75 mm loader, radio operator and driver, while in the Grant the 37 mm loader

A rear view of the prototype British turret on an M2 hull (note there is no separate commander's cupola) showing a good view of the engine and rear access doors.

Below
Early production version of the medium tank M3 with the British turret, which was known as the Grant.

doubled up as radio operator. The M3 was of course essentially a stopgap AFV and was soon superseded by the M4 Sherman. However, it did play a significant part in the battles in North Africa and when production ended in December 1942, many of the 6000 plus M3s which had been built continued to give good service all over the world for the rest of the war.

General Description

Relatively simple in design, the M3 was driven from the left front of the fighting compartment, with the driver's instrument panel directly below his vision port. His controls included both a foot accelerator (right foot) and a hand-operated throttle; a clutch pedal (left foot); gearshift hand lever to the driver's right (five forward, reverse and neutral); two steering levers which when pulled back simultaneously, slowed down or stopped the vehicle; a parking brake lever on the driver's side. To the right of the driver's compartment was the transmission housing, and it was the need to lead the transmission from the centre of the radial engine at the rear of the tank, to a gearbox at the front, avoiding the turret basket, that dictated the height of the tank. The radio set in the Lee was mounted normally in the left sponson to the left of the driver, about shoulder height. In the Grant, of course, it was in the turret bustle, behind the commander, while command and staff tanks which needed an extra radio set, had this mounted in the right sponson.

The 75 mm gun in its sponson was on the right hand side of the tank. The 75 mm gunner sat to the right rear of the driver, with his loader standing to the left rear of the breech of the gun. The 75 mm gun and mount was designed to give positive protection to the crew under all conditions of elevation and traverse, these limits being: elevation from 0 to 20 degrees; traverse 15 degrees either side. Fifty rounds of 75 mm ammunition were carried, forty one in boxes on the right-hand side of the floor of the crew compartment (directly behind the 75 mm gun), and the other nine in portable cartons as ready rounds.

The fully traversing turret with its 37 mm and co-axial .30-cal. combination gun mount could elevate to +60 degrees and depress to −7 degrees. It was offset to the left-hand side of the tank and its turret basket occupied most of the space in the fighting compartment. Inside the turret were the commander, 37 mm gunner and 37 mm loader (doubled as operator in the Grant), with their seats fixed to the sides of the turret cage. The gunner was

on the left, loader/radio operator to the right, with the tank commander sitting behind them and to the left. In the Lee he had his own cupola and .30-cal. Browning machine-gun, which added about 4-inches to the overall height of the tank (the Grant was 9 ft 11 in high, the Lee 10 ft 3 in). In the Grant he merely had a circular hatch with a split cover and a single periscope to see through when the hatch was closed.

Top
This version of the M3 had a welded instead of a riveted hull and was built by the Baldwin Locomotive Plant.

Above
Driver's compartment of the Lee, with the 75 mm breech just visible on the right of the photograph.

On either side of the fighting compartment was an entry door, with a revolver port and 'protectoscope', but on later models these doors were either welded up or completely

Variations between models

Model	Remarks	Numbers built
M3	The initial production model, with riveted hull, side doors and Wright radial engine.	4924 between April 1941 and August 1942
M3A1	Cast instead of riveted hull, but otherwise identical to M3 although later production models had no side doors or hull floor escape hatch.	300 between February and August 1942
M3A2	All welded hull, but otherwise identical to the M3 initially, but a new engine was introduced after two months production.	12 only between January and March 1942
M3A3	As for M3A2, but with twin General Motors diesel engines which increased the performance, but put up the weight to 63,000 lbs. Side doors were welded up or eliminated.	322 between March and December 1942
M3A4	Identical to the M3, but with the Chrysler 370 hp A-57 Multibank engine, which comprised five commercial truck engines coupled together on a common drive shaft. Weight increased to 64,000 lbs; the hull was just over 1 ft longer, as were the chassis and tracks. It had no side doors.	109 between June and August 1942
M3A5	As for M3A3, but with riveted hull. Side doors were dispensed with on late production models.	591 between January – November 1942

Specifications

	M3 – Lee I	M3 – Grant I	M3A5 – Grant II
Crew	7	6	7
Battle weight	61,500 lbs	62,000 lbs	64,000 lbs
Length	18 ft 6 in	18 ft 6 in	18 ft 6 in
Width	8 ft 11 in	8 ft 11 in	8 ft 11 in
Height	10 ft 3 in	9 ft 11 in	10 ft 3 in
Armor, max/min	2 in/$\frac{1}{2}$ in	2 in/$\frac{1}{2}$ in	2 in/$\frac{1}{2}$ in
Engine	9-cylinder Wright (Continental) R975 EC2	9-cylinder Wright (Continental) R975 EC2	12-cylinder General Motors 6046
Armament **primary**	75 mm Gun M2 or M3 37 mm Gun M5 or M6	75 mm Gun M2 37 mm Gun M5 or M6	75 mm Gun M2 or M3 37 mm Gun M5 or M6
secondary	One .30 coax with 37 mm One .30 in turret cupola One .30 in front plate (two in early models)	One .30 coax with 37 mm Two .30 in front plate (one in later models) One .30 flexible AA (optional) One 2-in mortar (smoke) fixed in turret	One .30 coax with 37 mm Two .30 in front plate (one in early models) One .30 flexible AA (optional)
Performance			
Max Speed	21 mph	21 mph	25 mph
Road Radius	120 miles	120 miles	120 miles
Vertical obstacles	2 ft	2 ft	2 ft
French crossing	7 ft 6 in	7 ft 6 in	7 ft 6 in
Fording depth	3 ft 4 in	3 ft 4 in	3 ft 4 in

omitted. Behind the fighting compartment was the engine compartment, the auxiliary generator (to run the power traverse, gyro-stabiliser, etc.) was mounted on the engine compartment bulkhead. The layout within the engine compartment varied with the type of powerpack fitted, but the fuel tanks were always on either side of the engine (there were four of these in all, giving a total capacity of 185 gallons), two vertical tanks located in the front corners of the engine compartment and two larger horizontal tanks on either side. A small separate fuel tank was also provided for the auxiliary generator. Access to the engine compartment was via doors in the hull rear and most day to day maintenance was possible through these rear access hatches.

Specifications and Models

There were basically six different models of the M3 whose details are set out in the adjacent table. However, to differentiate between the nicknames Lee and Grant is decidedly more complicated. In their excellent book on British and American tanks of World War II, Peter Chamberlain and Chris Ellis show them thus:

Grant I	The M3 with turret designed to meet British requirements.
Grant II	British designation for M3A5 with original American turret.
Lee I	British designation for M3.
Lee II	Designation for M3A1.
Lee III	Designation for M3A2 (none delivered to the British).
Lee IV	Designation for M3A3 with Continental engine.
Lee V	Designation for diesel-engined M3A3.
Lee VI	Designation for M3A4.

The specifications did, of course, vary with the model and whether it was a basic Lee or a Grant, so it is not easy to give standard specifications without resorting to a whole series of different tables. Three representatives examples have been selected.

The M3 in Combat

The first M3s to see action were those sent to the British Eighth Army in the Western Desert in 1942, while they were manning the Gazala Line — a long, deep belt of wire and minefields, interspersed with a number of fortified localities known as 'Boxes', which were generally held at not less than brigade strength. From Gazala on the coast, the line extended southwards, the southernmost pivot being the vital Free French strong hold of Bir Hacheim.

Rommel's second major offensive of January 1942, had reached the Gazala line fairly

A late production M3A4 which had no side doors and was fitted with the Chrysler A-57 Multibank 370 hp engine.

rapidly, but the DAK had by then virtually outrun its lines of supply. There followed a four month stalemate, while both sides rebuilt their strength before the Germans resumed the offensive. During this lull the British significantly improved their defensive positions along the 40-mile Gazala line. They also received tank reinforcements, including 167 new Grants from America and teams of American instructors to explain the new tanks to eager British crews.

One such British tank man was Jake Wardrop of 5th Royal Tank Regiment, and his thoughts about the new tanks are quite clear and unequivocal: 'The new tanks were arriving now and they were super, the finest things we had ever seen. They had a nine-cylinder radial engine, were quite fast and had a crew of six, Commander, gunner and operator in the top turret, and driver, gunner and loader down below. The gun was a 37 mm and the bottom one a 75 mm ...'. The new tanks were allocated to the 1st and 7th Armored Divisions, most of them going to the 4th Armored Brigade of the latter Division, in the ratio of two Grant squadrons to one Stuart squadron in each armored regiment.

The 'Desert Rats' (7th Armored Division) had previously reconnoitered defensive positions, to protect the Gazala line from a desert 'right hook' by Rommel, around the Bir Hacheim pivot, but sadly, due to the incompetence of their divisional commander who was totally lacking in experience when it came to using armor, the Division was 'caught with its pants down' by Rommel's attack and thrown into complete confusion. Divisional headquarters were overrun and the commander and many of his staff were captured (fortunately he managed to escape and rejoined the residue of his headquarters behind British lines forty-eight hours later). Not all the Division's armor was actually caught napping, however, as elements of 3rd Royal Tank Regiment got into their defensive positions in time, through the foresight of their Commanding Officer, Lt-Col. (later Maj.-Gen.) Pip Roberts, whose graphic account of the opening phases of the Gazala battle follows:

'Stand to at about 0545 hours passed off without incident so we repaired to breakfast. At about 0700 hours, Brigade HQ having been disturbed for some hours and now

General Grants, now with a British unit (cap badges have been censored for security reasons) moving up to the battle area. The Grants gave Rommel a severe shock when they were first used in battle (see Gen. 'Pip' Roberts battle aocount).

M3A4 LEE VI

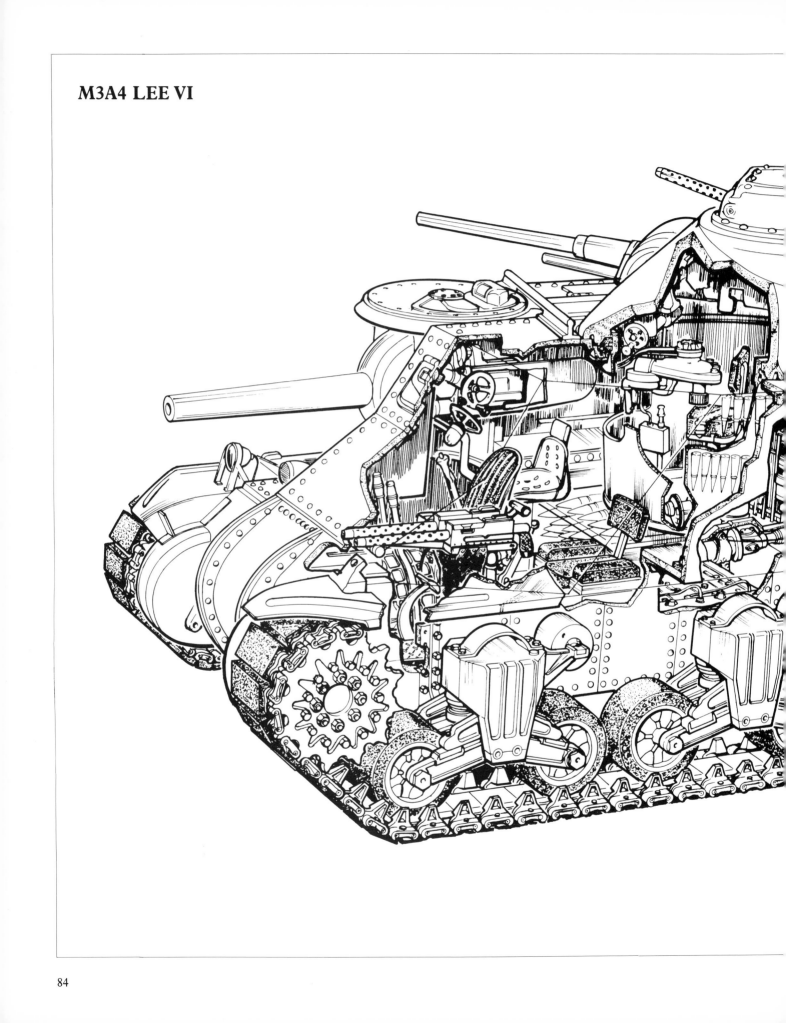

84

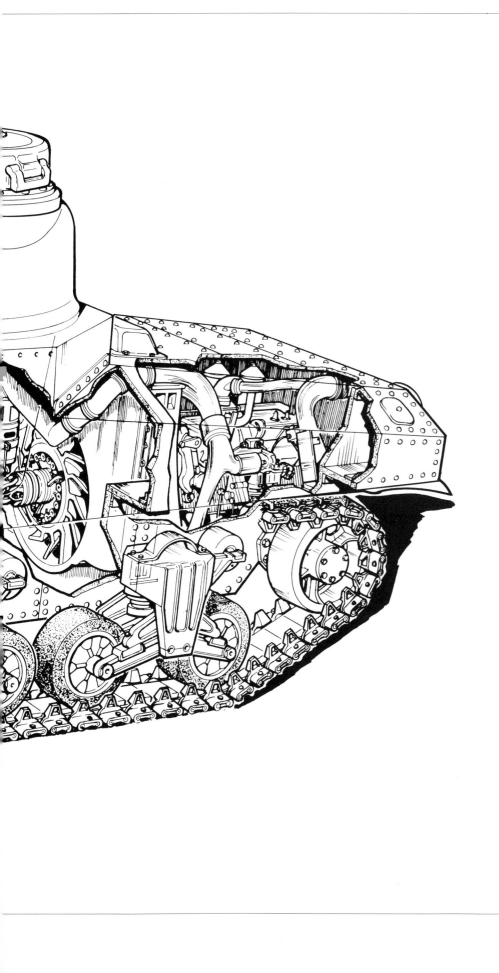

apparently without much on hand, rang up to request that we should furnish a full report as to why tanks numbered so-and-so and so-and-so were returned to Ordnance in a dirty condition. I sent for the shorthand clerk: Oh! I had such a lovely reply sizzling — all the facts, did but Brigade know it, were on my side. I was just itching to see it all put out on paper. However, I had only got the first two or three sentences off when the 'phone from Brigade rang again. "Enemy movement is reported towards Hacheim; the Brigade will take up the position *Skylark* (SE of Hacheim): the Brigade will RV and form up at point . . . (about three miles from our leaguer area on the route to the battle position), 3 RTR leading 8th Hussars left, 5 RTR right, Batteries 1 RHA move with armored regiments, KRRC in reserve; be in position at RV at 0815 hours." I cannot remember the exact order but that was the gist of it. "What sort of enemy movement do you think it is?" asked the Adjutant — "Sort of *Sinbad*?"[1] "Yes", said Brigade. "Something of that sort. We don't think its anything very serious." A sort of *Sinbad*, we knew the form! . . .

'We had been going about ten minutes, and the light squadron was about 2000 yards ahead, when they reported a lot of dust and unidentified movement three miles to their front. Perhaps the 8th Hussars. Then a report from Brigade came through that the Indian Motor Brigade just east of Hacheim had been overrun by tanks about 3–4 hours before. Perhaps it's not such a *Sinbad* after all! . . .

'We continue to move forward slowly, closing up on the light squadron and looking for a suitable hull-down position. Gosh! There they are — more then 100. Yes, 20 in the first lines, and there are six, no, eight lines, and more behind that in the distance; a whole ruddy Panzer Division is quite obviously in front of us! Damn it. This was not the plan at all — where the hell are the rest of the Brigade? However, no indecision is possible because no alternatives present themselves. "Hullo, Battalion — Orders B and C Squadrons (Grants) take up battle line on the small ridge 300 yards to our front. B Squadron right, C Squadron left. A Squadron [Honeys] protect the right flank from an outflanking movement and try to get in on the enemy's flank — leave one troop on the left to keep in touch with 8th Hussars who should be coming up our left at any moment."

'The Grant squadrons were instructed to hold their fire until the Boche tanks were within 1200 yards or had halted. Meanwhile our gunners, the famous Chestnut troop, had heard the situation on the wireless and were going into action close behind us . . . .

'The leading enemy tanks had halted about

A Grant tank in the desert cunningly disguised with painted canvas over a framework to look like a lorry.

1300 yards away; all our tanks were firing, there was no scarcity of targets, certainly two of our tanks were knocked out, but the enemy had also had losses. I could see one tank burning, and another slewed round and the crew "baling out" .... "Peter (my adjutant), tell Brigade we are holding our own, but I do not anticipate being able to stay here forever, and suggest that 5th Battalion should come up on our right. They would then prevent us being outflanked and might get a good flank shoot at the enemy." However, it appeared that the 8th Hussars thought it would be a good idea if the 5th Battalion came up between the 8th Hussars and ourselves; the 8th Hussars were fighting a battle in their original leaguer area against a large number of enemy tanks and had not had time even to get into battle formation. Our instructions were to hold on as long as possible.

'Further tank casualties had been inflicted on both sides, but as far as the Boche were concerned as soon as one tank was knocked out another took its place; they merely used their rear lines of tanks to replace casualties in the front line and attempted no maneuvre. On the other hand, from well in their rear a few tanks and some anti-tank guns were being moved very wide round our right flank and the light squadron was getting more and more strung out keeping them under observation.

'"Peter, tell Brigade we cannot hang on here much longer, either there will be nothing left, or we will be cut off, or both." "Driver, advance slightly into line with the other tank." "75 gunner, enemy tank straight ahead receiving no attention — engage. First shot just over — come down half a tank height. Still over — come down a whole tank's height! Good shot — that got him — same again." "Hullo! there is a dashing Boche on the left, he had come right forward against C Squadron who have withdrawn a little, just the job for the 37 mm. 37 gunner

traverse left, traverse left, traverse left — on; enemy tank broadside — 500 fire!' 37 gunner — good — have a couple more shots and then get ready with the co-ax."

'But C Squadron on the left are all going back, or what is left of them. "Hello C Squadron — what's the matter — you're going the wrong way." "Sorry," replied C Squadron Commander, "but I can't see a damn thing with blood in my eyes, and all my periscopes are smashed. I think the same thing has happened to my other remaining tanks. Also, I have no more ammunition."

'"OK, well done — carry on." It was found out afterwards that this tank had had 25 hits on its.

'But the situation was now getting serious .... On the right B Squadron seemed to have three tanks still firing, but they quite obviously could not have much ammunition left, no sign of the 5th RTR coming up on either our right or our left. There are certainly twenty Boche tanks knocked out in front of us, if not more, but if we are to reorganize at all we must go — and pretty quickly. I must see that the RHA troop does not get left all by itself . . . I give orders for the Battalion to rally on the high ground to the NE and then I look to the rear with the idea of reversing — it would never do to turn about here and expose the comparatively vulnerable side of the tank to the enemy with all the stuff there is flying about at the moment. As I look back I see at least two tank crews sheltering behind the tank, I signal them to climb up behind. "Driver, reverse very slowly, 75 and 37 gunners continue firing at suitable targets." If one reverses very slowly, no dust is raised and it will be some time before the enemy realizes that one is withdrawing.

'After about 100 yards of this funereal and agonizing movement — "Driver, speed up — right hand down — carry on . . . Driver, left hand down", it looks as if we are going to get away with it, but it's a good thing to do a bit of jinking. Two wounded men on the back are being given a little morphia. We have now gone in reverse for about 400 yards and the enemy do not seem to be following up! Now is the time to make a dash for it. "Driver, halt — rev up hard, turn about as quick as you can, then tread on it." An eternal few seconds — then we are going flat out for the rallying point leaving a cloud of dust behind us. Phew! that was a near thing. What ammunition have we got left — five rounds of 37 mm and no 75 mm. I hope the ammunition lorries will make the rallying point. There are four other tanks with me not counting the Honey Squadron, who have got away with it lightly, but are still reporting, most ably, the enemy's movements round our open flank.

'We reach the rallying point without further incident. There are seven Grants; I learn that three others have gone further back as they are unfightable, with both guns out of action. A certain amount of 'sorting out' takes place: B Squadron Commander, de-horsed, finds himself another charger. But no sign of the ammunition lorries. I get them on the wireless and learn that they are being shelled and will have to make a detour to get to us.

'At that moment one of the light squadron reports that six Boche tanks are approaching our rallying point and are even now climbing up the hill towards us. None of the Grants have any ammunition and the wadi behind us is full of French transport! I give out another rallying point a further 4 miles NE, hoping that there we will be able to join up with our ammunition lorries in reasonable peace, and at the same time tell the light squadron that they must hold up these enemy tanks while we and the French transport get clear. Most gallantly led by their Squadron

Commander [Major W M Hutton], two troops and Squadron HQ took up positions and held up the enemy; the Squadron Commander's tank was knocked out and he himself wounded — but was fortunately picked up by another tank under heavy fire and so brought back safely . . . .

'The ammunition and petrol lorries duly reached us, after a fairly adventurous journey. All the Grants were refilled with ammunition, and the light squadron was brought in a troop at a time to fill up with petrol . . . .

'Meanwhile orders had come through from Brigade that we were to join them in an area some three miles SE of El Adem. Thither we proceeded without incident, except that we passed large numbers of single lorries and groups of lorries all going in different directions, the resulting picture being of a somewhat disorganized musical ride . . . .

'The Brigade Commander had some interesting, if rather discouraging news. The 5th Battalion are practically complete — good — the 8th Hussars almost entirely incomplete — not so good — Advanced Div. HQ had been "put in the bag" including the Div. Commander — things must be very out of hand for that to have occurred and hence the interest shown by Corps in our movements! However, our guns are complete and the Motor Battalion is complete (except the CO who unwittingly drove into the enemy) so we have the where-withal to do a good deal more fighting — which we did.

'So ended one phase of a very busy day; it was now only just afternoon, lots more could happen, and did happen, but the past six hours had seemed like several days in one.'

Undoubtedly Rommel was very shaken by the success of the Grant tank; indeed, he wrote in his diary: 'The advent of the new American tank has torn great holes in our ranks. Our entire force now stood in heavy and destructive combat with a superior enemy.'[2]

Heinz Werner Schmidt, who had earlier been Rommel's personal staff officer, was commanding an infantry company in 15th Panzer Division at the time of the Gazala battle. He vividly recalled seeing the shells from his 50 mm Pak anti-tank gun bounce harmlessly off the Grants, while their return fire caused many casualties to his company.

In a recent letter to the writer, Gen. Pip Roberts enlarged on the battle. 'I must mention that the gunnery of 3 RTR at that time was very good . . . we had trained hard and it really paid off, but not for long, as we had so many tanks knocked out by 88s. I did not realise during this particular battle that

they were the cause of our casualties; when one is faced with a mass of tanks it is difficult to look beyond them. Perhaps if I had stood back I might have realised what was happening and could have got my Gunner battery to have shelled them. Incidentally, my tank had eight hits on it, including the very neat shooting away of the periscope which was incorporated in the turret lid, and when opened as it was, was upside down about one foot from my head — Tim Harvey, recently commissioned, lost his head completely within the first 10 minutes. . . . This was the one time that we had a superior gun to any of the German tanks — a few months later at Alam Halfa they had a long 75 mm in the Mark IVs and one complete squadron of Grants of the CLY (City of London Yeomanry) were written off in a few minutes. There is no doubt that the Grant 75 mm being in a sponson at the side was a disadvantage — one couldn't get hull-down. . . .

'I had an interesting experience a few days later when attacking a column of all arms at a certain map reference. . . . We, 3 RTR, found ourselves up against an escarpment with passes to the east and west, but on top of the escarpment were four 88 mms lined up! I sent the Honey Squadron out to the right to try a flanking movement, while, with six Grants, I tried the effect of HE both from the tanks and from our battery of 25 pounders . . . and finally knocked out three of the enemy guns. However, the time came when we had to move forward, the light squadron was to be prepared to move in from the right and we were only faced by one 88. So the Gunners put down smoke and the Grants started moving up the western pass. Of course the time came when we were getting out of the smoke and in fact I was plumb opposite the 88 — less than 400 yards away. It got off one round which went straight through my Grant — slap through the front, between the driver's legs, under the stand on which I was standing, through the engine and out of the back! Only casualty was the driver who got a small piece of gearbox in his leg, — and the other Grants got the 88 — so six Grants and a Gunner battery dealt with four 88s! One final point on the Grant — its comparatively simple mechanical arrangements and therefore its reliability came as a pleasant surprise after Crusader.'[3]

These early desert battles also gave the first American Grant crews their opening taste of combat. Three tank crews, under Maj. Henry C Lodge, were attached to 1st Royal Tank Regiment, when in early June 1942, they took part in the heavy fighting around Knightsbridge and Acroma, as they endeavoured to

First American Action

Within the Armored Force, the M3 was the first medium tank to be used on training maneuvers in any quantity and was widely employed in this role during 1941 and 1942. Before its arrival, light tanks were often designated as 'medium tanks' by marking their turrets with a large letter 'M', and labelling their 37 mm guns as '75 mm'! When units went overseas they normally exchanged their M3s for M4s. However, the only armored division which did not do so was 1st Armored. When 'The Old Ironsides' landed in Northern Ireland in May 1942, the medium tank battalions in their armored regiments still had M3s. And when they landed near Oran in North Africa as part of the centre task force of Operation Torch, just one medium tank battalion was included.

In a training pamphlet entitled *Tankers in Tunisia* the Headquarters of the Armored Replacement Training Center at Fort Knox, Kentucky, published many hints and tips which 1st Armored tankers had learned in battle. Soldiers who read the pamphlet were unanimous in their praise of its contents. Here are some extracts by the crews of M3s.

'1st Lt Thomas B Rutledge 751st Tank Battalion (M), Fondouk, 12 April 1943: "One thing that I have learned: The next time we move up, before we close up on the objective, it is a good thing to look down on the ground in front of the objective, and if you see anything that looks like the enemy or enemy guns, fire away at it with canister. We were so close that with keen observation, even two or three rounds of some machine-gun fire would have downed many machine-guns. I believe this would save us a lot of grief afterwards. We know there are lots of mines, but when approaching the objective we seem to forget those machine-guns. So instead of covering the ground in front of the objective with machine-gun fire, we thought only of the objective, which was on the hill."

'Did you see any anti-tank guns? "Not a great deal; only after I got behind them." How close were you then? "It could not have been more than thirty yards." Did you hit? "Yes, with the 75 mm gun. We had to get out in a hurry, as I figured he may do some more damage. It may have been useless expenditure of ammunition, but we had been expending it before. At a time like this we were always taught to shoot to kill and it being the first German I had seen, I thought to dispose of him was the main thing and we did. We wanted to get the gun out of action. I saw it before I left and it was burning, which satisfied me."

Tankers give an M3 a thorough check-up after day-long maneuvers at the US Army's desert training centre in California.

hold open the escape route area for the troops who had manned the Gazala Line boxes. In his definitive book on the history of the American medium tank, Richard P Hunnicutt says that in the fighting the three tank crews concerned claimed to have knocked out nine enemy tanks. After the battle they were sent home to Fort Knox to pass on their battle experience to other American armored units. Of the 167 Grants which had arrived from the USA, nearly half were destroyed, mostly by 88 mm guns, during the 'Gazala Gallop', but more continued to arrive in Egypt and by the time of the Battle of El Alamein in October 1942, there were 210 Grants in the Eighth Army, and 270 of its successor, the Sherman M4.

'Did you go back to the gun the next day? "Yes, it was out of action." Were you looking out of the turret? "Yes," You did not button up? "No sir, not yet. The driver was buttoned up, but three shots hit the top of the cupola. The enemy is known to try to pick off the tank commander when he is sticking out. You have to have good vision all around, but as soon as I stuck my head out I was fired on, but I did not know where it was coming from. We saw a dugout near the members of the enemy anti-aircraft crew, and we decided the fire was from there."

'Then what happened? "We put a 37 mm HE shell in the front of the dug-out, the next round went through that hole and it exploded. They had nice dug-outs, about five or six feet deep. I saw the position of an anti-tank gun when I had one of my tanks hit by them the day previous. I figured the gun was facing in the opposite direction to that one. I had in mind to go down there as I thought there may be other guns in the same place, when a call came through to go back to the rallying position. I told the driver we would be going back. I gave instruction that we might be fired on. I told him to keep zig-zagging which he did, when the anti-tank guns I had in mind, opened up. But it was not an anti-tank gun which got us. We found out the next day that we had hit a mine which was covered with the anti-tank gun fire. It was the first time I dealt with an anti-tank gun or a mine, and it was a bad guess. We rolled into a little roadway and I asked the driver if we were out of action. I knew the next minute that we were and I gave the order to abandon to the right because the gun was to the left.

'"We opened the door, the machine-gun fire started. I went to the front of the tank to see where it was coming from, and it was coming from both sides. We flattened out and started crawling. I stayed behind the rest with a Tommy gun. The driver was leading. One of those guns saw us and when one man raised up it hit him in the tail, and another man was hit in the back and another in the shoulder. Immediately I ordered everyone to freeze themselves flat to the ground. We stayed there until dark." What time was this? "It was about ten o'clock when we abandoned the tank." What happened then? "Well, during the day I heard the machine-guns behind us. They kept firing continuously. They never stopped. Then, there were two more which started firing from approximately the same position in our front. At dark we started crawling again and it took about two hours before we approached friendly troops. I was afraid that they would start firing at us, so I told one of my men to go within hearing distance and holler 'Friendly patrol'. We

An impressive line-up of late production M3s on exercises in England in December 1942.

could hear them now and then when they raised their voices. He did so, was recognized, told his story, came back to us and we moved up. The man that was hit in the back could hobble OK. We carried him across our shoulders. The man that was hit in the leg could not walk, but did crawl for those two hours. When this man was hit he just clenched his fist and said 'I'm hit' and I knew he was hit.

'"After I got in with friendly troops, I enquired as to how close the first aid station was for the three men. I reported to the aid station so that they would know exactly who they were and from which unit they came. We walked on further and I wanted to get to a telephone. They told me to go to the British

command car, but the line was not open, so I asked if we could sleep there. So we slept alongside his vehicle until six o'clock in the morning."'

Corporal Stephen J Ciracusa of Company B of the same tank battalion was a tank driver of an M3 and he was interviewed thus:

'Tell me how you drive the tank so that other men may get to learn something of it. "From the start you have to keep up your motor at all times to 1500 revolutions, and never let it get lower than that, because when she gets below 1500, the tank is no good as it has no pick-up." How do you know where to go? "The tank commander directs me." Do you pick the ground? "Yes, I pick the ground." Do you try to keep your front towards the enemy? "Well, we kept it towards the hills as much as we could." Have you ever picked up any targets? "I did not until we were behind it." What did you do then? "I stopped. You always stop when they fire."

What about stabilizers? "The stabilizers do not work on rough ground. Our stabilizer was in maintenance and they did not fix it in time." Did you worry about it? "No sir." What do you do yourself in the way of maintenance when you can't get help? "We drain the carburetor, grease the throw-out bearings and support rollers (on the suspension). We have steel tracks. The cactus juice and sand gum up the support rollers. We've burned out three of these steel tracks."'

Colonel Henry E Gardiner of Bozeman, Montana served with 1st Armored Division in North Africa as the Executive Officer and then as battalion commander of the 2nd Battalion 13th Armored Regiment, the one medium battalion which participated in the initial landings at Oran.

He writes: 'The Second Battalion was equipped when it landed in Africa with the M3, or as it was popularly known, the General Grant tank. While the M4s or General Shermans were being supplied to the armored divisions at home, we never had a full complement of them until after the fighting in Africa had ended. The M3 was a much inferior tank. It had a limited traverse on its 75 mm gun, which meant that the tank could only fire in the direction in which it was headed. Moreover, the gun was set so low that almost the whole tank had to be exposed before it could be brought to bear on a target. There was no slope on the side armor and the .30-caliber gun in the cupola, which was for defense against aircraft, was worse than useless.

'From Oran, the Second Battalion was rushed up into Tunisia. There we came under command of the British First Army and joined its forces in the drive on Tunis. We were within eleven miles of our objective before the mounting German resistance brought us to a stop. A period of confused and bitter fighting followed during which we were joined by the rest of CCB. When the battalion pulled out of the line on 10 December, it only had twelve tanks left, the other forty-two having been lost in actions around Djedeida and Tebourba.'

About the way in which he retained command and control of his battalion during tank actions Col. Gardiner writes: 'When we went into action I rode in my tank, I was tied in with the tank companies and my headquarters half-track by radio where my executive officer was located. He maintained the link between the battalion and the Combat Command. He would monitor my radio which allowed him to inform the Combat Command as to what was going on with the battalion and I was free to fight the battalion without interruptions from the next higher headquarters. He could of

This grimy crew and their strange looking contraption pose for the camera in North Africa. It was a mine clearance machine based on an M3 tank, which comprised a boom fitted at either end with a magnetically operated carrier. These carriers automatically picked up explosive charges as they rotated through the special superstructure. The boom then rotated, carrying the charge about 12 ft in front of the tank and 10 ft in the air. At this point the explosive charge was dropped until electrical wires attached to it pulled a firing trigger some 6 ft above the ground. The blast waves from the exploding charge then set off the mines. Initial results were promising, but unfortunately the power take off which operated the boom failed just before the demonstration was completed and could not be repaired.

course relay any orders to me, but I was free from all the requests for information that came from the next higher echelon. The other battalion COs for the most part directed their battalions from their command half-track.

'I used a throat microphone and my exec could hear not only what I was saying to the companies but also my orders to members of my tank crew. As was pretty much the general practice I operated with my head out, although if things were hot, at not much more than eye level. I gave my gunner the target, the range and the type of shell to be used and usually told him to fire when ready.

'In an attack I normally moved with the second company but if we were advancing in a line of companies I would be in the middle with the third company bringing up the rear in reserve.

'The first tank that I lost was in the operation around Tebourba, while I was a major and the battalion exec at the time. Once we really got into action my CO was rarely around, finding it necessary to go back to Combat Command for orders and I was left in charge. He was relieved after a short time and I took over, in fact, i.e. officially.

'We were rushed up into Tunisia from Oran where we had come ashore. Our first action which was just a skirmish was at Medjez-el-Bab, but two days later we got into it hot and heavy. We were very green and there was a great deal of confusion. In the attack which my CO led and in which I followed in the command half track we lost four tanks all of which burned. The colonel took off for the rear and from then on I was in charge. In this attack we had the Northamptons riding on our tanks, and many were killed when the tanks ran into anti-tank fire plus fire from enemy infantry. . . . . We gave the Northamptons fire support when they tried to take Bejedia the next morning after our advances was stopped, but they were beaten back.

American crews are seen here servicing M3s (Grants) before they were taken by tank transporter to join British units in the Western Desert.

'The Germans went on to the offensive and we were gradually forced back past Tebourba, this withdrawal taking three days during which we were continually bombed and strafed by the German Air Force. We were losing tanks and taking casualties every day and morale was far from high. Early on the third morning I was called to a tank of the 1st Battalion which had come into the area, to take a message from my absent colonel. This tank was up on a ridge and at a distance of 2 or 3 miles I could see a number of German tanks out in a flat, just sitting there. My orders were to attack these tanks which were moving between us and Combat Command. All the time my battalion was fairly closed up in an olive orchard. I hastily summoned the company commanders, gave them the situation and issued an order which, in retrospect certainly left much to be desired. It was in essence to follow me. A quick look at the terrain showed a low hill mass to the right of the enemy and in the back of my mind I had the idea of making for it and then trying to take the enemy in the flank.

'Told my 75 mm gunner that the moment we cleared the olive orchard to open fire at any targets he saw, or any huts, straw stacks etc. that might house enemy guns. Shortly after we emerged from the olive grove I turned to look behind me and to my dismay saw that there was only one tank following me which was the other headquarters tank which at that point was commanded by our liaison officer. We immediately came under fire from a direct fire weapon but at rather long range and it didn't score any hits as we raced across the open plain. After a run of about half a mile we pulled into another olive orchard and stopped. I was unable to raise anyone in the battalion on the radio and decided to return to them. On the way back we again came under fire and the other tank was hit in the engine compartment and burned. Fortunately none of the crew were injured.

'I found the battalion had taken refuge in and around a group of Arab huts. After an effort I got them out, lined them up in a battalion front and moved out in the direction of the enemy by leaps and bounds. As we crested a hill I suddenly saw a German tank to my direct front, down in a draw. Had shot off all my 75 mm ammo so ordered a round of AP from the 37 mm gun in the turret. Scored a hit and the crew started to bail out. I ordered them machine-gunned and they ducked behind their tank. Just at that point we were hit hard by what later proved to be an 88 fired from a Tiger tank that I had not seen. The M3 had a crew of seven. The driver and gunner were killed, the assistant driver badly wounded and I got some shrapnel in my

Opposite top left
A good photograph of a tank recovery vehicle T2 (M31) which has just pulled a 2½-ton truck out of a ditch. The ten-ton wrecker that was originally trying to get the job done is now lying on its side in the ditch and will no doubt also be pulled out by the T2s winch, which had a 600-lb pull.

Opposite center left
The M3 was also used in the Far East. Here a Grant moves into a burning village on northern Burma.

Opposite bottom left
The T36 40 mm Gun Motor Carriage, which mounted a 40 mm AA gun, never got further than the testing stage, because it was found to be too complex.

Below
A steel treadway bridge being put into position over a gap by a Tank Recovery Vehicle T2 belonging to 1st Armored Division in the Mignano area of Italy in February 1944.

Bottom
The full track prime mover M33 was used to tow heavy artillery guns. It was a 1943-44 conversion of the M31 Grant ARV (*i.e.* a turretless medium tank).

Opposite top right
Coming ashore from a tank landing craft in Italy is this Grant Scorpion III flail mine clearance vehicle. This was a British conversion (the 75 mm gun had to be removed).

Opposite center right
Mine Exploder T1, mounted on an M3, showing the twin roller disc units which were pushed along with one roller in front of each track. Each comprised four heavy steel discs about 40 inches in diameter. A third roller with five such discs was towed at the center rear of the tank to give complete path coverage. It was unsatisfactory.

Opposite center right
Cargo Carrier M3. Standardized as the M30 Cargo carrier, it was in fact identical to the M12 GMC — a 155 mm gun mounted on an M3 chassis — without the gun and recoil spade at the back. It had a rear tailgate and was used as a limber vehicle, carrying ammunition, stores and the gun crew.

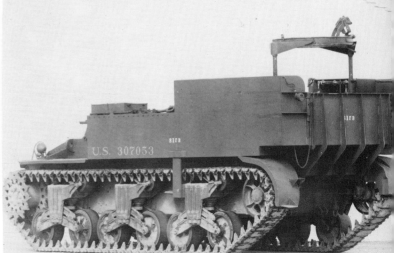

left arm. The other three men escaped without injury. Our tanks took up a position along the ridge and exchanged long range fire with the German tanks until dark. We were then withdrawn and joined CCB and its other units. The next day I went to a temporary hospital at a French mining camp up in the Atlas mountains. From there I was evacuated to a British tent field hospital near Bone where most of the shrapnel was removed from my arm and after a week I rejoined my battalion.'

Although larger numbers of Shermans came to 1st Armored Division to replace battle casualties, many M3s fought on throughout the campaign. At the end of hostilities in North Africa, there were still fifty-one M3s on the strength of the division. These were handed over to the French who later used them for driver training. The M3 was not used again by American forces in action in either the Mediterranean or European theatres, although it did see action in late 1943 in the Pacific theater. The 193rd Tank Battalion, which took part in the seizure of the Gilbert Islands, in November 1943, used its M3s there in the support of the 27th Infantry Division. In Burma, the British Fourteenth Army under General Bill Slim, had both Lees and Grants in small numbers throughout their hardfought but successful campaign against the Japanese, long after the tank had actually been declared obsolete (April 1944). It performed much useful work mainly 'bunker-busting' and supporting the infantry, due to the virtual absence of enemy armor. Over 1300 M3 tanks were also assigned to Russia under the lend-lease programme and saw action against German armor in that theater.

Variants

The Lee/Grant chassis was used for a number of other rôles, some variants being more successful than others. One of these was hailed at the time as a revolutionary 'secret weapon' described below. The most notable of the others were:

M33 Prime Movers A most valuable use for elderly M3s was to use them as artillery gun tractors, with their guns and turrets removed. An air compressor and outlet lines were added to operate the brakes on the gun carriage, and normally there was a .50-cal. AA machine-gun mounted on top.

M31 Armored Recovery Vehicle This was a standard M3 with its guns removed (replaced by dummy wooden barrels) and a rear-mounted boom and winch added: the winch had a 60,000 lb pull.

Grant Scorpion III and IV Scorpion minefield clearing device (flail type) fitted to a Grant from which the 75 mm gun had been removed to give the necessary clearance of the rotor frame. The Scorpion IV had an additional Bedford engine fitted to provide a more powerful drive for the rotors.

The 'Secret Weapon'

There were, of course, just as with nearly every other British and American wartime tank, a large number of other conversions, mounting flame-throwers, assault guns, AA guns, etc, but none were particularly successful, and did not have the wide appeal of the M4 Sherman chassis. However, one 'Gizmo' did gain quite a reputation for itself, yet it went by the innocuous title of the 'T10 Shop Tractor' of which 355 production vehicles were produced, mostly being converted M3A1s. Britain called these AFVs by their more obvious name of 'Grant CDL', the initials standing for Canal Defence Light, which gives a clue to their use.

Roy Millard of the 740th Tank Battalion, who were equipped with this new 'secret weapon', told the writer about the project which was one of the most closely guarded secrets in the US Army in World War II. All the men of his battalion and the others involved were first sworn to secrecy and then behind closed doors at Fort Knox, Kentucky, they were shown the new 'wonder weapon'. Certainly it didn't look like much at first meeting. It was basically an old General Grant tank still with its 75 mm gun, but the rotating turret had been replaced by an armored searchlight housing, including a ball-mounted machine-gun (later vehicles also had a dummy 37 mm gun barrel added to the front of the turret).

The searchlight was of course the 'Gizmo', and it was a carbon arc lamp of some 13 million candle power, similar in design to carbon arc lamps and to carbon arcs used for welding. It was mounted in a steel box resembling a movie projector, inside the turret. The power to work the light came from a generator, and it shone through a slit (2 ft by about 2 in, which was shuttered by a steel plate. Canvas covers were used to hide the turrets and the tanks were kept in a specially guarded enclosure. Then the whole outfit was moved to Bouse, Arizona, for training.

In an article published in *The American Weekly* in 1957, another member of the 'Gizmo Force', Capt. Stuart L Daniels of 748th Tank Battalion, tells a very similar story. He explains how they trained together by companies (fifteen of them), their lights making the desert nights seem like day, over a five mile area. Tactical uses of the lights were

Below
Men of the Chemical Warfare Service use a gas decontaminator during training in England.

Right
Close-up of a camouflaged M3 CDL, (Canal Defence Light), known in the US Army under the cover name of the Shop Tractor T10. One of the most secret inventions of World War II, it was never used to anything like its full potential.

Below right
Crews mount! Canadian tankmen mount their Lees during training 'somewhere' in England, February 1942.

After training hard the force was alerted for overseas duty in March 1944. They moved to Wales under strict security and established contact there with British units who had undergone similar training in Cumberland and Westmorland. In an article entitled 'The Secret Tanks of Lowther castle',[4] Peter Connon told a similar story of these 'death rays' and gives a very good description of the workings of the CDL. The turret had two compartments, with the operator sitting in the left-hand side one, while the optical equipment was housed in the other. The 13 million candle power came from a 'slimly built carbon arc, mounted on a cradle at the rear of the turret, the power being provided from a generator driven by the tanks own propulsion unit. The intense light was picked up by a parabolic elliptical mirror at the front of the turret and transferred to an alloy reflector at the rear; the addition of this reflector prevented the mirror from being shattered by MG or light arms fire.'

The focal lengths of the beams produced had been calculated so that they intersected at the vertical slit, the angle of beam dispersion being about 18 degrees. This meant that with the CDL tanks in line abreast and 30 yards apart, the first intersection of light fell about 90 yards ahead, and at 1000 yards the beam was 340 yards wide by about 34 yards high. On the order 'Scatter' being given, the armor plated shutter was oscillated about six times a second thus flickering the light, so that it was impossible for the enemy gunner to lay accurately on it. The effect on the observer was a blinding headache, while the power was such that it was possible to read a newspaper in the streets of nearby Penrith when a squadron of these tanks was operating!

Sadly, the wonder weapon was never properly used. The D-Day landings were successfully achieved without the 'Gizmos', and while the CDLs could have assisted in a night breakout battle, they lay instead in tank parks near Cherbourg and Caen, waiting in vain for the word to go. Later, one squadron of British CDLs was used during the Rhine-crossing, where they proved invaluable for locating floating mines sent down the river to destroy bridge crossings and in providing artificial moonlight. However, this was an ignominious role for their highly trained crews. Various military historians have said that the failure to use the CDL properly was 'one of the greatest blunders of the war'. Certainly their potential was never realised, the CDL tanks sinking into the mud of the Cherbourg dump, while their crews went back to normal tanking.

A T2 (M31) belonging to 2nd French Armoured Division waits under a tree near the English port of embarkation, prior to being taken to France, some weeks after D Day.

worked out at Bouse, coloured filters were developed, and a blinking technique to confuse the enemy was perfected. During this training some of the troops acted as enemy infantry and all those involved were exposed to the blinding rays for more than a year.

However, at the time no ill effects were noted.

Since those days, and this was the real point of Capt. Daniels' article, various members of the force have claimed that they were genetically harmed by the light rays. At the time, however, the men were full of pride at being members of an elite force, so it was a great disappointment to them that their new wonder weapon was never really used 'in anger'.

9
The Tank that Won the War: The M4 Sherman

The M4 Sherman was the most widely used tank of the World War II, and, while it was not up to the best German tanks in firepower or armored protection, it was without doubt the most important Allied tank of the war. The Sherman was produced in such quantity as to dwarf the production of any other single AFV, a staggering total of 49,234 Sherman gun tanks of all types being produced by the United States. The only other AFV to approach this gigantic figure was the Russian T-34. If one appreciates that there were more Shermans produced than the *total combined* tank output of Britain and Germany during the whole of World War II, then the magnitude of this achievement can be seen in perspective. The Sherman made up for its deficiencies not only by sheer weight of numbers (remember the significance of the German tanker's remark "You always haff eleven.'), but also by its straightforward design, ease of maintenance, ruggedness and reliability. Probably its most worrying feature was the way it caught fire — hence its nickname 'The Ronson Lighter' — but it was simple to manufacture and simple to operate, two factors which counted for a great deal in a country with little pre-war tank building experience and a large conscript army to train from scratch.

Origins

The Sherman began life as the T6 Medium Tank, which was built in mock-up form in May 1941. It was the result of an Armored Force requirement for a successor to the M3 which, as we have already seen, was only meant as a stop-gap AFV. The new tank would, it was hoped, make up for the four major shortcomings of the M3, namely the limited traverse, and the limited performance of the main gun; its high silhouette; and its poor armored protection. Sensibly, it was decided to use as many components of the M3 as possible, so the same basic chassis, suspension, transmission and engine were employed

initially. The major difference was the completely new hull top in the centre of which was a fully traversing turret, mounting an improved 75 mm gun and co-axial .30-cal. machine-gun (the 37 mm had been disposed of completely). Crew was to be five men, three in the turret (commander, gunner and loader/radio operator), and two in the hull (driver and assistant driver/bow gunner). It can be seen that the Americans had adopted the British idea of having the radio in the turret, thus, when necessary, saving a crewman, although the fifth man, the assistant driver, was extremely useful as both bow gunner and a 'jack of all trades'. The modern tendency of reducing tank crews first to four and now in some cases to three men, by fitting an automatic loader is fine in theory, but an automatic leader does not make a very good sentry, nor can it clean a gun, repair tracks or even make a cup to tea!

Certain changes were made to the mock-up which included the removal of the commander's cupola, thus reducing the overall height, and approval was then given for a pilot model to be built, with a cast hull, and this was completed in mid-September 1941. It was at this time that President Roosevelt dropped his 'bombshell' by ordering the doubling of tank production, so that 2000 medium tanks would

Mock up of the medium tank T6, built in June 1941 at Aberdeen Proving Ground. Note that in addition to the bow gunner's machine gun, there are two .30 fixed machine guns similar to those on the M3. Also, the commander has an M3 type (Lee) cupola.

Pilot model of the medium tank T6, with cast upper hull. Photograph was taken in September 1941. Note the side doors, and 75 mm M2 gun with double counterweight which were necessary as the gun mount had been designed for the new long barreled 75 mm gun T8 (M3) and was badly out of balance with the M2 gun.

be built each month in 1942, along with 800 lights. This meant not only finding more existing plants to build the new tank, but also building from scratch another purpose-built plant (the Grand Blanc Tank Arsenal at Grand Blanc, Michigan). In all eleven plants would produce their quota of Shermans, the M4 pilot model being built at the Lima Automotive Works in February 1941.

The major difference between the pilot model and the T6 was the elimination of the side doors, although the very first one built at Lima used a T6 upper hull casting with the holes welded up. The second, with a new hull casting, was sent to United Kindom with the name *Michael* on its side (Richard Hunnicutt, biographer of the Sherman tank, thinks this was in honour of Michael Dewar, head of the British Tank Mission. The tank, still with its unusual nameplate, is now on show in the British Tank Museum at Bovington Camp, Dorset). Both these tanks were armed with the short barrelled 75 mm M2 gun, fitted with counterweights, because the new M3 gun was not yet available. They were the first of the enormous run of Sherman gun tanks and associated AFVs that would be used by every Allied nation, in just about every role one can associate with armor, in every theater of operations.

Models

By the time production ceased, there had been six basic models of the gun tank, designated M4 through M4A6, whose main differences are summarised in the adjacent table. (The missing **M4A5** was the US designation for the Canadian-built Ram 1 which resembled the Sherman because it was also developed from the M3 series.) To these basic models must be added the seven gun models in the lower half of the table. When HVSS and 23-in tracks were introduced later in the war, the suffix 'Y' was added to the designation of tanks so equipped. The British also used the following nomenclature the types of main armament: 75 mm — **Sherman**; 76 mm — **Sherman A**; 105 mm — **Sherman B**; 17-pdr — **Sherman C**.

General Description

For a short general description of the Sherman, I am going to use an extract from a privately published book called *The Little Picture*, written by Maj. Herbert F Hillenmeyer and sub-titled *Tales of World War II for my children*. Herb Hillenmeyer wrote his book in 1953 after his children had '... listened to my ridiculous after-dinner stories of how your mother and I met in Italy;[1] and never were the stories the same. You have

Model	British Name	Main Characteristics	In service	Quantity
M4	Sherman 1 (late production with cast upper front hull: Sherman Hybrid 1)	Welded hull; Continental R-975 engine. Early vehicles had three piece bolted nose and narrow M34 gun mount: very late vehicles had a combination cast/rolled hull front.	July 1942	6748
M4A1	Sherman 2	As for M4, but with a cast hull. First model into full production. Early vehicles had M3 type bogie units, M2 75 mm gun and counterweights, twin fixed machine-guns in hull front (later eliminated and M3 75 mm introduced). Nose altered from three piece bolted to one piece cast. M34A1 mount and sand shields added later.	February 1942	6281
M4A2	Sherman 3	As for M4 but never had cast/rolled hull. Twin General Motors 6–71 diesel engines due to shortage of petrol engines.	April 1942	8053
M4A3	Sherman 4	Welded hull and one piece cast nose: 500 hp Ford GAA V-8 petrol engine. Most advanced of series with 75 mm gun. Mostly retained for US use.	June 1942	1690
M4A4	Sherman 5	Three piece bolted nose. Chrysler WC Multi-bank 370 hp engine, requiring hull to be lengthened to 19 ft 10½ in, but increasing speed to 25 mph.	July 1942	7499
M4A6	—	Final basic model with M4A4 hull and chassis and 450 hp RD-1820 Caterpillar radial diesel engine. Cast/rolled front.	October 1943	75
			Sub Total	30,346
M4(105)	—	Mounted the close support 105 mm howitzer M4 in an M52 mount in the turret.	February 1944	1641
M4A1(76)	—	The W stands for 'wet stowage' —	January 1944	3426
M4A2(76)W	—	the ammunition was stowed in water	May 1944	2915
M4A3(75)W	—	protected racks below the turret	February 1944	3071
M4A3(76)W	—	instead of in the sponsons e.g. ten boxes on the hull floor held 100 × 75 mm rounds and needed 37.1 gallons of water, with a further gallon to protect the four ready rounds. The water contained both ethylene glycol, to prevent freezing, and a corrosion inhibiter, known as 'Ammudamp'.	March 1944	4542
M4A3(105)	—	CS howitzer as for M4(105)	May 1944	3039
Assault tank M4A3E2	—	Heavily armored version (thicker armor put weight up to 84,000 lbs), including a more heavily armoured turret, 7 in on gun shield. Tracks had permanent grousers fitted to improve the ride. Nicknamed Jumbo.	June 1944	254
			Sub Total	18,888
			Total	**49,234**

Left
Standard production M4A1, but fitted with half-track suspension (called Centipede), 1943. Note that it has two half track suspension units and three support rollers.

Below left
M4A2 which was fitted with twin GMC diesel engines. It had many welded components. The pistol port had been omitted on this particular vehicle.

Bottom left
The M4A4 had a lenghtened hull in order to accommodate the Chrysler A57 multibank engine which comprised five engines, giving a total of 30 cylinders!

laughed, and no doubt wondered how much you could believe. Now, you are old enough to appreciate a few tales of your parents' younger days . . .'. He did not have the manuscript printed until 1979. Hillenmeyer was commanding Company H of 1st Armored Regiment, 1st Armored Division, and fought with 'The Old Ironsides' in Tunisia and Italy.

'There were various models, but the General Sherman, or M4, as we knew it, was the backbone of armored formations in World War II. . . . It weighed thirty tons, and had armor plate from an inch and a half to three inches thick. There was a crew of five. There were four entrances and exits to a tank. The driver had his hatch, the assistant driver had his hatch. There was a hatch in the turret and an escape hatch in the bottom of the tank. The last was more useful than you would suppose. More than once a tank has turned over, and the bottom escape hatch became the only means of exit. Many tankers also used it as a more or less protected avenue of exit if it became necessary to abandon a tank, say, that was burning, and still subject to enemy fire. Since the war, they have developed tanks to such an extent that driving it is child's play, but at that time it took a real man. The assistant driver didn't have much to do, and his seat was the warmest spot in the tank. We used to take turns in that seat during long cold night marches. He had a gun to fire — a machine-gun, but it rested in his lap on a ball and socket mount, and there was no way he could aim it. About all he could do was to sort of spray the bullets around much in the same manner as you would use a garden hose.

'The gunner, loader, and tank commander were in the turret. The turret could be traversed 360° by the gunner, either by a handwheel or with a power mechanism, but the latter lacked the fine adjustment he needed to bring his gun on the target. He fired the gun, and also a machine-gun which was co-axially mounted alongside. There were two foot switches which fired these guns electrically. He could fire them singly or together. The big gun was a 75 millimeter or about 3 inches in diameter. A "basket" was hung from the turret, and in this the gunner, loader and tank

Left
Marguerite was an M4(105), built in 1943 and armed with the L/25 105 mm howitzer.

Below left
The *Flying Scot* is an M4A3E8, which was the prototype for, and identical to the M4A3 (76 mm) HVSS, 1445 of which were built by the Detroit Arsenal between August and December 1944.

Bottom left
Jumbo, the assault tank M4A3E2, which was 42 short tons in weight (due to added armor, etc). It had 100 mm of armor on the hull surface, and grousers permanently fitted to the tracks to improve the ride, but retained the 75 mm gun. Built by Grand Blanc in May–June 1944 and rushed into service in Europe to 'breach the Siegfried Line'.

commander revolved with the turret, which had a .50-caliber machine-gun mounted on top for mostly AA use. All around this basket were racks containing ammunition, for both the machine-gun and the 75. Needless to say, this ammunition was a constant source of danger in case of a direct hit on the tank.

'The tank commander had his hands full. He usually had a map to follow. He had field glasses he had to use. He had to direct the gunner on to targets. He wore earphones which were plugged into a jackbox on the side of the turret. He had a microphone through which he could talk to any member of his crew, or, by flicking a switch over the radio to other tanks in his formation. He had a push-button FM radio, through which, by punching various buttons, he could listen or talk to other units in his "net". The tank commander stood directly behind the gunner, usually with his head sticking out of the turret. When in a combat area, we usually operated "buttoned-up", that is, with all hatches closed. However, we learned long before we got into battle that the tank commander just couldn't see enough buttoned-up, and consequently he usually peeped out, even when under direct fire. Each hatch had a periscope through which the occupants peered when buttoned-up; thus they were not exposed to direct fire. The gunner had a telescopic sight in his periscope. We carried about 180 gallons of gasoline, and that was good for about 100 miles of operation. On a clear highway we could run at forty miles per hour, but twenty was more nearly the usual speed. Various types of engines were designed for use in a tank, but the trouble was that any engine which was hefty enough to do the work expected of it was so bulky that by the time you got it into the tank, there was no room to work on it without taking it out! So we used aircraft engines during most of the war, nine-cylinder radial air-cooled Continentals, with about 400 horsepower. We had a honey in our light tank, though (20 tons). It used twin Cadillac engines with hydramatic drive, and this was at a time when automatic shift was unheard of, even in light-duty civilian cars.

'Our tank was superior to the Germans, but theirs had a better gun. In the flat desert country where there was no cover, that hurt. It was merely a matter of who had the longest reach, and the Germans had it. You get a sinking feeling when you poop around out there and see it bounce off the enemy tank, and about that time you see his gun wink, and the tank next to you bursts into flame. When we later got into country where we could sneak around in the hills, our better manoeuvrability paid off. German prisoners we captured were bitter after holing up in the hills only to have a tank run right up the mountain after them. They felt it wasn't fair to send a tank after one man! Our tanks had a tendency to catch fire easily when hit, or "brew up" as the British said. We always had a private opinion that it was because we used gasoline whereas the Germans used diesel fuel. Regardless of the reason, I knew we lost no time in "bailing out" when the tank went up in flames. Very few men could tell you how they got out. The first thing they remembered was that they were on the ground and running. This was such a common occurrence that one of our soldiers, Tommy Stinsill, carried on his belt what he called a "bailout kit" — a little packet containing razor, toothbrush and a change of socks.'

Herb goes on to recall an occasion when his tank was engaged by a well hidden anti-tank gun while his tank company was trying to rescue some American troops trapped by the Germans.

'The first shot penetrated the turret of my tank, killing my gunner immediately. That red-hot slug of tungsten steel banged around and came to rest on the floor of the turret spinning on its point like a top. It was bouncing up and down making a terrible racket, and others later told me they could hear it as I talked over my radio. I remember looking down at it and wondering if I would burn my foot if I stepped on it. However, I didn't have time to give it much thought, as the next shot hit down in front stopping the tank, breaking my driver's leg, and setting the tank on fire. We bailed out, leaving the dead man, but pulling the driver, Freddie Blair, out with us. We huddled behind our tank and watched three more of our tanks go up in flames before somebody finally got the gun. Four out of five tanks were knocked out in a matter of minutes, here I was on the ground, with no means of communication. We dragged Blair back to a spot which we thought was protected from enemy fire and sent for stretcher bearers. We finally worked our way out through a wadi and got our man back safely. I

took over another tank, but it was getting dark by then, and I regret to say we never rescued the trapped men. The next day the Germans withdrew. I counted twenty-five hits on my burned-out tank. I lost two lieutenants that day — one killed and one wounded. I have fought that battle over many restless nights since.'

First Combat

As with the M3 it was the British Army who first used the Sherman in action. Following the Gazala battles, Rommel had continued his advance and on 21 June 1942 his forces captured Tobruk, which had long been a persistent thorn in his flesh. The Fuhrer was so delighted that he made Rommel a Field Marshal. After pausing for a short time to regroup, the DAK continued their advance, driving the British back across the Egyptian frontier. At the time of the surrender of Tobruk the British Prime Minister, Winston Churchill, was in Washington visiting President Roosevelt so it was only natural that Roosevelt should offer to try to help the embattled British. The first proposal was for the 2nd Armored Division to be sent to assist.

In his book *Hell on Wheels*, Donald E Houston recalls that on 20 June 1942, the Armored Force ordered that all armored units should be ready to expect orders to move

overseas at any time and that they must '. . . be prepared to execute these orders expeditiously and efficiently'. However, when General Marshal, Chief-of-Staff of the US Army, looked at the situation more closely, it was clear that the division would take four to five months to reach Egypt, by which time it would be too late to be of any use in stopping Rommel from reaching the Nile Delta. He therefore offered to withdraw 300 Shermans that had already been issued to units under training and send them immediately to Egypt.

This generous offer was accepted with alacrity and the convoy carrying the Shermans, together with 100 new M7 self-propelled howitzers left the USA on 15 July. En route one of the ships was sunk by enemy submarines, but a special fast replacement ship was immediately despatched with a further fifty-two Shermans. By 11 September a total of 318 Shermans had arrived in Egypt, not in time to take part in the Battle of Alam Halfa (31 August–1 September) in which the British managed to halt the German advance on the El Alamein line, but in plenty of time for the preparations that followed for the British counterstroke which was to prove the turning point in the desert war.

The Shermans were mainly M4A1s, but included some M4A2s, and as soon as they were unloaded work began to modify them for desert warfare, sandshields, for example,

M4 Specifications

With so many models it is impossible in a short space to give the specifications of all of them, so I have chosen three, the M4 (mid production), the M4A2(76)W, and the M4A6 (late production), as examples of the series.

Model	M4	M4A2(76)W	M4A6
Crew	5	5	5
Battle weight	66,900 lbs	73,400 lbs	70,000 lbs
Length	19 ft 4 in	24 ft 10 in	19 ft 10½ in
Width	8 ft 7 in	8 ft 9 in	8 ft 7 in
Height	9 ft	9 ft 9 in	9 ft
Armor max/min	3.5 in–0.5 in	4.25 in–0.5 in	4.25 in–0.5 in
Armament	75 mm Gun M3 in	76 mm Gun M1A1,	75 mm Gun M3 in
primary	M34 or M34A1 mount.	M1A1C or M1A2 in M62 mount.	M34A1 mount.
secondary	One. 50-cal. AA machine-gun; two .30-cal. machine-guns (one coax and one in bow mount); one 2-in Mortar M3 (smoke) fixed in turret.		
Engine	Continental R975C1 9-cylinder radial.	General Motors 6046 12 cylinder twin inline.	Ordnance RD 1820 9 cylinder radial.
Performance			
Max speed	24 mph	30 mph	30 mph
Road radius	120 miles	100 miles	120 miles
Vertical obstacle	2 ft	2 ft	2 ft
Trench crossing	7 ft 6 in	7 ft 6 in	8 ft
Fording depth	3 ft 4 in	3 ft 4 in	3 ft 6 in

Above
The first Shermans to see action were with the British Eighth Army at the battle of El Alamein in October 1942.

Left
At a tank camp in Oran, Algeria, 1st Armored Division tankers prepare their tanks for action on the Tunisian front.

being added, before they were issued to units. The tank strength of the British Eighth Army just before the battle was 1351, including 285 Shermans, 246 Grants and 167 Stuarts; of these 1136 were with units in forward areas and 1012 were fit for action.

The official orders for Battle for the Eighth Army at 2200 hours 23 October 1942 (forward area only), show the breakdown of Shermans to have been as follows:

X Corps
2 Armoured Brigade, 1st Armoured Division — 92 Shermans split between the Bays, 9th Lancers and 10th Hussars.
8 Armoured Brigade, 10th Armoured Division — 31 Shermans split between 3 RTR, Nottingham Yeomanry and Staffordshire Yeomanry.

24 Armoured Brigade, 10th Armoured Division — 93 Shermans split between 41, 45, and 47 RTR.
XIII Corps
Nil
XXX Corps
9 Armoured Brigade, 2 New Zealand Division — 36 Shermans split between 3rd Hussars, R Wiltshire Yeomanry and Warwick Yeomanry.

This makes a total of 252, leaving thirty-three unaccounted for and presumably unfit for some reason or another.

General Montgomery's outline plan was for the main thrust to be made by XXX Corps in the north with the task of forcing two corridors through the enemy minefields, then X Corps would pass through. In the south XIII Corps would mount two diversionary opera-

tions. The first casualties to Sherman tanks were thus in 9th Armoured Brigade who were supporting the infantry during the initial assault, from mines and enemy anti-tank gunfire. This was also the case, when the leading tanks of X Corps tried to deploy out of the cleared lanes through the enemy minefields. Richard Hunnicutt records the first encounter by a Sherman with an enemy tank as occurring the following morning, the 24th, shortly after sunrise, when leading elements of 2nd Armoured Brigade, tangled with Panzer IIIs and IVs of the 15th Panzer Division. It was a long range action, commencing at some 2000 yards and both sides suffered casualties before the enemy tanks withdrew to the north. 'Thus began the battle career of the Sherman which, in one form or another, was to last for more than 30 years.'[2]

First American Action

This also took place in North Africa, with the 'Old Ironsides' in Tunisia. One of the tankers of 1st Armored Division was Bill Haemmel, of Waynesville, North Carolina, who was a loader in a Sherman M4, in 3rd Platoon, H Company, 1st Armored Regiment. Here is how he described those early days in North Africa in a privately published manuscript entitled *A Tank Soldiers' Journal*, which he wrote in 1974. They had landed at Mers-el-Kebir, just north of Oran on 21 December, moving eastwards into Tunisia after helping with the capture of Oran.

'On 31 December 1942 376 men and the tracked vehicles of the 3rd Battalion moved from the bivouac area to Oran and went aboard landing craft and the following day departed from the harbor. The Germans were in evidence; a Junkers 88 flew over on a reconnaissance mission and that night a torpedo bomber attacked the convoy but it suffered no casualties. On 4 January they completed the 400 mile voyage and landed at Phillipville and moved six miles to the south. Two days later they moved to another assembly area at Oued Seguin, a village located about 20 miles southwest of Constantine, and close to the main road from Oran. The wheeled vehicles moved overland, departing from Oran on 8 January, and moved to Oued Seguin. Some of the tracked vehicles also made the trip by railway.

'On 19 and 20 January the battalion travelled 95 miles south-eastwards to Ain Beida. On the 20th and 21st another 73 miles were covered to Bou Chebka, immediately east of the Algerian-Tunisian frontier; the march was completed at 2 am. On the 21st another 60 miles were covered; they arrived at Sbeitla at 3.45 pm. On the 22nd they moved into an olive grove bivouac area to the east of Sbeitla. CCA under Brig.-Gen. Raymond E McQuillen, was concentrating around Sbeitla. CC A's major elements were the 1st Battalion, 6th Armored Infantry and Col. Peter C Hains' 1st Armored Regiment, less the 1st and 2nd Battalions. The balance of the 1st Armored Division was back at Bou Chebka.

'As II Corps and the 1st Armored Division completed the move into central Tunisia, the Germans attacked Faid Pass, over 30 miles to the southeast of Sbeitla. As the Axis forces in Tunisia expanded, they carried out a series of attacks upon the mountain passes which cut through the range of mountains running generally north and south. The Eastern Dorsal mountain range is pierced at one point by Faid Pass and almost four miles to the south by Rebaou Pass. The village of Faid is on the road which passes through Faid Pass.

'A French garrison had taken up position at Faid Pass about 1 January. Early on 30 January the Germans attacked the French, who resisted stubbornly. They called for help and McQuillen was directed to counter-attack Faid Pass but not to weaken his defense at Sbeitla. He moved a reconnaissance company toward Djebel Lessouda and Faid and started other units across the straight road between Sbeitla and Faid Pass.

'In the afternoon H moved in a column toward Faid Pass. The company had been underway some time when the *Luftwaffe* brought it under strafing attack. The German pilots came in low from out of the east and they scored upon one of the company's thin-skinned vehicles. Throughout all but the very last weeks of the Tunisian Campaign the *Luftwaffe* posed a constant and ever-ready threat to the Allies. The *Luftwaffe* was present in large numbers and was extremely aggressive; at times they completely dominated the sky. The US Army Air Corps was present in small numbers and suffered the disadvantage of having to adjust to the forward movement of its bases. It was only in the very last stages of the Tunisian fighting that the Allied airmen were able to contest the German command of the air. Late in January the German air arm was so strong in southern Tunisia to the eastward of Sbeitla that the roads could be used by trucks and other thin-skinned vehicles only at night. During the time the battalion was in bivouac in the olive grove it was subjected to several attacks and retaliated by firing the anti-aircraft .50-caliber machine-guns mounted on the top of the tank turrets. The battalion suffered no casualties and neither did the German aircraft. The tank soldiers were constantly on the alert for the sudden approach of low-flying enemy aircraft.

'The attack on the advancing company column brought about the first casualties and caused the death of Pvt Lester A Torgerson and the wounding of Pvt Donald H Mertens. Mertens received a flesh wound and returned to the company several weeks later. They had volunteered for the Canadian Army and joined the US Army after service in England.

'The company was also subjected to attack by the US Army Corps, by both A-20 attack bombers and P-39 pursuit planes. While the US air arm was under orders to attack only to the east of Faid Pass and the company was miles to the west, the American pilots attacked the American tank soldiers. Fortunately, no casualties were suffered.

'The air attacks caused confusion and delay and McQuillen decided to put the attack off until the following morning. He established two task forces, the northern under Col. Alexander M Stark, Jr, CO 26th Infantry, 1st Division, attached to CCA, and the southern under Lt-Col. William B Kern, CO 1st Battalion, 6th Armored Infantry. Stark was to attack Faid Pass and Kern was to attack Rebaou Pass. Stark assembled his force around Poste de Lessouda and Kern at Sidi-Bou-Kid. I, 1st Armored Regiment was to be in reserve and H was to work with Stark until Faid village was secured and then go to aid Kern's attack.

'After dark on the 30th H assembled at Lessouda, about seven miles from Faid village. 1st Lt John T Jones, Jr of Houston, Texas, departed on a jeep reconnaissance patrol to the south. About an hour before dawn orders were received, settling the attack for 7 am. The maintenance officer, 1st Lt Hillenmeyer took command of the 1st Platoon in Jones' absence; he took over Jones' command tank.

'The company began to move eastward at about 6 am. As the tanks moved eastward on the pass, four German airplanes suddenly erupted from Faid Pass, flying low and firing hard. Sergeant William A Tretter of the 3rd Platoon was able to bring down one of the attackers by expert use of his .50-caliber machine-gun.

'The German defenders had spent the night to good advantage. They had placed eighteen tanks in defilade and had dug in anti-tank guns, heavy machine-guns and mortars. The Germans' elevated position provided excellent observation. The attacking tank soldiers were greatly handicapped as they had the early morning sun shining directly into their eyes. While the tank movement had begun at 6 am, the attack started slowly and communications proved difficult. It was 8.30 am before the attack got under way and the tanks crossed the line of departure. The 1st and 2nd Platoons moved forward on two lines; each platoon had three tanks on the forward line and two each on the rear line. Initially, the 3rd Platoon was in reserve and somewhat to the rear but as the attack developed Capt Stepro ordered the 3rd Platoon to move up on the right and extend the company line. The Germans opened fire with artillery and mortars and the attacking tanks returned the fire. Stuka dive bombers hit the tank force and the supporting artillery, firing from positions east of Djebel Lessouda. As the tanks came within range, the Germans opened up with anti-tank fire and in short order ten of the seventeen attacking tanks were hit and disabled. Of the ten tanks, eight were stopped and began to burn. Additional shots scored upon the tanks as they came to a halt. The tank of 1st Lt Gilder S Horne, Jr, of Charlotte, North Carolina, and the 2nd Platoon was hit and began to burn but continued to fire. As the flames finally shot out of the turret the cannon finally fell silent.

'Gordon F O'Steen of Florida was a sergeant tank commander in the 1st Platoon during the attack upon Faid Pass. He recalled that the attack progressed in accordance with regulation training: the tanks moved up, halted to fire and then repeated the cycle. His vision was obstructed by the direct rays of the sun and by heavy clouds of dust. When the

M4A3 SHERMAN

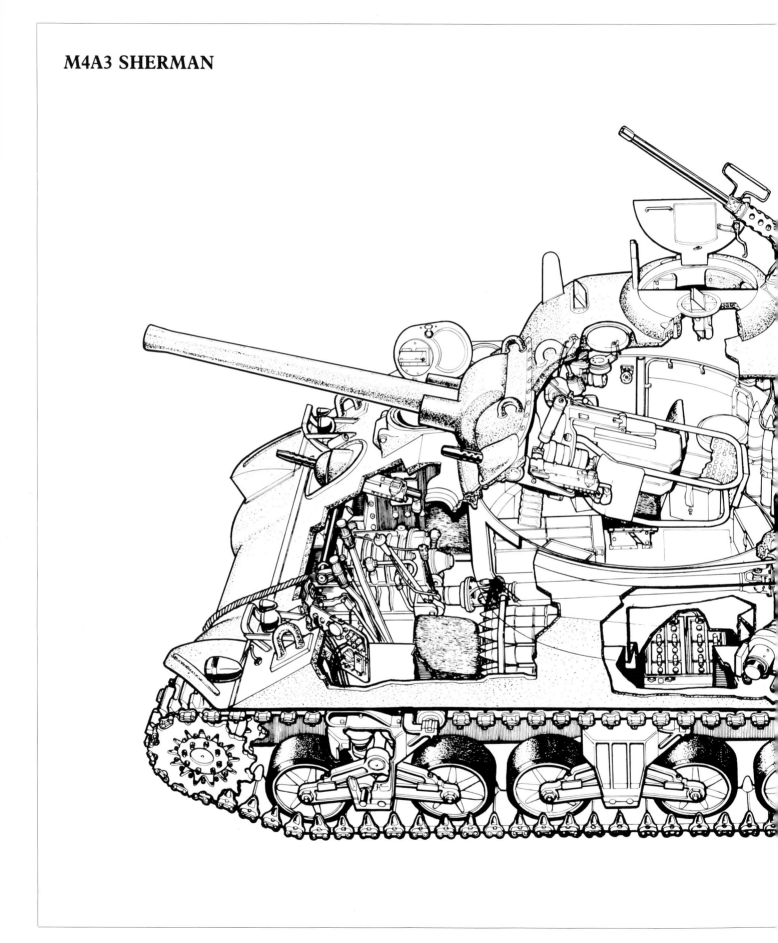

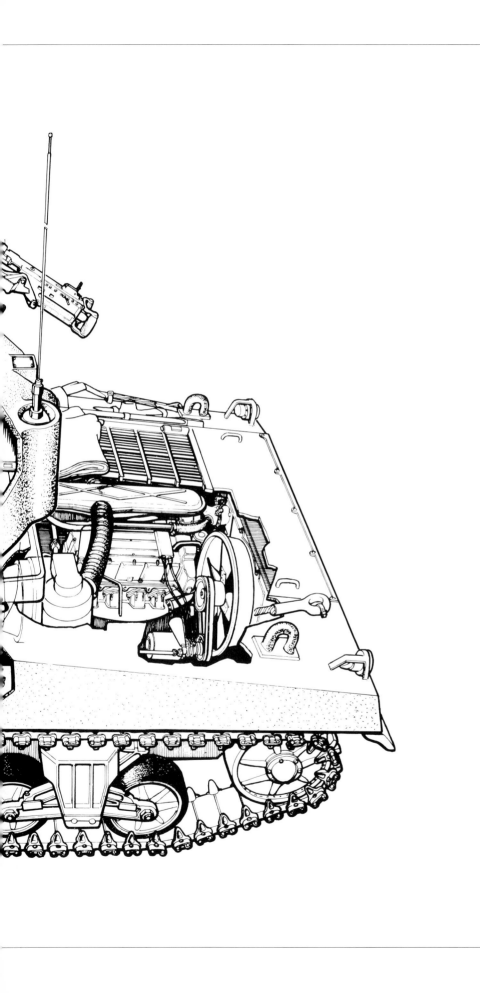

platoon was about 800 yards or less from the enemy position, O'Steen expected to receive the order to move in upon the Germans. At that moment he glanced to the south toward the rest of the company and he was able to dimly see what looked like the rest of the tanks in the company all burning! When he observed several tanks moving back, he decided he had better join them and he gave orders to his driver, T4 Ernest O Brown of Kentucky to back up the tank. The reverse movement was not fast enough and O'Steen finally directed Brown to turn around and move to the rear. The tank stopped several times to pick up survivors.

'While the infantry was able to make some headway in their attack in the mountains north of Faid Pass, they were finally stopped and it appeared the attack was repulsed. At 11 am he was ordered to withdraw to a rallying point at Djebel Lessouda. The retiring tanks picked up the surviving crews of the burning tanks and carried them off the battlefield.

'As 2nd Lt Laurence P "High Pockets" Robertson of the 3rd Platoon and New York City sought to disengage, his tank backed into the bed of an intermittent lake and was quickly bogged down in the thick mud just under the hard surface crust. As the German gunners found the range his crew "bailed out" and the tank was soon in flames.

'Of the seventeen tanks which started the attack, nine burned and were a total loss and two were disabled but were able to withdraw. Stepro's command tank was undamaged and in the 1st Platoon four tanks escaped. Of the ten tanks in the 2nd and 3rd Platoons only Sgt Glen E Hinzman's 3rd Platoon tank was not damaged. The two disabled tanks were hit and severely damaged but were able to back away; both were salvaged and later joined to make one tank. Sergeant Lyle W Smith's 1st Platoon tank hull was split by an armor piercing round; the drive sprocket was displaced. The turret of Sgt Andrew B Stone's 2nd Platoon tank was hit and penetrated.

'The remaining tanks retired to the southwest, toward Sidi-Bou-Zid, rather than to the northwest, the starting point of the attack. At the end of the engagement Hillenmeyer's tank threw its right track. A German artillery shell broke one side of the track, but it held together long enough for the tank to get out of range. . . . The tank had stopped to let some of the riders dismount from the outside and when the tank started up the track parted. The crew repaired the track immediately.

'The casualties included three men killed in action in the turret of Sgt Stone's tank: Stone, gunner Cpl Ralph D Barber and leader Pvt

Herbert W Baird. Three men were missing in action, all in the turret of Lt Horne's tank: Horne, gunner Cpl Richard W Glenn and loader Pfc Robert I Earle. Included in the four wounded were Horne's driver, T4 Elmer C Farmer and Sgt Von Staden's loader Pfc G J Goliash who was wounded by mortar fire as he left the tank; he was hit in the arms and lower parts of his legs.

'Elmer J Farmer was the driver and Pfc Edward L Stieren was the assistant driver or bow gunner on Horne's tank. They had been trapped in the tank because the turret had been swung around and the radio bulge in the rear of the turret prevented them from opening their hatches more than a few inches. The tank was burning and could explode at any minute as both men frantically pushed up their hatches — all to no avail. Farmer was pushing his up once again when another German projectile hit the tank, shearing off his hatch and smashing the little finger on his left hand. Farmer lost the finger.... Both Farmer and Stieren escaped from the tank, and Farmer returned to fight another day.

'The German defence made the tank forces of both Stark and Kern turn back.

'During the night of 31 January/1 February, H received new replacements and was supplied with some new tanks. Tank crews were reshuffled to insure that experienced personnel were present in all tanks, and early on 1 February the company moved south to support an infantry attack upon Rebaou Pass. The company engaged in some direct and some indirect fire in support of the infantry attack for several hours before the attack was broken off. That night the company withdrew to a bivouac area with the battalion in a cactus patch east of Sidi-Bou-Zid. On 1 February, S Sgt Hugh D Preston, platoon sergeant of the 3rd Platoon was injured. The tank commanders had assembled for discussion when Preston was shot. He was climbing up the front of the tank when the .30-caliber machine-gun was discharged. Sgt William A Tretter of the 3rd Platoon was made platoon sergeant and Sgt Bernard F Schilling, the driver of the 3rd Platoon command tank, was made a tank commander.

'Three men in the company received the Army's second highest decoration, the Distinguished Service Cross, for bravery during the January action. Horne received the DSC posthumously for his bravery in continuing to direct the fire of his tank and the operations of his platoon after his tank was hit and began to burn. Sgt Bowser dismounted from his tank during the course of the fighting and by use of his ramrod removed a jammed shell from his tank cannon. Pfc Glendon F Davis, a draftee from Missouri and loader on Sgt Ben-

nett's 3rd Platoon tank, along with the other two men in the turret, evacuated their disabled and burning tank and ran several hundred feet away when Davis realized that both the driver and bow gunner, T5 James W Dennis and Pvt Thomas F Costello, were not present. Davis raced back to the burning tank under heavy enemy fire. The turret radio bulge blocked the hatches and Dennis and Costello faced sure death in the burning tank. Davis climbed back into the turret of the burning tank and turned the turret around, enabling Dennis and Costello to escape. Lt Hillenmeyer and Sgt Tretter received Silver Stars for their aid to their comrades under fire on the battlefield.'

This action was only the beginning of 1st Armored's blooding and there was worse to follow as their history relates. 2nd and 3rd Battalions of the 13th Armored Regiment attempted to stop the German attack on Sidi-Bou-Zid on 14/15 February 1943. It was a disastrous battle in which the Americans suffered heavy casualties. To illustrate what happened I have chosen two accounts of the action, one from the German side, which is taken from a private history of Machine-Gun Battalion 8, who were the 3rd Battalion of Infanterie Regiment 104 in twenty-one Panzer Division; the other is from the Old Ironsides battle history.

To begin with the German narrative; 'Our battalion marched off on 13 February with 21 Panzer Division who had been relieved of the Faid Pass by 10 Panzer Division. We pushed through Gunifidia southwards, swinging around Sidi Mecheri, then northwards to Bir el Afey on the main road from Gafsa to Sidi-Bou-Zid. Moving on from there we reached a dried out wadi west of Zaafria (about 14 km west of Sidi-bou-Zid) by the early morning of 14 February. Our division had gone round Sidi-bou-Zid far to the south and stood west of it on the lines of communication between two American concentrations at Sidi-bou-Zid and Gafsa. On the edge of this wadi the division took up a position facing north. In front of the position all was quiet. Indefinable noises drifted down to us from the distance. At about 0100 hours our eyes "jumped out of their sockets" and we caught our breath as a huge wedge of tanks came towards us. Undaunted, 1 Company's new 7.5 cm anti-tank gun started to engage them. Unfortunately it had not been very well camouflaged and gave away its position as soon as it opened fire. It was knocked out after a short exchange of fire by two direct hits. Now the Americans knew our positions and they halted. Either they over-estimated our strength or lacked aggression. Our artil-

lery used this hesitation to lay down a barrage during which the tanks of 5 and 7 Regiments (the latter from 10 Panzer Division) pushed right and left of the thickly bunched American tanks, under cover of tall cacti. Then all hell broke loose!

'Our Panzerschutzen fired shot after shot; yelling and explosions filled the air; tanks were burning, enveloped by dense clouds of black smoke, while others exploded, and some turned in circles, with one track destroyed, aimlessly firing all the while. Then the *Luftwaffe* joined in the attack and the inferno mounted — a picture of hell right before our eyes ... '

In the middle of this 'picture of hell' was Sgt Clarence W Coley, who was the radio operator of a Sherman tank named *Texas*. It was the battalion command tank of the 3rd Battalion, 1st Armored Regiment, which was commanded by Lt-Col. Louis V Hightower. He recalled that fateful day thus: '14 February 1943 started off just like any other of those beautiful African days we had been having there in the "cactus patch" near Sidi-bou-Zid for the past week or so. We had been taking it easy, knowing the enemy was over there, somewhere the other side of Faid Pass. The evening before, at officers' call, we had been instructed to dig holes, deep holes, to sleep in because of reports of big guns moving into position to shell us. I, like the rest, slept as well as ever because everything was quiet that night.

'When daybreak came on that fatal morning we crawled out of our holes for our first "stand-to" which meant checking equipment, motors, radios, and guns. I climbed into the turret of the Battalion command tank, an M4 named *Texas*, the vehicle of which I was a crew member. I turned on the SCR-508 radio, checking it for operation, and it checked out OK. I then got out of the turret and into the assistant driver's seat, and turned on the SCR-245, which was mounted in the right sponson. It was OK also. In the meantime, Clark, the driver, had started up the motor, and about that time, here comes Col. Hightower with brief case in hand. Climbing into the turret, he tells Clark to move out.

'The Colonel told me to get into the CCA net. I proceeded to report into the net and took over from the set which was installed in the Battalion command track as Battalion command station. We moved out and after a short time, stopped near CCA Headquarters tent, leaving us sitting there wondering what it was all about. In the meantime, Companies H and I were pulling out of bivouac area and getting in position on the road. I think that is about the time when I learned that the Germans had attacked Company G, which was in position at a place called the "Oasis".

'After a short time the Colonel came out of the Headquarters and mounted the tank and we moved out. He got the company commanders of H and I Companies lined out, and we took off towards the "Oasis". We hadn't gone very far when we ran into blistering fire from many guns, including a lot of "Eighty-eights", I suppose. I didn't see too much and didn't know much about what was going on, but I did see many of our tanks get hit. Sometimes two or three men got out. Sometimes no one got out. Most of the tanks burned when hit. The artillery got so hot and heavy, and we were losing so many tanks due to being outranged, that the Colonel decided to withdraw. So we started backing out, keeping our thickest armor toward the enemy. The Colonel told Clark to back and zig-zag and when we reached a suitable place, to turn fast and get going. I remember that two men got on our tanks to ride out of the battle area — but I guess we were moving too slow for them because pretty soon they jumped to the ground and took off on foot.

'We moved on back towards Sidi-bou-Zid, and learned by radio that the Germans had put up a road block there and we were expecting to have to fight our way through it. I loaded my .30-cal. machine-gun and was ready to fire at anything that looked suspicious but the road block did not materialize, so I did not get to fire. Back in Sidi-bou-Zid we pulled in beside a building and the Colonel left us on foot to check the situation. As we had started before breakfast that morning, Clark, Bayer, Agee and I warmed up some C-rations and had us a feast. It was around noon, anyway.

'Pretty soon the Colonel came back to the tank. We mounted up and moved out towards the desert. I didn't know in what direction but away from the enemy, which had all but wiped us out. The *Luftwaffe* paid us many visits that day. They seemed to have about a 20 minute schedule, just time enough to go back and load up again. It was getting up in the afternoon now, and was pretty hot and smoky in this whole area. As we were moving along, we could see many other vehicles moving in the same general direction across the desert, half-tracks, peeps, motorcycles, and trucks. About five tanks of Company H had moved on out ahead of us. As far as we knew, we were the only tank back there, and the Colonel seemed to want to bring up the rear, keeping between the enemy and our withdrawing forces.

'As we were moving along, I suddenly got a call on my SCR-245 set. I answered telling Capt Green to go ahead with his message. His

Crew of an American Sherman in Italy (Fifth US Army) display an interesting mixture of tankers uniform. Note the differing headgear — tank and steel helmets, 'flyer's' helmet, and tank crash-helmet (second from right). The middle man is wearing the padded overtrousers with a bib front which extended up to the mid-chest, and the driver on his left wears the tank windcheater.

message was to the effect that a bunch of German tanks were shooting up the column, knocking out trucks and half-tracks, one after the other. I put the message on a message blank and passed it up into the turret to Col. Hightower, who immediately got on the SCR-508 set and tried to contact the tanks of H Company, which he knew were ahead of us. But no luck — he could not raise a peep from any of them.

'The Colonel then said we would just have to take them on by ourselves. He immediately rotated the turret until the 75 mm was pointing over the left rear fender at the German tanks. I don't remember when I first found out that there were seven of them. Perhaps Larry Green had it in the message. But anyhow, Cpl Bayer, the gunner, started firing at them. Col. Hightower was observing the fire with field glasses. I could hear him complimenting Bayer on getting hits. Clark, the driver, was craning his neck trying to see the action. Agee, the loader, was busy keeping the 75 loaded. All the time we were firing at the Supermen, they were not wasting any time. We were getting it hot and heavy. I did not keep the count on them, but we received many hits on our tank. I could feel the shock and hear the loud noise as those projectiles bounced off.

'We had done quite a bit of firing that morning over towards Faid Pass, and the rounds were running out in the turret racks, but we had a few rounds left in the racks underneath the turret. So I took off my headphones, laid them up on the BC-312 receiver, took the back of the assistant driver's seat out, and placed it up front under the .30-cal. machine-gun, very deliberately. I

had no fear, and was calm and collected. It is when you have nothing to do that you are afraid. Sitting backwards on my seat, with my feet on the escape hatch, I began pulling the rounds from the racks underneath the turret, and passing them up to Agee, the loader. I remember that other times when I had needed to take rounds from these racks it was very hard for me to get them out because I was afraid of hurting my fingers, but believe me this time these rounds came out easy. I didn't worry about my fingers. In fact, I wouldn't have given two cents for our chances to get out of that mess alive. I kept passing the ammo, Agee kept loading, and Bayer kept firing that 75. Every once in a while I could hear the Colonel tell Bayer that he had hit another.

'Our luck finally ran out. A round got stuck in the gun, wouldn't go in or come out. I remember that I had about three rounds lying on the turret floor when the round got stuck, so I got straightened back up in my seat. The Colonel told Clark to move on out, and about the same time, one of the enemy guns got a penetration in our tank. The projectile came in the left side, passing through the gas tank, richocheting around, and winding up on the escape hatch just behind my seat. Thirty seconds earlier I was bent over in that space pulling ammo from the racks. I remember it well — sitting there watching that bit of hell standing on end, spinning like a top, with fire flying out of the upper part of it like it was a tracer. Our tank was on fire inside.

'I heard the Colonel say: "Let's get the hell out of here." So we started bailing out. I distinctly remember trying three times to raise my hatch, but it wouldn't go up but about four inches on account of that part of the turret which contained the radio overhanging the hatch. The Colonel, Clark, Bayer, and Agee were all out of the tank while I'm trying to get my hatch open. I finally gave up trying to get my hatch open and got across the transmission like a snake and up through the driver's hatch, diving head first out of that burning vehicle. Hitting the ground on my shoulders, I rolled over and before I got to my feet, I noticed the tracks were burning also. I jumped to my feet and took off after the rest of the crew, who were not letting any grass grow under their feet. When I was between 25 and 50 yards away, I heard an explosion. Looking back, I could see fire shooting skyward from old *Texas*, ammo or gas blowing up, I suppose.

'I caught up with the other fellows in short order. The Colonel instructed us to scatter out a little, but I can't remember if we did or not. My total equipment at that time consisted of a tank helmet, a pair of coveralls, and a combat jacket with a busted zipper. I had left my pistol in my foxhole that morning when I had gone to check my radio never dreaming that we were going to get into the worst battle of all time that very day. We moved on across the desert on foot, sweating out small arms fire from the German tanks, but I guess it was so smoky and dusty that they couldn't see us. We were also sweating out the Arabs because, although I may be wrong, I don't believe any of us were armed.

'We tried to signal some passing vehicles but no luck. They were quite a distance away. After a half hour or so of walking and running, we came across two half-tracks, one of which was broken down. The Colonel advised the crews of the situation and suggested that they had better load up and get out of there because the German tanks were not far away, and heading in our direction. A member of one of the half-track crews had a very nasty wound in his side, and had been bleeding a lot, but they had already put sulfa powder and bandages on the wound, and he was going OK. We stripped the broken down track of its machine-guns, and took the men's personal belongings and put them in the other track, along with the wounded man, and all climbed aboard and took off, leaving the broken down track sit. We didn't burn it because we had expectations of coming back and picking it up, so they said. You can't prove it by me. We made it on back beyond Kern's Crossroads

Top
A US Tank Division 'gasses up' just before embarking for the 'trip across the water'.

Above
Excellent shot of a Free French Sherman engaging an enemy target in a ruined town in Italy. The commander observes through his binoculars, while the empty shell cases and the open side port tell their own story.

(which had not been named yet) to an assembly area on a piece of high ground.'

The German narrative closes the day's action: 'In the evening thirty-four Shermans lay burnt out and still smouldering redly. We combed the area and took three officers and seventy-four men prisoner, most of whom were from 1st Armored Division and were in action for the first time. They sat down in holes in the road and immediately went to sleep.'

In fact, before it was destroyed *Texas* had knocked out at least four enemy tanks and its intervention on the south west flank had delayed the enemy sufficiently to allow the rest of CC A to escape, but there was no doubt that 1st Armored had suffered grievous losses and as they admitted, had been taught a number of lessons the hard way. However, they were lessons that would not be forgotten, as 1st Armored proved time and time again during the remainder of their operations in North Africa and Italy.

Ubique

The motto of the British Royal Artillery is *Ubique*, Latin meaning 'Everywhere' and a similar motto could well be applied to the Sherman which, once full production had

Top
Preparing for the Second Front. A line of Sherman tanks belonging to the Free French firing on the open range.

Above
Roadside scene in southern England, as a long line of Shermans waits to proceed to its embarkation port.

commenced, quickly became the most widely used tank in the Allied armies; for example, 15,153, 1993 and 656 Shermans had been supplied to Britain, Russia, and the Free French respectively by the end of 1944. Some of the most important attributes of the Sherman which made it so widely used were its 'vital statistics'. The Sherman had been designed deliberately as a tank that would have to be shipped for thousands of miles before it could be landed on hostile shores (it is doubtful if any tank designer in America for one moment contemplated the war actually reaching the continental United States). Landings might be via a port or over the beaches. Once ashore the tank had to be able to cross countless water obstacles on temporary bridging so the tank had to be not too wide and not too heavy. US tankers also favored the policy of using armor boldly for deep, long range thrusts — witness Third Army's 'Gallop across France' — so endurance and mechanical reliability were put above armored protection.

This inevitably led to the Sherman being outclassed in tank versus tank engagements with the larger German tanks, such as Tiger 1 and Panther. In the history of *The Lorraine Campaign* by H M Cole, which forms part of the *History of the United States Army in World War II* compiled by the Historical Division of the Department of the Army, there is an interesting piece about the Sherman and its performance versus German tanks.

'Lorraine was a good testing ground for the American medium tank, the M4. The army commander was a student of tank warfare; moreover, he was willing to give his armored formations a free hand. The two armored divisions that continued with the Third Army throughout the campaign had won recognition even before they reached the Moselle. Patton employed his tanks under favorable and unfavorable conditions alike. They fought in large scale armored battles, tank against tank, and supported the infantry in an assault gun role. So varied was the armored experience in Lorraine that at first glance it would seem possible to give an accurate and final evaluation of the combat characteristics of the M4 tank as opposed to the German Mark IV and the Panther. But the battles in Lorraine were not fought under conditions conducive to a clean-cut decision on the relative merits of the opposing armor, even when, as in September, tank was pitted against tank. In the first place, the American tanks always outnumbered those thrown against them. Second, in the largest armored battles the enemy was forced to employ untrained tank crews against the veteran Americans and French. Finally, the German tanks had to operate with no air cover and with very limited artillery support. The competing claims for German tank kills made by the Allied armor, fighter-bombers, and artillery give some clue to the crushing weight of this combination of arms when hurled against tanks fighting almost unaided.

'During the Lorraine Campaign General Patton and a few of his armored commanders were called upon to furnish "testimonials" as to the efficacy in action of the M4 tank. These "testimonials" may have had some value in building public confidence in American armored equipment, but they should not be taken as a critical evaluation of the American medium tank. The M4, mounting a short-barrelled 75, was outgunned by the Panther (Mark V). The M4, was less adequately protected by armor than was the Panther. The American medium tank, however, had some important points of superiority. It was more mobile than either the Mark IV or the Panther, although less maneuverable than the latter. Its gyrostabilizer and power traverse permitted a greater flexibility and rapidity of fire than the enemy tanks could attain. It may therefore be said that, while the American tank at this period of the war had been outdistanced in the race to pile more armor and heavier guns on the tank chassis, certain features of mechanical superiority and weight of numbers kept the M4 in the running. During 1944 higher American headquarters made various attempts to redress the balance in armament and weaponing. Experiments were conducted with an eye to improving the American armor-piercing projectile. A number of modified M4s with heavier armor were sent to the European Theater of Operations, but only a few specimens of the new model reached the Third Army. The 76 mm tank gun began to replace the short-barrelled seventy-five as the Lorraine operations progressed and the new 105 mm howitzer mounted in headquarters tanks proved to be very useful (particularly when fired in battery). Nonetheless the Americans fought the Lorraine tank battles with a relatively obsolescent weapon.'

Marine Combat in the Pacific Theater

In the war against the other Axis opponent, the Japanese, the situation was markedly different. The Japanese did not consider that tanks were an arm of decision in their own right, but rather subordinate to the traditional arms in a similar manner to the view held by the United States after World War I. Consequently, large numbers of Japanese tanks were never encountered, so no large tank versus tank battles took place and Allied armor was more used in the support of its own infantry rather than in great armored 'swans' which the terrain prohibited in most places anyway. The one exception must be the race for Rangoon, by the armored elements of British Fourteenth Army, which has been described as being one of the greatest pursuits in the history of British arms, with the two tank brigades going hell for leather along the two main routes, as they tried to reach the capital before the monsoon broke.

The Sherman was, therefore, invaluable on the Far East battlefield and was also used extensively by the US Army and US Marine Corps from early 1944 onwards, taking part in nearly every battle of the island-hopping campaigns in the Pacific. Its gunpower was often supplemented by various special weapons, such as flame-throwers and rockets which will be dealt with later. However, the gun tank was normally adequate to get the basic job done. It was vulnerable to the Japanese 47 mm anti-tank gun which could penetrate the sides of the tank, so additional protection was often added, as the photographs show.

Lt-Col. R K Schmidt, of Woodland Park, Colorado, is a retired USMC tanker who served in the Pacific. He writes: '... we all made various mods to our tanks which weren't authorised by the arsenals or by Marcer, but which were very practical e.g.: extra track blocks and bogey wheels carried on turrets,

glacis plates, and sponsons as added protection; rotating turret hatches so that the cover opened towards the bow to provide some protection for turret occupants in case they had to bail out. Affixing regular tank turret hatches to retriever turrets so retriever commanders would have some protection; we had 2 in × 6 in oak planks on our sponsons with a 2 in space between the wood and armor — sometimes the space was filled with sand to protect against magnetic mines and to detonate AT shells outside the sponson armor — it worked; we had sandbags on the rear deck armor as protection from mortars; we modified our escape hatches so that they could be opened and released from inside the tank. This allowed us to pull wounded into the

Top
Excellent view of a Sherman splashing ashore from the gaping doors of an LST. The photograph was taken in late December 1943 during the invasion of Cape Gloucester, New Britain.

Above
Shermans assemble around Hollandia on the northern coast of New Guinea, to mop up Japanese snipers in April 1944.

tank, drop off ammo, medical supplies, full canteens and rations; on Saipan we had puncture proof (rubber) auxiliary fuel tanks from the M5s mounted on the rear of the M4s filled with water and with a spigot so the gravel crunchers could fill their canteens. During the course of the battle all of the water tanks were destroyed; we had metal grids over the bot-

tom half of our fording gear, so that when the top half was jettisoned, the Nips couldn't lob grenades into that inviting hole; we installed stabilising "feet" on the front of our retrievers so they could lift heavier loads without tipping.'

Nile E Darling of Salmon, Idaho, was another USMC tanker who served on Shermans. He writes: 'Our main combat tank was a Sherman with 75 mm gun and machine-guns. We as crewmen felt rather safe and secure about our tanks.... We never spent nights close to the front combat lines as the enemy would spot the tanks during the day and lay a heavy artillery barrage on us which created a problem for the infantry. During the day we worked ahead of the front lines and in close contact with the infantry. We had an outside phone on the rear of each tank that the infantry could use to direct our fire . . . I was a driver, assistant driver and loader of the 75 mm and machine-guns. I was a crewman in a regular combat tank, a Sherman with a bulldozer blade on the front . . . one day while going down the runway of an airfield and while I was driving, we took a direct hit from an enemy 47 mm anti-tank gun. It hit the front slope plate of the tank and right in front of me. Since they were using smokeless powder and leaving no dust, we had trouble

spotting their emplacement. My tank commander gave me the order to put the tank into reverse gear, my hand on my lap and not touch a brake lever, which I did and we backed up a few feet and then they hit us again. We then moved straight forward a few feet and they hit us for a third time. We took five hits — none of which penetrated — before we could locate their gun and destroy it. ... Since the Japs had lost their airfields they proceeded to landmine them, using 1000 lb bombs upside down with a landmine on top. We had a couple of tanks hit these and it cost us the tanks and all the crewmen. ....'

A graphic account of the Sherman in battle in the Pacific area comes from Brig.-Gen. Robert L Denig of Los Altos, California, who has sent a great deal of excellent information. I have chosen extracts from his letters home during the assault on Okinawa, the Marines last big battle of World War II, in which teamwork between tanks and infantry reached the peak of its development for the entire Pacific War. Bob Denig, was then a Lt-Col. commanding the 6th Tank Battalion. He had been given the job of both organising and training the new battalion on Guadalcanal, the three combat companies coming from three separate tank companies from three different tank regiments of a disbanding brigade.

'As each tank Co. had been operating separately and as they saw fit, it took some salesmanship to get them to operate in one fashion. We all eventually saw eye to eye and developed a good team. Up to this point tank Cos were attached to the infantry regiments.

Consequently, when the Regiment was in reserve the tanks just sat around. Col. Stuart, who had the 1st Tank Bn on the Russell Islands to the north, and myself decided that we wanted to control our own tanks and to use them in support of the division's main effort rather than regimental. I was lucky, as the Div Commander went along with me. ... Training on Guadalcanal — Stuart wanted diesel tanks, I wanted gasoline ones as they were newer and had self-flooding ammo boxes to cut down on fire. I was happy as the gas tanks were new. We gave Stuart all our diesel jobs. Our gunnery practice with the 75 mm was a lot of fun as there was an ammo dump on the island that was being worked over by an Ordnance Co. Serviceable ammo that wasn't considered good enough for combat was given to me in large quantities, especially AP shells as they were worthless against Jap tanks — explosive shells penetrated their thin armor just as well. My tank companies trained with each infantry regiment so that all commanders would know each other. Before embarking for Okinawa, the division had a modified landing exercise with a two day ground maneuver. This was a big help . . .'

L Day for the Okinawa assault was on Sunday 1 April and the night before Bob Denig had written home. The following extracts are taken from this and subsequent letters:

'Saturday 31 March — This will be my last letter from shipboard. The next will be written from the target which you will know when you receive this note will be Okinawa Shima.

USMC Shermans about to start engaging targets on another Palau group island north of Peleliu in September 1944.

As you have already heard on the radio that initial landings have already been executed with success on a group of islands some few miles to the westward. Our trip to the target has been quite nice and our stay at the staging area Uthill was pleasant. As Dad already knows, we are a part of the Tenth Army. It appears as if the III Phib Corps was given initially the most difficult task of rapidly seizing the main airport for our ground air support.

'It appears as if the task for the Corps during the past year or so is to seize airfields but this time it is for Marine aviation. The III Phib gave the 6th Div the main task of seizing the field while the 1st Div aids us. It was decided by Shepherd that while the Nips were disorganised from preliminary bombardment we should rapidly advance and seize the edge of the field some 1100 yards inland. That would give us a good beachhead for the next day's operation. So you can see where the 6th Tank Bn enters the picture. For the first time tanks are landing in an assault wave. In the past they have come ashore on call. This then will give the infantry immediate tank support so that the impetus of the attack will not slow down due to organized centers of resistance. If we can do the job as planned, I know that Shepherd will have a soft spot in his heart for us. We are getting various reports concerning defenses etc from time to time and it appears that the Nips haven't been idle during the past years in fortifying the joint. But fortunately the island is a large one with numerous landing beaches so they will have a tough time in defending all of them. So it won't be another Iwo Jima. For the first time since Cape Gloucester we will have

enough elbow room. The terrain looks favorable for tanks so initially, for the 1st week anyways, we will play a big role. That is why I said in my last letter that I wasn't going ashore in a tank. I took all of the Battalion Headquarters armor (five tanks) and have thrown them in with the companies. That will, I hope, add to the punch necessary to overrun the Nips. Instead I am in a ''call'' wave with my staff etc and we will hit the beach about the same time as Gen Shepherd which is estimated to be at H plus 4 hours or about 1230. The beach at that time should be relatively safe so you have nothing to worry about. The troops are getting a "boot" out of this expedition as it is the first one to land in Nip territory, the Ryukyu-Rette.

'Tuesday 10 April — As you know, the Division landed on 1 April. The first tanks hit the beach at 8.50 am and ran into no opposition. Before I knew what had happened "B" Company radioed back to my ship LSD 13 (Casa Grande) that they were on Yontan Airfield. Things progressed so rapidly that boat schedules got rather mixed up so I didn't get an LCVP until 2.30 pm to come ashore. I got ashore about 3.30 or 4 pm and the beaches were quiet as the devil. Not even a rifle shot was heard. My forward element of the Battalion Command Post was already ashore and had picked out an assembly area for the Battalion. So we dug in and spent the night there, about 600 yards from the beach and about the same distance from the airfield. The next day, 2 April, the attack progressed rapidly forward and we had two tank companies with the two assault regiments. My Bn-3 and myself took two command tanks about two hours after the 2nd day's attack shoved off and we meandered all over the landscape and ran into nothing. So we went to Div CP and recommended that tanks with infantry take to the roads and that a reconnaissance in force be

made to find out where the Nips were. The Div didn't do exactly that but tanks with infantry, up until yesterday, have been whipping out to limited objectives on reconnaissance missions. So far, the resistance in our zone of action has been negligible; as a matter of fact, the tanks have hardly fired a round of ammunition. Our biggest worry is fuel. Two days ago three of the tanks traveled 70 miles each and burned 300 gallons of gasoline each. We haven't been able to figure how many miles our tanks have gone on the average. I am now in our 4th assembly area and are 35 miles by road from our initial beaches. Another worry has been louzy roads, blown bridges and the lack of trucks. However, we have managed to keep going somehow. We are now in about the center of the island with the 29th working out on a large peninsula. There are three roads but to the end of the peninsula. Each one had a large bridge which the Nips blew, so we are stuck. Also today it started to rain so we are, in addition, bogged down with mud. The soil here is red gumbo like Quantico, so you can see we are having grief. I have grounded all trucks with hopes that it will clear up and dry out, thus saving the small trials that we have in the vicinity. The gooks here are poor as the devil, live in horrible shacks which smell to high heaven. Worse than China, I would say ... We are so far ahead of the remainder of the Corps that we have lost contact with the others so I don't know what the 1st Div is doing.'

'Sunday 15 April—An officer from the 1st Tk Bn popped in last evening and said that he had spent a couple of days with the Army and that they were doing nothing expect looking at the Nips and wondering when the Marines were going to relieve them as they figured that they had done enough which totals up to nothing as they haven't advanced an inch during the past 10 days. However, I doubt if the Army will call for help as they have plenty of dogfaces on the island. Gen. Buckner visited the Division the other day and said that we had been doing fine. We advanced some 30 miles during the first six days against limited resistance which is quite good for a Marine Division with its limited transportation. Since then, the Division has been chasing Nips all over a peninsula (Motobu).

'The few that were on Yontan Airfield withdrew up the island to the north and are now on a piece of ground to their own chosing. On the main road up the island they blew numerous bridges but it didn't slow down the advance. After the first two days, when the Div overran the airport and the approaches thereto, the tanks tried to support the infantry over the entire front but the only good tank country was captured by noon of the first day, when one of my companies sat on the far edge of the airfield and blasted at caves. My other company went to the north of the Airport. Neither saw a Nip as far as I can determine. By noon the next day, L plus 1, the troops and tanks had advanced so far that I recommended armored patrols and a fast pursuit idea. However, about L plus 3, they decided that it was a good idea, so the tanks with infantry on them and on foot made a series of rapid advances up the island. Then on this peninsula the Nips blew two large bridges which we couldn't by-pass so the tanks had to go to interior roads but they were so poor and the terrain so rugged that we had to quit. On the way up the peninsula we used the bull-dozer attachment on five of our tanks (we lost one on L Day) and they did good service fixing roads, covering bomb holes, making by passes, etc. (One of my officers just phoned in from a sentry post and said that a sniper is taking pot shots at him and another lieutenant. So out goes a ten man patrol; as it is 1430 we have four hours to root him out prior to darkness.) I don't think that we could have made such a rapid advance if we didn't have one of these dozer tanks at the head of each tank column.

'On Thursday (12 April) it was decided that the 22nd (one Bn) should seize the north tip of the island some 38 road miles from my Bivouac area. One of my companies went along and they made the trip in two days. The advance elements of the infantry rode on the top of the tanks. The others followed by motor. My Co. Comdr reports that his tanks are the nearest the Tokyo. (They can't find the sniper in the immediate vicinity so an organized patrol must set out. Can't have my sleep disturbed tonight.) I went up there by jeep yesterday. An all day trip it was. The road went along the coast, had tunnels, etc. It was quite pretty. The tank company is bivouaced on the tip of the island which is very high ground with hills in the center. Plenty of Japanese pine trees that are flat on the top. Rather nice and they would like to stay there and I don't blame them. During the entire trip, they only saw ten unarmed Nip soldiers. As for the 4th and 29th on the Peninsula, the 29th has been chasing Nips over the landscape for a week and having some pretty stiff fire fights. The 4th went in yesterday (Col. Shapley) to assist the 29th Marines and they did more in 24 hours, so they say, than the 29th did all week. Our operations are more or less completed when I withdraw my company from the north. Tanks can't operate where they have the Nips pinned down, as the mountains go straight up and down and the roads peter out to trails. The operation has been damned useful,

however, in as much as it has shaken the Bn down and allowed them to operate under combat conditions. We have air alerts but the Nips haven't bothered us any, as the Airport and shipping is more inviting.

'Wednesday 23 May — Haven't had a chance to write since I left our nice camp on the Motobu Peninsula. We left there and assembled in a rear area and got our tanks in first rate condition. Then we displaced forward into a service park near Jeb Stuart's Bn about a mile and a half behind the lines. The 6th had already taken over the lines on the ASA-Kwa or just to the rear of it. The infantry had already been in action, that is the first day of it when we moved up. Rain ruined the roads and they ruled us off, hence the delay. We arrived in our park late in the afternoon and the next morning saw one of my companies up trying to cross the river, but there was no bottom to it so we had to give up. Consequently during the night and forenoon of the following day the engineers threw up a Bailey Bridge for us. I sent two companies across to support the infantry who couldn't advance on the other side. The arrival of the tanks turned the tide and they assisted in the seizure of the high ground. From then on until today (12 days) we have been in action. Rain, with its muck, has stopped our employment for today and if it keeps up it will be for quite a few days. It has been quite rough on my troops and on our tanks themselves. At first we were using companies but as we began to run out of tanks and also began to find out more about the Nips we started in using the battalion as such to support any operation. By getting our tanks behind "Sugar Loaf Hill" and getting at the caves there, we finally "processed" the hill enough for the infantry to take it. The artillery has been a joke as they can't get the Nips out of their caves or hurt them. But the tanks shooting at point blank range, 100 ft to really fix them up and pave the way for the Infantry. I got rather peeved today when the news sheet said that the 6th Div supported by Art and Air did so and so, so I called up Popham. About an hour later he had an agent down to get the big picture on what we have been doing. Our casualties have been nearly as high as the infantry and in addition, each tank has been damaged at least once, repaired and put back in action. The 1st Tanks have been doing about the same work. We are certain that without our tanks we wouldn't have gotten as far as we did. Close tank-infantry did the trick. Now we have an Artillery Bn in direct support of the tanks with forward observers in the tanks, so when we want covering fire for either ourself or the infantry we can get it right then. We don't know how much longer this show will continue

M4A3 tanks belonging to C Company 4th USMC Tank Battalion on the beach at Iwo Jima, 1945. Note the sandbags, oak planking, grids over periscope housings and other additions to improve the Sherman's protection. Lt Col. R K Schmidt, USMC (retd)

as the Nips really have the hill masses at SHURI well defended. So it is going to be a tough job to wipe them all out, and may take longer than expected. Someone said that the casualties here per Regt during a fighting day exceed Iwo.

'It has been such a struggle, up to 2 am making plans then up at 6 am or 7 to get things going so that you can see that I have had little time for writing. So much has happened during the past 12 days that it is impossible to write about it. Wouldn't know where to start. The main thing about the show so far is the anti-defenses that the Nips have set up against the tanks. Their mainstay is the 47 mm gun but we are [devising] and have devised means to take most of the sting out of it. The next worry are mines and those jokers have put them all over the place. We have run over about 25 of them but only one tank was destroyed because of the mine. The remainder just blew off the track or something and we fix them up when we can work on them without fear of artillery fire. The Nips even shoot single 15 cm guns at the tanks, sniping at them if you will. So far they have only hit one and that was on the front slope where it is thick and only one man was wounded and they drove the tank away and back to the park. Other tanks have been hit by large sized shells but managed to survive. (What we have done is put extra armor etc. (irrespective of what the Army Ord says) all over the tank or else they wouldn't have turned the stuff so well.) Then those characters jump out from behind houses, ditches etc. with satchel charges which consist of a box with a lot of explosives in it. They have damaged some of our tanks with those. Those satchel boys are a suicide outfit, so we are always on the lookout for them. We found out that they always travel in company (two or three) so we fix them right up.

'Saturday, 26 May — Am slowly going through letters etc., trying to catch up with everything. Today is more or less a day of rest for my outfit. Last night about midnight it really began to rain. The stuff that we had during the daylight hours was nothing. What is, I think, the tail end of a typhoon. Anyhow the place is really wet with the fields flooded etc. Our road is a sea of mud so the chances of getting in and out are poor as far as tanks are concerned. We can't even run a jeep for they get stuck. Right now it has stopped raining hard so I figure that the storm center is passing and by nightfall we will have another hard rain. My tent is in a hollow surrounded by rock walls on two sides, one of the Okinawan tombs on the other and a low wall on the third. So we are trapped in our own "fish bowl". Fortunately, the ground is porous (coral formation) so the water seeps through quite nicely except when the income is greater than the outflow. The rain really affects our operations and I doubt if we can do much for quite a few days. The infantry can't seem to gain any ground without the tanks being with them unless they are willing to accept terrific losses, which, of course, they can't do. So it appears as if things will come to a halt until it dries out and we can take off again. It will give everyone a rest if you can rest in the mud and rain. In one of your letters you said that by press accounts the Army is having a tough time. They were and so are we but it is the same stuff like Iwo except on a larger scale. I don't think that the Army was prepared for such a thing. They thought that they would sweep southward and roll the Nips back. But as the Nips are in caves and prepared gun positions it is hard to roll them back unless you roll a mountain at the same time. So again this has resolved itself into a war of closing up caves or burning them out. That is where the tanks come in. The Nip defenses are in depth and they have plenty of machine-guns. The tanks both with the regular gun and the high capacity flame-throwers can work around to these caves paying particular attention to mine fields, AT guns and suicide experts and blast these caves shut, so you see it is a very slow process of neutralization, and destruction of Nip installations before the infantry even has a chance of occupying any ground. Our method of attack must be working for we have gained ground but in addition, the Nips now snipe at our tanks with 15 and 12 cm guns in their attempt to get out tanks. Our Bn maintenance is excellent and the Nips must be worried for they hit our tanks plenty but the next day more tanks roll out into the field and work them over. If we didn't have men at the service park when the tanks rolled in in the evening to swarm over them and get them ready for the next day plus a good maintenance section, we would have been dismounted before this ... The picture of the tank that fell through the bridge doesn't tell the whole story. (I am not in the picture.) One passed over it just prior ... an engineer told me later that the bridge should have sustained under American standards, 60 tons, but the Nips obviously didn't use as good a grade of cement. We got it out by digging with a dozer in front and putting a small charge to blow the forward wall away that the bow was resting on. Then with three tanks pulling together, out she came and is now in operation as good as new.

'Wednesday, 13 June — This is the first chance that I have had to write since I came over to the Oroku Peninsula. The landing was made on 4 June (Monday), and after the assault tanks were landed the craft came back to our loading area, but a storm came up so I was left on the beach. The Navy didn't return until Wednesday and that is the date I came over here. This phase of the campaign is now over and it was quite tough. Luckily the Nips thought we were going to enter the peninsula from the landward, instead of from the sea. Consequently, they didn't have their sea coast defenses manned as they should, so they were caught off base. We supported the attack as a Battalion and had tanks all over the landscape blazing away. As it had rained badly prior to the landing, we at first were restricted to roads. But the Nips had done such a good job at wrecking the roads that we were rather in a bad spot trying to get anywhere. Finally we got an Engineer Liaison Officer and the services of the entire battalion. After that we went to town fixing roads for ourselves and finally got the tanks where they were needed to blast caves, etc. Finally the Nips were compressed into a small pocket with three regts and tanks surrounding them. Today a few are giving up but most of them are killing themselves much to the amusement of the Marines who are perched on surrounding hills watching the show. Fortunately, our casualties have been very low in this action which was a big help as we were loosing people at a fast rate during the first part of May ...'

'Thursday, 14 June — The weather continues fair and we are putting tanks back together as fast as we can just in case our services are needed elsewhere. We are hoping that our blitzing is over as far as this island is concerned but as you know the joint hasn't been secured yet... Am glad to see that all the papers are carrying pictures of the 6th Tanks. All pictures taken of flame-thrower tanks with us belong to 1st Plat Co. "B". Lieutenant Bennett commanding, who four years ago was an all American guard (I think) at Fordham. Quite a fine lad and we get a book out of him. "Fippo" is what we call him. An oversize cigarette lighter. Everyone here is wishing that the 1st Army would hurry over here and take charge. We could use a few experienced hands. Even the Army says that they are going to learn the hard way out here as things are different. However, the sooner they get here the better for the quicker they will catch on and get organized. I got a letter from Lt-Col. Walseth who was in the past the Tank Officer at Hdq. He now has the 4th Tk Bn. It seems as if they operate their tanks as three companies of the three regiments. He is wondering how we are doing any other way. We have supported each regt in turn as an entire Bn and in that way Naha was finally taken. Over here we supported the Div's main effort with the bulk of our armor and in other spots used a few tanks to maintain pressure on the Nips. If we had had the one company system then the regts that needed tanks would have been out of luck as after two days I managed to get a fresh and rather strong company over that I pushed into the line to help out another company that had it hands full, and I mean just that. We had 25% of our tanks destroyed when it was all over. Fortunately, we had only one killed and about ten wounded. Lucky I calls it. To prove the point on our value as a Bn, we had an engineer Bn, in direct support of us so we could push our tanks forward over nearly impassable roads. The First Tanks are operaring like we do and are in turn having great success. So the day of the RCT is over, especially when operating on a large land mass where maneuver is possible. All of the above is to give you a background on how we operate. Am certainly glad that Gen. Shepherd lets us operate as a Bn and treats us as a tactical group, in that manner we are able to support the infantry more effectively ... also we are never attached but are in direct support. That allows the officers on the spot to either do the correct thing or walk away. If they were attached they would have to do what the infantry wanted whether it was correct or not.

'Friday, 22 June — You seem to be mixed up with the tanks of the two Divisions. The 1st Div uses the Company letter followed by a number, example: A-6, B-1, C-12 etc. Our tanks are marked differently: "A" Co. has red markings; "B" Co. has white markings; "C" Co. has yellow markings.

'Each platoon of each company uses the following figures: 1st Plat a square; 2nd Plat a circle; 3rd Plat a diamond; 4th Plat a triangle; Co. Hdq tanks a clover; Bn Hdq tanks a heart.

'The number in the center of the figure represents the tanks squad or crew. So: A red clover with a one in the center is the "A" Company number, *One* command tank or the Co. Comdr of "A" Co. A two in the center would be the executive officer.

'The tank that Dad saw that hit a mine had a white square with a "2" in it, was: The second tank, 1st Platoon of "B" Co.

'The reason why we have such a complicated marking is for communications and the handling of tanks in the field. It makes it easier to distinguish tanks at a distance so as to find out whose they are. Also the Company Commander if he wants a platoon or sees them doing something wrong knows who had the square or circle platoon and can jump down their throat faster. Evans the other day took some pictures of a mass tank formation that we put on. We employed 42 tanks at one time with the 4th Regt. Two companies in the assault with one delivering overhead fire support to furnish a base of fire. After the two assault companies gained the objective we moved the 3rd company out to work over the right flank. The field we were operating in was in our zone about 2 miles long and a mile to a mile and a half deep. At the far end of the field was a steep ridge. There is where we expected the Nips to fight it out and they did in isolated spots but not as they had done in the past. We rolled out each and every tank we owned that day that could make it down to the jump off. We figured that the Nips were hard up and the more armor there would help matters no end. We also figured that they were out of AT guns so tanks that aren't fixed up with extra protection were okay to use. We guessed right and I think helped bring the conclusion of the battle with a lesser loss of life. Our flame-thrower tanks really have been having a field day for the past three days burning up caves and pockets of Nips that won't quit. They are out today with a couple of platoons of "A" Co. doing some mopping up with the 4th and 29th Regts. I suppose that this mopping up will last for a week or so.

'The island was officially secured at 1305

Excellent shot of a Sherman Firefly with its formidable British 17 pdr gun, capable of knocking out both Tiger 1 and Panther. Fireflies were issued on the basis of one per troop.

yesterday and it certainly is a big relief to all hands. An unusual thing is the number of POWs that are being taken. The Div has taken about 2000 so far. Civilians are coming out of caves and holes by the thousands and they are a pretty sorry lot. The Nips had filled them with propaganda so they were scared as the devil when the Nip defenses collapsed and we moved in.'

Improvements to the Design

As the M4s began to be used in combat by tankers all over the world, ideas for improving them were passed back to Armored Force Headquarters for evaluation. Approved modifications were then put up to the Ordnance Department for incorporation into future Shermans as they came off the assembly lines. The main improvements covered the three vital areas of firepower, protection and mobility.

Firepower Clearly, the most important requirement was to upgun the Sherman and so the Ordnance Department developed the 76 mm gun T1. This was similar to, but not as heavy as, the 3 inch gun M7 which had been designed for the heavy tank project (described later) and used the same ammunition with a smaller diameter cartridge case. This gave it a muzzle velocity of 2600 ft per second when using the APC M62 projectile, as compared with 1930 ft per sec for the 75 mm M2 gun and 2030 ft per sec for the

75 mm M3 and M6 guns. The new gun was tested in August 1942 and standardized as the 76 mm gun M1. Tanks reequipped with the new weapon had (76M1) added after their normal nomenclature. However, further testing showed, that while it was perfectly possible to fit the new gun, the long barrel badly unbalanced the turret and made it very difficult to traverse on a slope. A counterweight at the rear of the turret was proposed and twelve M4A1 (76M1) were built and sent for evaluation in early 1943. The Armored Force was distinctly unhappy with the results and rejected them on the grounds that the turret was of a rushed design with insufficient space for proper crew working. This led to the design of a new cast turret — it was actually a pre-production version of the turret developed for the T20/T23 medium tank which was to be the successor to the Sherman. The new model, designated the M4E6, had other good features in addition to giving more space and a better gun mounting for the 76 mm gun, these included safer ammunition stowage through the use of water jacketed ammunition racks. 'Our morale went up when we began to receive the Shermans with the long barrel 76 mm,' Colonel Bill Lovelady told the writer,'... the gun had more firepower and greater velocity.'

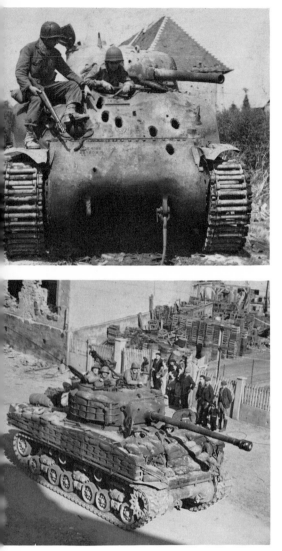

Top
This photograph illustrates well the problem which Sherman crews had to face when taking on opposition such as Tiger and Panther.

Above
Sherman with HVSS and 76 mm, well protected with concreted sandbags, held in place with metal grids, in an attempt to increase its protection.

The main advantage of the 76 mm was that it would penetrate about one inch more armor plate than the 75 mm, although its HE projectile was not as effective and consequently the Armored Force decided, initially, not to drop the 75 mm completely. Unfortunately, despite its improved performance, the new gun was still not a complete match for enemy armor. Soon after D Day, 138 Shermans with the new gun were sent to Normandy, but much to everyone's chagrin, it was soon discovered that they still would not penetrate the frontal armor of either the Tiger or Panther.

'You mean our 76 won't knock these Panthers out?! General Eisenhower exclaimed angrily, 'Why, I thought it was going to be the wonder gun of the war.' 'Oh, it's better than the 75,' replied,' General Omar Bradley, 'but the new charge is much too small. She just hasn't the kick to carry her through the German armor.' Ike shook his head and swore. 'Why is it that I am always the last to hear about this stuff' Ordnance told me this 76 would take care of anything Germans had. Now I find you can't knock out a damn thing with it!'

That conversation appears in Bradley's autobiography, *A Soldier's Story*, and epitomises the profound anger and frustration which the discovery must have engendered. Much later on in the war a high velocity AP round was perfected that increased the muzzle velocity to 3400 ft per sec (HVAP M93 Shot (APCR-T)) but this could still only penetrate the thick frontal armor of the Panther at less than 300 yards range.

There was, however, one type of Sherman that could deal effectively with the heavier German tanks and this was the British version which mounted a high velocity 17-pdr gun, making it probably the most powerfully armed British tank of the war. Known as the Sherman Firefly, the conversion was effective in early 1944 and top priority was given to the upgunning programme. The upgunned tank was issued on the basis of one per troop initially, although towards the end of the war they became more plentiful. There were three models: the Sherman IIC (Firefly) which was the British designation for a Sherman M4A1 with a 17-pdr gun; the Sherman IVC (Firefly); an M4A3 with a 17-pdr, and the Sherman VC (Firefly), an M4A4 with a 17-pdr.

The Americans, once they discovered the inability of their 76 mm to get the job done, tried to get the British to equip their Shermans on a similar scale, with one per tank troop, but unfortunately British Ordnance were already too swamped with British orders, while combat units could ill afford to part with their tanks to send them back to the United Kingdom for refitting. Bradley summarises the unhappy situation by remarking that 'our tank superiority devolved primarily from a superiority in the number rather than the quality of tanks we sent into battle.'

George Stimpson of Kidderminster, Worcestershire, was a sergeant tank commander in 5th Royal Tank Regiment and although he did not command a Firefly, he told the writer that the rest of the troop would not move forward one inch without it. 'The main reason for this was that we had seen the 17-pounder anti-tank gun in action in Tunisia and were well aware that it could knock out a Tiger front on. Tied up with this we were issued with a silhouetted diagram showing that the only places the 75 mm gun would penetrate the Tiger or Panther were the Commander's cupola or the bottom plate at ranges up to 200 yards; this chart which I think originated at Lulworth[3] was as you may well imagine, a terrific boost to morale. The long barrel of the 17-pounder like the 88 mm on the German tanks was at some disadvantage in the Bocage country when it was quite often impossible to traverse and I once saw two Tigers pass broadside on to a Firefly at no more than 200 yards range but neither could traverse to fire at the other. The Cromwells did manage to register hits but I think that in the heat of the moment the gunners forgot to aim at the cupola or floor plate because the shots just bounced off, but as one wag put it, it did prove that they were at least partly right at Lulworth.' George did, however, point out, that a Firefly was never a true match for the Panther or Tiger, because although it had a gun capable of knocking them out, its own armor plating could not even keep out the German 75 mm let alone the 88 mm.

Protection It was important to improve the protection of the Sherman, especially for assault operations and this meant adding in more armor. Perhaps the outstanding example of up-armoring the Sherman is the assault tank 'Jumbo', which weighed in at 42 tons, some six tons over the average M4 combat weight. First to be developed as an assault tank was the T14, the pilot version of which was completed in July 1943 and weighed about 47 tons. Its extra wide tracks came from the heavy tank project and it had a top speed of about 25 mph. The first pilot went to Fort Knox, the second to Britain, which had stated a requirement for a need for up to 8500 assault tanks, and it is now display at the Tank Museum at Bovington Camp. The Armored Force did not like the T14 and the project was therefore canceled.

Nevertheless, the requirement for a more heavily armored tank to support infantry still remained. The danger from such lightweight hollow charge weapons such as the German *Panzerfaust*[4] resulted in all sorts of 'in the field' improvisations to make the Sherman armor better. The T14 had been canceled and the new heavy tank would never be ready in time for D-Day, and so it was decided to modify the Sherman M4A3 model by adding on armor to all hull-surfaces to give a maximum thickness of 4 inches. A new cast turret with 6 inch thick armor on front sides and rear was designed. This all put the weight up to about 42 tons which reduced the maximum speed to about 22 mph. Permanent grousers (known as 'duckbillls') were fitted to the tracks to improve the ride. A total of 254 of these assault tanks, designated as the M4A3E2, were produced in May and June 1944 and shipped over to Europe, arriving that autumn. They were used most effectively and considered by all to be very successful.

Mobility No fewer than five different engines were standardized for use in the Sherman — the GM 6046 diesel, the Chrysler A57 multibank, the Ordnance RD 1820, the Continental R975, and the Ford GAA V-8. The last of these was the one most favored by the US Army and they would have replaced all other types, had there been enough production capacity. Unfortunately, this engine and the Continental R975 both needed a modified hull which would have considerably complicated production, especially as regards the manufacture and supply of spare parts, so it was decided to drop the project. The other engines were all subject to continual development to improve their efficiency. For example, the power of the Continental R975 engine was improved from 400 to 460 hp (at 2400 rmp), while better cooling, engine lubrication, and increased fuel capacity all added to its greater efficiency. In January 1943, the Chrysler Engineering Division installed an A65 petrol engine into a Sherman, the engine having been developed at their own expense, while General Motors developed the V8-184 diesel in a similar manner. Considerable work was also done to improve the transmission, running gear and tracks. Nor was this development all confined to the manufacturers. Combat terrain problems which limited the tanks effectiveness in battle had to be dealt with on the spot. Such a problem was faced in the bocage country of Normandy, where the thick hedgerows which bounded the narrow, sunken country roads greatly hindered tank movement. They were just too thick and strong to burst through and a tank became dangerously exposed if it managed to climb over the top. This led to the invention of a hedgerow cutter, nicknamed the 'Rhinoceros' for obvious reasons, as it was made of steel angles which when welded to the front of the tank formed a tusklike structure. The 'tusk' cut into the base of the hedge and the tank was then able to push its way through taking part of the hedge along with it and completely burying any enemy with a *panzerfaust* who happened to be lurking behind! The invention was also known as the 'Culin hedgerow cutter' after its inventor, Sergeant G Culin of the 102nd Cavalry Recon Squadron who later received the Legion of Merit in recognition of his brainwave. Over 500 tanks were fitted with the Rhinoceros in time for the Norman-

Towards the end of the war plastic armor was fitted to try to improve the Sherman's protection. The M4A3E8 pictured here at Aberdeen Proving Ground in September 1945 has HCR2 plastic armor installed which could defeat the German Panzerfaust 100 or the 8.8 cm rocket.

dy breakout, much of the steel used coming from German beach defence obstacles.

The Sherman in Combat in ETO

Although, as we have seen, the Sherman was used in combat all over the world, by far the greatest concentration of M4s was in North West Europe. Here the American Army alone had fifteen armored divisions and 37 separate tank battalions deployed by the end of the war — representing over 15,000 medium tanks. If all the mediums in British and other Allied tank units plus all the other Sherman variants are included, the total number in the Theater is enormous.

Typical of the actions they fought are those described in *Five Stars to Victory*, a privately published history of the exploits of 'Task Force Lovelady' which comprised the 2nd Battalion (Reinforced) of 33rd Armored Regiment of 3rd Armored Division. The Task Force commander was Bill Lovelady. The history was written by his battalion surgeon, Capt A Eaton Roberts, MC, who had administered to the sick and wounded throughout the five campaigns (Normandy, Northern France, Rhineland, Ardennes, and Central Europe). 3rd Armored Division ('Spearhead') was activated and trained in Louisiana and sailed to England in autumn 1943. They landed in Normandy on 23 June 1944 and 'came of age' in the bloody hedgerow fighting of the Normandy bocage.

'Who will forget that first day? The bowgunners joining the infantrymen to spray every tree from top to bottom, the platoon of tanks dashing a few yards to a confining bank which enclosed every field; the great lumber-

ing tank dozer carving a crude driveway into the next field followed closely by infantry lookouts who would peek around corners to point out tank targets, crawling on their bellies and shooting snipers, real and imaginary out of trees; the tanks pouring through the narrow gap to disperse hurriedly in the tiny field beyond, monotonously like the ones they had just come from; the piercing urgent cry of "Medic!" when one was wounded. These memories come back today with a vividness that can be retained only by the frightful uniqueness of high adventure . . . Admittedly we were green, inexperienced troops. But we showed promise and got the job done, with all our mistakes. Lt Lipman's D Company platoon, together with some tanks from E Company, performed exceptionally well by knocking out five Mark VI tanks, almost before dawn of their first day of combat. In addition, they destroyed two enemy pillboxes, and killed several enemy soldiers armed with bazookas. Only one of his Shermans was hit. This belonged to Staff Sergeant Triola. It was quickly repaired and fighting again before the day ended. . . . The night of 11 July cannot be forgotten by Captain George Stallings (now Lt-Col.) commanding D Company. This was the first of a long series of examples of his leadership, devotion to duty, courage and cool-headedness. Rightfully he was awarded the Distinguished Service Cross for his bold action. The night was dark as his tank returned alone towards the front lines following

an officers' meeting. Without warning, a mass of fire belched down the hatch and all its occupants scrambled out looking like human torches. The acrid fumes of asphalt filled the air, and they realized that they had been attacked by flame-throwers. Sgt Lewis and Tec/4 MacHumphrey perished from their burns. Tec/5 MacLaim and Corporal Miracle escaped and crawled back wounded, to our lines. Capt Stallings threshed the flames from the burning clothes and body,

Left
An American armored column advances inland through a small French village on 11 June 1944. Note the Tricolour on the railings.

Below
Lifting the damaged engine from *Hurricane* in France in August 1944 is a 10-ton 'Wrecker' fitter's lorry. Another fitter prepares the new engine — note the pin ups on the lid of his tool-box! The damaged engine will then be repaired and reused.

Bottom
A squad of GIs advance into a Belgian town, making full use of the cover afforded by the accompanying Sherman. Note the Culin hedgerow cutter on the front of the tank.

Right
Sherman DD (Duplex Drive), with the screen fully raised just entering the water. Invented by Nicholas Straussler, a Hungarian naturalised Briton, who first put forward his ideas to the War Office in 1940. Before then most swimming devices had comprised some type of cumbersome pontoon. Having waterproofed the AFV the collapsible canvas screen was raised around it, using rubber tubes carrying compressed air. Struts then held it in place. The propellers (clearly visible at the rear) were driven by a power take-off from the main engine and provided for a speed of approximately 4 knots in the water. A complete brigade of Sherman DDs was used on D Day in the British and Canadian sectors and they were the only gun tanks which managed to get ashore to support the assault. In the US sector most of the DD tanks launched foundered in the heavy seas and never reached shore. This undoubtedly had a major effect upon the size of the initial bridgehead achieved. DDs went on to be used in assault crossings over the Scheldt, Rhine, and Elbe, the latter being the last time they were used in the North West European campaign (29 April 1945). The existence of DD tanks was not made public until September 1945.

Far right
Shermans of 9th US Army push forward on the offensive into Germany, on 19 November 1944, despite the deep recaptured on 24 January 1945.

Opposite Center left
The swimming device shown here (the T6) was one of a number tested by the Ordnance Department who did not like the Sherman DD because of its lack of seaworthiness. Compartmented steel floats were attached to the tank — front, rear, and sides — then filled with plastic foam covered in waterproof cellophane. Propulsion was by the Sherman's tracks and twin rudders at the back were controlled by ropes from the turret. It achieved 4 mph in the water. Overall length was 47 ft 8 ins and width 11 ft. The photograph shows an M4A1 fitted with the T6 device on the island of Bougainville on 27 October 1944.

Opposite Center Right
This Sherman was captured by the enemy and used during their attack in the Ardennes. It was then recapture on 24 January 1945.

Opposite bottom
Gun towers. Various 'war-weary' tanks and SP artillery guns were converted into either APCs or gun towers. These included Priests, and Ram and Sherman tanks. As APCs they would carry a section of ten men plus two crew, or as gun towers they would carry the gun crew and ammunition, while towing the gun behind. These particular vehicles were photographed advancing towards Zundert in Holland.

ending up head downwards in a deep wet ditch. Gutteral voices of the German tank-hunting patrol warned him to simulate death. Not daring to move, scarcely breathing and with the pain of second degree burns on his forehead and arms, he lay motionless. The intruders gathered round talking and examining their prize. Once they approached Capt Stallings, decided that he must be dead and after an hour, their voices dissolved in the chill night air. The Captain alternately crawled, walked and ran back to the vicinity of our task forces command post. He arrived at dawn, covered in black asphalt spots in his hair, face and uniform. He remained on duty and retained his suggestion of cool dignity, which was to hold the respect and admiration of all who fought with him during the bitter months which followed.

'*Northern France.* ... On the day Paris was freed, we reached the banks of the Seine River some twelve miles south of the capital . . . We thought the German army might make a definite stand at the Seine, but the crossing at Tilly was entirely uneventful and we leaguered the night of the 25th of August on the eastern bank. The following day we knocked out four Mark IV tanks and four trucks and were driving hard over historic land, for we were approaching the Marne River, where American blood was spilled so abundantly during the First World War. By starting our drives a little earlier, stopping a little later and going a little faster, we were apparently straining the enemy's ability to coordinate his units and maintain his own lines of communication. At any rate even his usually brilliant rearguard action was failing,

Top left
Sherman fascine carriers seen here in Italy. They were also used by 79th Armored Division in ETO.

Above
Sherman Twaby Ark bridge had trackways fitted fore and aft over the hull top (the turrret had, of course, been removed). The AFV would be driven into the river or ditch needing to be spanned and the ramps released. They were then hoisted by a second vehicle.

Top right
A concentration of infantry and armor 'marrying up' before moving forward during Montgomery's drive on Goch, 18 February 1945, which was one of the main towns of the Siegfried Line. The odd M5A1 light tank can be seen among the Shermans.

Above right
Tanks of First US Army advancing towards Samree in Belgium where victory came only after a 48 hour battle in a blinding snowstorm in January 1945.

Right
Shermans of the Seventh US Army are used in an indirect fire mission against enemy counter-attacking in the Gambsheim area, north of Strasbourg, on 20 January 1945. Note the tactical sign on the side of the tanks which denotes A Company 3rd Platoon (three dots above the chevron) of 23rd Tank Battalion, 12th Armored Div.

for on the 27th of August we captured, intact, two selfpropelled guns, two armored cars, including their crews, knocked out several personnel carrying trucks and killed and captured many infantrymen. More important we reached the Marne River at 1500 hours, crossing it on an unblown bridge which required only a few minutes to reinforce it sufficiently to allow our column to thunder over it. ... Exhilarated by lack of effective resistance at the river, we continued full speed reaching the outskirts of the sizeable city of Meaux at 1700 hours. Quickly planning an attack and rendering the essential orders, Col. Lovelady and Capt Stallings drove into the city with the leading tank companies, seizing it immediately and securing it completely by 2000 hours. ... Hunting was fine indeed on the roads to Soissons, which we reached within twenty-four hours after crossing the Marne. Behind us that day were 69 miles of unbeliev-

ably brilliant fighting. We knocked out three Mark V Panthers, four Mark IVs, two self-propelled guns, three scout cars, eight half-tracks together with an uncounted number of trucks and smaller cars. The price we paid, in addition to two light tanks, were the lives of two infantrymen with eight others wounded and three wounded tankers. ... These were mad days. There were no two of them alike. Each was filled with new thrills, new adventures. These were Panther hunting days and it was unusual if we didn't knock out two or more of these massive German tanks, along with smaller Mark IVs, armored cars, trucks, command cars, SP guns, and dual-purpose 88s. Almost daily we would capture 40 or more prisoners and now we were beginning to contact many horse-drawn vehicles of enemy cavalry.'

Later in the history there is a short account of a successful engagement of a Panther with the new 76 mm gun in the Rhineland near the Siegfried line.

'Knowing that we must come to the top of the hill in single file, the Germans waited for us and had a field day of their own for a while costing our task force four Sherman tanks and a half-track but wounding surprisingly few. The enemy did not have long to revel in his early successes, for by late afternoon the tables turned and we knocked out a Mark V Panther, two 88 mm dual purpose, three anti-tank and seven well dug-in 20 mm AA guns. We headed down hill now, looking into the narrow valley, on our left, a Panther crept stealthily towards us. Sharp eyes caught it, lurking in the long afternoon shadows of evergreens. S/Sgt Stanko (later to be honored by a battle-field commission) expertly trained his new 76 mm gun on the target, firing a round of high-speed armor-piercing ammunition at the enemy colossus. True as an arrow the missile found its mark, incapacitating the offender by penetrating under its final drive. Firing six more rounds in rapid succession, Stanko and his crew of veteran tankers left the Panther burning. Little did he realise that stars were watching him. Maj. Gen. Rose (CG 3rd Armored Div) and Brig.-Gen Boudinot (Comd CCB) were nearby having come forward to help plan the next day's operation. Both of these commanders had seen at first hand the type of marksmanship that helped to make Task Force Lovelady a great team.'

Another tanker of Spearhead was featured in an article in the Army weekly newspaper Yank.[5] He was a lanky, one-time Golden Gloves boxing champion from Sinton, Texas, by the name of S/Sgt Lafayette G Pool, whose CO said of him: 'Pool is the tanker of tankers; he can never be replaced in this regiment.' Hardly surprising that he should be thought of so highly when he was definitely credited with the destruction of 258 enemy vehicles, 250 German prisoners taken and over 1,000 dead '... before the guns of his Sherman tank In The Mood.'

'When the division — it was the "Bayou Blitz" then — was activated at Camp Beauregard, Louisiana, back in 1941, Pool, a skinny lad from Texas, was right there in the ranks. He came from the old 40th Armored Regi-

ment, medium tanks, which was famed for its cadres, and he was a rugged Joe. He was over six feet tall, wiry, with the sloping shoulders of a boxer and a twisted nose to remind him of the golden gloves. There was the beginnings of a legend about Pool even then. He'd won the sectional 165 pound crown at New Orleans, Louisiana, that year, but turned down an offer to go to Chicago and the national final golden gloves tournament. The reason? Pool was a tanker first and a boxer second; his outfit had just been alloted a few of the latest tanks!

'In action, as in the ring, Pool punched hard and accurately. He hated German theory and believed that he could beat the Wehrmacht, gun to gun and man to man. He wanted tough assignments. He asked for the dubious honor of leading those powerful armored attacks that knifed through the Nazi legions during our summer offensive.

'Pool's crew was ideal for the task. Besides Richards and Close (Cpl Wilbert "Red" Richards was the driver and Pfc Bert Close the assistant driver), there was Cpl Willis Oller of Morrisonville, Illinois, gunner, and T/5 Del Boggs, of Lancaster, Ohio, the loader. Boggs fought with special fury; he'd had a brother killed in the war. Oller, gunner of In the Mood is alleged to have seen all of Normandy, France, Belgium and the Siegfried Line through the sights of his gun! He was very quick and alert. Richards recalled a night when the spearhead had driven deep into German lines from Origny in France. It had become quite dark when the order finally came to halt and coil. Pool opened his mouth to say — "Driver halt", but found himself looking at a big Jerry dual purpose AA gun in the gloom ahead. He said: "Gunner, fire!" And Oller, with his eye perpetually pressed into the sight, squarely holed the enemy weapon before the crew could recognize the American tank.

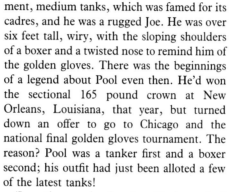

Top
Shermans of Eight Armored Division, First US Army, line a quiet lane in Bergerhausen, Germany, soon after the town had fallen to First Army in their drive for the Rhine, 6 March 1945. Note the tanks' extra protection.

Center
Sandbagged Shermans, supporting the 17th US Airborne Division, moving forward through the battle-scarred streets of Munster, some 50 miles Northeast of Wesel on the Rhine. Munster was cleared of enemy forces on 3 April 1945.

Above
The snow-capped peaks of the Bavarian Alps and the gaily decorated chalets of the famous ski resort of Garmischpartenkirchen, provide an incongrous background to this column of 10th Armored Division Shermans, Seventh US Army, on 11 May 1945.

'Night actions were commonplace to the crew of *In the Mood*. At Colombrier, in France, Pool's leading tank almost collided with a Jerry Mark V Panther, pride of the Wehrmacht. The Panther fired twice and missed. Pool's single projectile tore the turret off the big German vehicle. Again, at Couptrain, the armored column reached its daily objective deep in the night. Beseiged on all sides, unable to send help forward, Col. Richardson listened to the radio report of the battle from Pool's vehicle. He heard the Sergeant say joyously: "I ain't got the heart to kill 'em ..." And then, over the airwaves came the mad rattle of the .30-caliber bow gun. And again the fighting Sergeant's voice "Watch them bastards run. Give it to 'em Close!" Surrounded by dismounted enemy troops, Pool and his crew fought steadily until morning brought reinforcements.

'The amazing score compiled by the Texas tanker and his gang is fully authenticated. At Namur, Belgium, they knocked out a recorded 24 hour bag of one SP *Sturmgeschutz* gun and fifteen other enemy vehicles. It was great stuff for Pool. He was proving to himself, and to the world, that the American soldier is more than a match for Hitler's "supermen".

'Again, at Dison, in Belgium, as the spearhead neared the great city of Liege, Pool distinguished himself. Acting as platoon leader he characteristically decided to use one tank, his own, to clean out an annoying pocket of resistance on the left flank of the route they were travelling. After finding and destroying six armored infantry vehicles, Pool discovered that the head of his column had been fired upon by a German Panther tank. Hurriedly he gave orders to his driver to rejoin the column. Upon arriving at the scene of action he immediately observed the enemy tank, gave a single estimate of range to Oller. The gunner fired one armor-piercing projectile at 1500 yards to destroy the Panther. The column went ahead again, Pool at his accustomed place in the lead.

'Although Lafe Pool lost two tanks to

enemy action, he remained as nerveless as a mechanical man. The crew drew added confidence from his bearing under fire and as a result they worked beautifully together. From the day of the great breakthrough in Normandy, they had smashed the Wehrmacht before them, burned its vehicles, decimated its troops. These men seemed impervious to German shells. Twenty-one times they had led the irresistible drive of the American armor and remained unscathed in this most hazardous task of total war. Now, after crossing France and Belgium, smashing the famous outer fortifications of the Siegfried Line and taking part in the action which resulted in the capture of the first German town to fall to US forces, Pool and his crew turned their faces toward greater Germany and the last round.

'The town was Munsterbusch, south of Aachen. Desperately, as the west wall crumbled into ruin, Panther tanks came out to duel with Shermans of the 3rd Armored "Spearhead" Division.

'Pool's tank strangely enough, was working as flank guard of the task force that day. Watchers including his Colonel, who also rode in a tank, saw the bright lance-shaft of German tracer hit the turret of *In the Mood*. The big Sherman faltered. Inside, Pool said calmly, "Back up Baby". And, as Richards backed the tank slowly, the second shell hit them well forward.

'To Close, Oller, Boggs and Richards, there was only the space-filling, bell-sound of the hit, the acrid stench of powder and the shower of sparks. They didn't know that Pool had been thrown clear, his leg bleeding profusely from a splinter wound. Richards continued to back the tank, carrying out his last order from the Sergeant.

'Col. Richardson saw *In the Mood* slowly reach a cut bank, tilt, and with the agonizing slowness of a nightmare, topple almost upside down.

'At that monent Oller felt the hot blood on his legs and knew that he had been wounded. Richards, Boggs and Close were unhurt. All four men crawled out of their tank. Medical aid men had already reached Pool, now two of them came forward to attend Oller.

'Pool cursed the Germans bitterly as the aid man bandaged his wound. As they placed him on a litter he twisted suddenly and said: "Somebody take care of my tank."

'Exit, for the time being, Lafe Pool, ace of American tankers. He thought he could beat Jerry. He did. He proved it so often that the record is almost an unbelievable document of total victory. In the arena of armored warfare, S/Sgt Lafayette Pool, golden glover from Sinton, Texas, bowed out at a climatic

moment. From the beaches of Normandy to the dragons teeth of the Siegfried Line he had been the point of the "Spearhead".'

Specialised Equipments

A wide variety of specialized equipment was fitted onto the basic Sherman chassis by both the American and British armies, examples of which are illustrated. They can be broken down under the following headings: armored recovery vehicles; earth moving equipment; mine clearing equipment; gap crossing equipment; amphibious equipment; miscellaneous engineer equipment; flame-throwers; rocket launchers; gun mounts (not including artillery howitzers or tank destroyers); armored personnel carriers, load carriers and prime movers.

79th Armoured Division

One of the greatest concentrations of these specialized equipments was to be found in the British 79th Armoured Division, or 'Hobo's Funnies' as they were sometimes irreverently called. The 79th Armoured was a very special ized formation, larger than any other armored formation in 21st Army Group. However, because of the unique nature of its AFVs it never fought as a complete division; elements fought with *every* brigade, division and corps in both the British and Canadian Armies, from the Normandy D-Day onwards through France and North West Europe. The success of the division and its skill in handling the complexities of these strange devices was due in no small measure to just one man, Maj.-Gen. Sir Percy Hobart — 'Hobo'. Before raising and training his 'Funnies', Hobo had been responsible for the training of two of Britain's finest armored divisions—the 7th and 11th Armoured. 79th Armoured did, of course, contain a very large number of specialized armored vehicles which were based upon other AFVs than the Sherman. However, large numbers of Sherman DD swimming gun tanks and Sherman Crab flail minesweepers were employed by the division. If one takes the planned D-Day landings as an example, then the specialized armored vehicles were scheduled to precede the infantry during the landings, so that they could deal with beach obstacles, pill-boxes, clear gaps through minefields, etc, and establish points of exit from the beaches using bridging tanks. They would be led in by DD tanks and followed by normal gun tanks. However, due to the exceptionally high seas most of the DDs were unable to swim ashore from their LCTs and so the Sherman Crabs, which had been landed from beached landing craft, were the only gun tanks available ashore in the early

stages of the landing. Nevertheless, the landings in the British and Canadian sectors were successful, and by the end of D-Day the beachheads were firmly established and troops were already moving inland. In the American sector, the situation was not so good. The Americans had decided against the use of specialized armor, apart from DD tanks and armored bulldozers. In the high seas most of their DD tanks had foundered, so the infantry landed virtually unsupported by armor. This led to them being confined to the immediate beach area and they suffered heavy casualties as a result, before they could eventually manage to get off the beaches and strike inland. Thereafter, specialized armor was used on numerous occasions as the Allied armies fought across North West Europe. For example, at the time of the Rhine Crossing, the strength of the division was nearly 2000 specialized vehicles and gun tanks, plus nearly 5000 soft-skinned vehicles, and hundreds of motorcycles. It is interesting to note that the very existence of this special force was not announced publicly until after March 1945, while details of some of the AFVs (*e.g.* the DD tanks) were kept secret until after the end of the war.

'Georgie's Boys'

It would be unthinkable to write a book about American armor in World War II without mentioning the exploits of Gen. George S Patton's magnificent Third Army. Even when reduced to cold figures the feats which he and his tankers achieved in 281 days of campaigning make incredible reading. In that time the US Third Army liberated or captured 81,522 square miles of North West Europe, containing an estimated 12,000 cities, towns and communities, including 27 cities of more than 50,000 people. They killed 144,500 enemy, wounded a further 386,200, and captured a staggering 1,280,688. No fewer than six corps and 42 divisions were at one time or another under command. These included some of the finest armored divisions in the US Army — for example, 4th, 5th, 6th and 7th Armored Divisions were all in the Third Army Order of Battle when they landed in France in July 1944.

Here are a few battle stories from units of Patton's Third Army. The first appeared in War Department General Orders published on 30 July 1946, and tells of Company A, 68th Tank Battalion's action in Landroff, France in November 1944.

'*Company A 68th Tank Battalion*[6] is cited for extraordinary gallantry, indomitable courage, tenacity of purpose and high *esprit de*

Top left
The Sherman Scorpion IV used equipment very similar to that developed for the Grant Scorpion IV mounted on a Sherman III. The two auxiliary engines which drove the chain flail made the tank very wide and difficult to maneuver across bridges, etc.

Top right
A Sherman Crab Mk 1 in Normandy. The flail is raised in the road travelling position. There were 43 flailing chains on the rotor which beat the ground just ahead of the vehicle to explode enemy mines. Note the station-keeping lights on the rear. Troops of five Crabs were usually allocated for clearance operations.

Above left
Sherman with Lulu (photograph shows it in the operating position). Lulu was an electrical mine detecting equipment — there were mine detector coils in each of the three wooden drums which registered on an indicator inside the tank if they passed over a mine.

Above right
Sherman with AMRCR (anti-mine reconnaissance castor roller) Mk 1a. The rollers were carried on a frame in front of the tank and exploded the mines by pressure. A similar device was fitted to the Churchill tank.

corps displayed in accomplishment of an unusually difficult mission during the period 14–15 November 1944 in Landroff, France. On 14 November 1944, at about 1300 hrs, Company A, 68th Tank Battalion, reinforced by elements of the 44th Armored Infantry Battalion, launched an attack against enemy forces holding Landroff. By 1800 hrs, the village had been secured and outposted although enemy artillery and self-propelled guns maintained continuous heavy fire on the village and reconnaissance elements reported approximately ten enemy tanks and heavy reinforcements of infantry maneuvering to join enemy forces on the high ground dominating the village. At 1900 hrs, under the protection of direct fire from eight enemy guns, an enemy force of company strength, with two self-propelled assault guns, counterattacked, broke the outer defenses, and entered the village. Enemy armor was allowed to enter the village and then ambushed and destroyed by tank destroyer and tank fire. Enemy infantry pushed the attack vigorously and in the desperate hand to hand fighting the attack was beaten back only after the entire crew of a self-propelled gun was killed and the supporting infantry decimated.

'Another enemy counterattack was repelled about 2400 hrs by effective defending tank and automatic weapons fire, maneuvering rapidly from one threatened point to another. A third counterattack at about 0110 hrs was halted in a similar manner. After intense artillery, assault gun and mortar concentrations, lasting for 30 minutes, had been directed on the village another coordinated enemy attack, employing an estimated force of battalion strength in the assault wave, was launched at 0200 hrs. Despite strong friendly artillery support, the enemy, heavily armed with rocket launchers and automatic weapons, continued their fanatical attack. Although the extreme darkness prohibited effective employment of the 75 mm guns of the tanks, the enemy was beaten back three times in the bitter fighting which lasted until 0430 hrs. Enemy infantry managed to infiltrate and, at one time, encircle and isolate the defenders, taking up positions with machine guns and rocket launchers in buildings and streets within the defensive perimeter and were repeatedly routed out by the courageous defenders in hand-to-hand fighting with pistols, knives, and grenades. Prior to daybreak, another force of enemy armor and infantry was observed preparing to attack, but was

neutralized by fire from friendly artillery. After the artillery preparation, a platoon of medium tanks maneuvered into firing positions at close range and inflicted heavy casualties on the remaining enemy in the assembly area by direct fire. This action turned the enemy flank and forced the remnants of the unit into the fire of a friendly task force. It was estimated that the force before Landroff was of division strength and, in the bitter fighting, the bulk of one regiment was completely destroyed. During this action, Company 68th Tank Battalion sustained casualties amounting to 13 killed and five officers and 79 enlisted men wounded. The fortitude, tenacity and indomitable will displayed by Company A, 68th Tank Battalion, are in keeping with the highest traditions of the military service and reflect great credit on the armed forces of the United States.'

One of the members of the beleaguered tank company was Master Sgt Howard A McNeill, who was then a member of a tank crew in 1st Platoon. He wrote: '. . . the official order tells you how fierce the fight really was.

However, except for the intense artillery fire, both friendly and enemy, the 1st Platoon didn't get hit by the attack as much as the rest of the company. 1st Platoon outposted the east end of town, next to the graveyard. We wouldn't have had so far to go had we got it. Sgt Foutch took over our tank and remained with us overnight. Foutch called for artillery to fire on our position. They obliged, so did the Germans. Next morning, the tank and surrounding area was completely covered with a two to three inch depth of black powder. The in-coming mail must have been mightily close. Some of the tanks ran out of ammo and men were killed while taking ammo from tank to tank. Sgt Moore's tank was well out in front and the direction from which the main German attack came. He called Sgt Burger and told him they were out of ammo and the Germans were almost on top of them and wanted to move back into town. Burger came back with: "You come this way and I will blow your A.. Off!" Sgt Moore's tank remained in position. The next morning Shunk couldn't get the tank started, so he had Sgt Sucharski's tank pull us to start the tank.

Top left
Aunt Jemima, the mine exploder T1E3(M1) was developed in 1943. Some 75 were built and it was the most widely used of the American mine exploders, seeing operational service both in Italy and ETO. Sometimes it needed a second tank to help push the equipment along.

Top right
Mine Exploder T10. This strange looking remotely controlled mine exploder device initially comprised three roller units in an articulated tricycle layout which was controlled from a following tank. This was then modified so that the tricycle unit was powered and driven from a M4 hull and turret, mounted above. It proved too unwieldy and was canceled in late 1944.

Above left
Mine Exploder T8, known also as *Johnnie Walker*. It comprised steel plungers/exploder units carried on a pivoted frame in front of the tank. The original model had three units but this was increased to six. Tests proved it impossible to steer and the project was abandoned in March 1944.

Above right
Mine Resistant Vehicle T15. Extra belly and side armor was fitted, the turret was removed, and heavy duty tracks and suspension units reinforced by armored brackets were fitted. Two other models, the T15E1 and T15E2 were also built, but all were very similar in appearance. Work started in September 1944, but was abandoned when the war finished.

Top
A POA-CWS-H5 flame-thrower, mounted with a 105 mm gun during tests in Hawaii in July 1945. The fuel container was carried inside the turret.

Above
The M3-4-3 bow mounted flame-thrower replaced the .30-cal machine gun in the bow ball mount. It had a range of about 60 yards. In the photograph the gun is being used to fire thickened gasoline fuel in a demonstration.

In doing this it put Sgt Sucharski's tank in the position we had occupied and later that morning the tank was hit, causing injuries to Dutchy Walters and others in the tank which partially burned. We continued to receive artillery all that day and most of the next two days. We could see German infantry in the woods and hills east of us. We tried to get some artillery fire onto them, but they wouldn't give us any. We remained in Landroff a few days and had Thanksgiving dinner there.'

On leaving Landroff, the company moved on and a few days later McNeill's tank was hit by *panzerfausten*. He gives this account of the incident: 'We had been told to expect fire from rocket launchers from the ditches along the road to Metzing and as we were just starting toward the town, I was keeping an eye open for German infantry when all of a sudden Kratzer yelled "Bail out". First round hit Shunk and also hit Kovaleski, knocking him over to my side. We were both trying to get out of the tank at the same time but couldn't, so as I dropped back down onto my seat to enable Kovaleski to get out, another hit was made on the loader's side. This round cut the machine gun in half and completely destroyed both the radio transmitter and receiver. How I got out I just don't know. Anyway, the next day my left side and shoulder was black and blue. The assistant driver pulled on the lever to get the tank off the road and it went into a field and on toward Metzing and finally stopped when it hit a large tree — *The Stars and Stripes* had an article in it about this incident with the heading: "Phantom tank chases Germans"! The assistant driver had never been inside a tank until the day before. How he knew which lever to pull God only knows. ... Just a note about Kovaleski, what I believe saved him and he agreed, was a pistol he was wearing on his left hip. The first projectile hit the gun and of course slowed down, only knocking him across to my side. We found out about the gun the next day, when Kratzer, who was holding our pistols until we returned from the medics, told us the gun had been bent so badly by the hit it received, that the receiver could not be pulled back.'

McNeill also relates that, during the battle of the Bulge, the weather was so cold that the only way to get the grease and oil out of the 76 mms of the newly issued tanks, was to pour gasoline into the barrels, strike a match and let the fire melt the grease enough to clean the bore. As he remarks: 'It's a wonder we weren't blown to Hell and back'.

4th Armored to the Rescue

It was of course the 4th Armored Division that relieved the battered Bastogne garrison of paratroopers, who, under their gallant commander, Brig.-Gen. McAuliffe (whose reply 'Nuts!' to German surrender demands is part of American folklore) had held Bastogne against the full weight of the last German offensive in the Ardennes. 4th Armored were the only armored division not to adopt a nickname, (although they were occasionally called 'Breakthrough') because they felt that to be called the 4th Armored was name enough. As their famous commander Maj.-Gen. 'Tiger Jack' Wood explained to newsmen when they asked him what the name of his new command would be: 'They shall be known by their deeds alone'. That phrase is now the byword of the 4th Armored. The relief of Bastogne came after Third Army had executed an amazing 90 degrees turn from the Saar, to help deal with the enemy breakthrough in the First Army sector. The news that 'Georgie's Boys' were coming to the rescue was typically greeted with remarks such as the one made by a sergeant of the equally beleaguered garrison at St Vith, when told by his commander Colonel (later General) Bruce C Clarke, that Gen Patton's army had turned north and was attacking the southern side of the German 'Bulge': 'The Sergeant thought for a minute and said: "That's good news. If Georgie's coming we have got it made". I know of no other senior commander in Europe who could have brought forth such a response.'

It was the 37th Tank Battalion who were leading on the final run into Bastogne and their privately published history tells of these last dramatic moments.

'The final assault was launched from the far edge of Assenois, the last village before Bastogne. In the lead was Company C of the 37th Tank Battalion, followed by Company C of the 53rd Armored Infantry Battalion. Lt-Col.

126

Creighton W Abrams, then commander of the 37th Tank Battalion, clinched a cold cigar in the corner of his mouth and said: "We're going in to those people now." With that, he swept his arm forward and the charge was on.

'The command tank of Company C, 37th Tank Battalion moved out first. In the turret was 1st Lt Charles Boggess, Jr. "The Germans had these two little towns of Clochiment and Assenois on the secondary road we were using to get to Bastogne", he recalled later. "Beyond Assenois, the road ran up a ridge through heavy woods. There were lots of Germans there too. We were going through fast, all guns firing, straight up that road to bust through before they had time to get set. I thought of a lot of things before we took off. I thought of whether the road would be mined, whether the bridge would be blown, whether they would be ready at their anti-tank guns. Then we charged and I didn't have time to wonder."

'Meanwhile, four American artillery battalions were slamming barrages into enemy-held Assenois and the edge of the woods beyond it. The 22nd, 66th and 94th Armored Artillery battalions of the 4th Armored dropped in 105 mm shells and a supporting battalion lobbed 155 mm howitzer rounds. Under the artillery support, Lt Boggess' medium tank advanced through shell bursts from the enemy positions. The ground pitched and houses spilled into the street, but the undaunted American forces kept going.

'"I used the 75 like a machine gun" said Boggess' gunner, Cpl Milton Dickerman. "Murphy (Pte James the loader) was plenty busy throwing in the shells. We shot 21 rounds in a few minutes and I don't know how much machine gun stuff. As we got to Assenois an anti-tank gun in a half-track fired at us and threw dirt all over. I got the half-track in my sights and hit it with high explosive. It blew up."

'Dirt from the enemy shell burst had smeared the driver's periscope. "I made out OK, although I couldn't see very good," explained Pte Hubert Smith. "I sort of guessed at the road. I had a little trouble when my left brake locked and the tank turned up a road we didn't want to go. So I just stopped her, backed her up and went on again."

'The armored infantry was also in the thick of the fighting and one of the infantry men distinguished himself gallantly enough to become the third Congressional Medal of Honor winner in the 4th Armored Division. He was Pte James Hendrix, a 19 year old rifleman with Company C, 53rd Armored Infantry Battalion. His citation read: "Pte Hendrix dismounted and advanced upon two 88 mm

One of the greatest armored commanders of all time, General George S Patton, Jr, whose ivory handled revolvers and immaculate appearance were as much a part of his 'War Face' as Montgomery's double badged baret was his special trademark. Patton was the first commander to lead American tanks into action in World War II and earned a tremendous reputation for dashing leadership. Controversial in World War II through such incidents as the slapping of a 'malingerer' in Sicily, Patton was still a superlative field commander, probably the general most feared by the Germans, who rated him as the best Allied commander. His profanity and larger than life character are probably better remembered than his sensitivity and compassion for the wounded. He was a complete mixture of opposites, however, on one point no one could disagree and that was his ability to lead armored forces in battle. Gen. Patton was killed in a traffic accident in Germany in December 1945. Mike Province

gun crews, and by the ferocity of his actions compelled the German gun crews first to take cover and then surrender."

'Hendrix, a red-haired, freckle-faced farm boy from Arkansas, later explained, "We ran up on them yelling 'come out' but they wouldn't. One poked his head out of a foxhole and I shot him through the neck. I got closer and hit another on the head with the butt of my M1. He had American matches on him. Others came out with their hands up."

'The citation continues: "Later in the attack this fearless soldier again left his vehicle voluntarily to aid two wounded soldiers threatened by enemy machine gun fire. Effectively silencing two enemy machine guns, he held off the enemy by his own fire until the wounded men were evacuated."

American armor on parade in Berlin. 2nd Armored Division (Hell of Wheels) on parade for the Secretary of War, Henry L Stimson on 20 July 1945. With him in the leading half-track is the unmistakable figure of the 3rd US Army Commander Gen. George S Patton, Jr. US Army.

'"I just shot at the machine guns like all the .50s on the halftracks were doing," Hendrix said. "A halftrack had been hit pretty bad and these fellows were wounded and lying in the ditch. Machine gun fire was mostly toward them, but some bullets were coming my way."

'Continuing the attack, Hendrix again endangered himself when he ran to aid still another soldier who was trapped in a burning halftrack. Braving enemy sniper fire and exploding mines and ammunition in the vehicle, he pulled the wounded man from the conflagration and extinguished his flaming clothing with his body. Hendrix explained it so: "A grenade exploded between his legs and everybody got out. But he was hollering help. I pulled at him and got him out on the road, but he was burned bad. I tried to find water to put out the fire, but the water cans were full of bullet holes, so I beat out the flames as best I could. He died later."

'The four lead tanks in Boggess' column drew ahead as the halftracks were slowed down by German shells and debris. The tankers rolled along, sweeping the wooded ridge with machine gun fire. Finally, they burst through the German defenses and into the 101st Airborne perimeter. Lt Boggess ordered the roaring Sherman tank down to a crawl. In the open fields beyond he saw red, yellow and blue parachutes spilled over the snow like confetti. Some of the colored chutes, caught in the tall pines, indicated where ammunition, food and medicine had been dropped to the besieged troops. The column halted.

'Standing up in his turret, Lt Boggess shouted, "Come here, come on out," to khaki-clad figures in foxholes. This is the 4th Armored." There was no answer. Helmeted heads peeped suspiciously over carbine sights. The lieutenant shouted again. A lone figure strode forward. Lt Boggess watched him carefully. "I'm Lt Webster of the 36th Engineers, 101st Airborne Division," the approaching figure called. "Glad to see you". The time was 4.45 pm, December 26th.'

'Georgie's Boys' had done it again.'

Top
Loading 4.5 in rockets into the 90 in long plastic tubes of the T34 Rocket Launcher. There were 60 tubes arranged in a double bank of 36 on the top and two double bank of twelve below (one on either side of the elevating arm). After firing the launcher could be jettisoned if necessary.

Left
The T34 launcher was nicknamed *Calliope* (probably because it slightly resembled a steam organ rather than the chief of the nine Muses!). This graphic photograph of it firing by night is an awesome sight.

Action on Hill 91

Of course, some soldiers of arms other than tanks found themselves as 'part-time tankers', manning Shermans in order to carry out their particular task on the battlefield. A perfect example is that of Forward Observer (FO) of an armored artillery battalion. Lieutenant Ralph Balestrieri, of Eatontown, New Jersey, was an FO for the 58th Armored Field Artillery Battalion of 1st US Army, and supported the 3rd Armored Division for most of the war in Europe. The Shermans which the FO parties manned were fighting tanks and he told the author about some of the occasions when they had had to fire their guns 'in anger'. For example: '. . . when approaching the Siegfried Line a truck-load of enemy troops was spotted in a nearby town. The FO tank was the only one with a clear shot and took them under fire. . . . About 11 September 1944, the leading elements of CCB, 3 Armored Division were scattered by an anti-tank gun. The FO-2 tank of the 58th Armored FA Battalion got caught on a ridge line and suppressed the enemy anti-tank gun with seven of the fastest shots anyone had heard, the task force commander even commented about their rapidity. . . . The 58th were moving up to join the 28th Infantry Division east of Bastogne when it came under fire from an enemy spearhead, east of Longvilly (Bastogne). Led by the three FO tanks, the eighteen M7 Priests held off the German attack for fourteen hours until the 9th Armored Division moved in. All FO tanks were lost along with half the M-7s. . . . S/Sgt Ben Throneburg of Hudson, North Carolina, received a Silver Star.'

Ralph sent the writer various graphic accounts of his experiences as an FO in a Sherman, including the following one of an action on Hill 91, near Haute Vents, France:

'It was not my first limited objective attack (one of the many designed to take some of the pressure off Monty). It was the first I was able to make a decent contribution in. It was bad, very bad, but didn't seem so at the time.

'I was attached to CCB (Combat Command B), 3rd Armored Division CCB was supporting the 30th Infantry Division and was split up so badly and battered enough so that I never knew who I was with. My orders were to stay with the lead elements on the attack of Haute Vents. We all learned much during this battle. We were up against the best, the Panzer Lehr Division.

'The task force attempting the attack was led by Col. Dorrance Roysdon with assistance from Task Force King (Lt-Col. Rosewell H King), the task force assigned to make the

initial assault. (The 3rd was a "heavy" armored division, two regiments of tanks and one of infantry, and was always divided into a variety of task forces or battle groups. A battle group was a company of tanks, a company of infantry, and — if operating away from division — a battery of artillery. Otherwise the attached FO called for fire from his battalion. A task force was anything larger than a battle group, but not the whole Combat Command (CC)).

'We started up the hill on 10 July and got to within 300 meters of the top by the time darkness had fallen. We paused before making the last dash while a battalion (391 Armored FA Battalion) fired a preparation concentration. Although the 3rd had not been

Top
The T105 rocket launcher comprised a single 7.2 in rocket projector in a box-like case which took the place of the main armament on this M4A1. It was more likely to be used for demolition purposes, but did not get past trials stage.

Above
A British rocket system was this 60 lb aircraft rocket, mounted on a launcher rail. The angle of the rail was such to ensure that the rocket would hit a target about 400 or 800 yards ahead of the Sherman V, but they were relatively inaccurate.

in combat very long they were already defying "the book" and continuing armored assault after dark — a technique that was to work successfully for them later. The concentration fell short causing the tanks to fall back about 50 yards while I called for a cease fire to give a correction. The original concentration was

Multiple Gun Motor Carriage T52, in its firing position. This was one of a number of different combination mounts of AA guns tried out on the Sherman. A 40 mm gun was flanked by two .50-cal. heavy machine guns, but unfortunately the traversing arrangements proved too slow and the project was ended in October 1944.

fired from the map on orders from someone in command. Meanwhile, my tank was stalled with a dead battery and a very obstinate "Little Joe" (the battery charger driven by a two-cycle lawn-mower type engine) on the edge of the still falling 105s. While my crew worked to get "Little Joe" running I watched the 105s bursting and remarked at what a beautiful sight it was. The bursts were above ground and "cutting grass" unlike the incoming Jerry mail which dug in too much before it exploded throwing the fragments up in the air — a break for us as we often got hit with spent fragments. When the firing stopped I began to worry, though. We were out there alone and my gunner and loader were busy with "Little Joe". After much cussing, the rope pull breaking and needing fishing out, and what seemed to be a liftime, "Little Joe" finally decided to cooperate and start. With its help we got the main engine started and pulled back with the rest of the tanks.

'By the time we got back it had been

decided to call off the final assault until dawn. We fixed coffee and I dug out the Scotch from the grenade box and added a short ounce to my coffee and that of Sgt Ben Throneburg (FO Sgt — gunner) and T/5 Severyn Helmin (tank driver). The bow gunner T/5 Ward turned down the offer. T/5 Ward (FO Radio Op-loader) was taking the first turret watch.

'As we drank our coffee and were getting settled for the night one of the tanker sergeants walked over and remarked that it was a brave thing we had done staying up there to cover their withdrawal. I looked at him for a moment and replied drily, "Yeah." (Later I would realize that is how some heroes are made.)

'After a relatively uneventful night we had a short briefing before dawn. The attack was to be led by Recon Troops, M-8 and M-20 Scout Cars with some "How Tears" (half-tracks). That made me the first M-4 (sic) tank in the column, which put us on edge a little. For the first and last time in two wars I was about to participate in that overworked dramatic "dawn attack".

'We took off up the road precisely at dawn. Somewhere at a 9th air Force airstrip a P-47 Thunderbolt took off at the same time carr-

ying with him, no doubt, our last known positions. Our lead vehicles drove steadily up those last 300 meters taking care of a few Jerry outposts on the way with 37 mm cannon, .50 and .30 machine gun fire. The four P-47s steadily flew toward Haute Vent — they were to be our umbrella. Our lead vehicles passed through a row of trees at the edge of the flat clearing on the hilltop; a "How Tear" was proceeding through the trees; our tank was still about 50 yards down the slope; and the lead P-47 was in his dive. The P-47 came out of nowhere from our rear and tore up the half-track very badly with his eight .50s. Fortunately the other three P-47s didn't follow him down and instead remained up high to give cover.

'Immediately everything broke loose. The recon troopers started firing up flares and tossing smoke grenades (including red — used to identify a target for an air strike by our 'planes on the enemy). My mind was racing remembering something one of the old FO's, with experience in Africa and Sicily, told us replacements during informal training talks while in England. He said to always fire on a white flare fired in the air because it was Jerry infantry signaling his own artillery to lift their fires as the rounds were landing too close. (I was to use that later with great success, even getting a second flare to help me adjust on target). I was thinking Jerry is stupid — he would do the same thing. I yelled to Sgt Throneburg to get the tank moving up as I climbed out and started running toward the half-track screaming for the people around it to stop firing flares and lay out panels instead. As I was running and yelling (completely forgetting I was only a second Lieutenant and there was much more rank ahead of me) I jumped over a couple of mounds of earth almost landing on a couple of dead Jerries. Though that was the closest I came to contacting dead bodies up to that point they made little impression on me. I just wanted to get the firing of the flares stopped! I do not know if anyone heard me over the noise, the ammo exploding in the half-track and another nonfiring pass by the P-47, but finally a couple of men started laying out panels and were telling the others to do the same. When I saw that and the firing of flares cease I turned around and headed back for my tank motioning them to double time up to me. After I got back in the tank we continued to the top of the hill.

'(From that point on the 3rd Armored Division — and very quickly following, the rest of the forces — carried orange panels on the rear deck of armored vehicles and other vehicles at least kept them very handy. Some enemy tanks also did that to escape our air attacks while retreating across France later. They would hang just ahead of one of our columns to work that successfully.)

'Upon reaching the top of the hill I was dismayed at what I saw — or, if you prefer, at what I could not see. We were in an open flat clearing a bit larger than a football field. On our left the slope was very shallow and heavily wooded. To our front could be seen three successive rolling hills, also heavily wooded. Possible observation of enemy activity was nil.

'I was *not* surprised by the volume of machine gun and small arms fire coming from the wooded area on our left already, along with an occasional high velocity 77 mm round. Fortunately the 77 seemed to be firing up one alley. Nor was I surprised at the volume of 105 mm and 150 mm rounds that started landing as I was calling in my position (in code) to FDC. I doubt the enemy in the woods could see us since the firing appeared wild and few hits were scored. On the few vehicles we had on the hill a couple were knocked out apparently by accident. Certainly the enemy artillery did not need observation to drop in on us. Jerry was on the ball and another *big* lesson had been learned

Prime mover M34 converted from the M32B1 Recovery Vehicle from which the turret was removed and a special rounded turret with an open top and a rounded hatch in front fitted. There was also a split hatch on the bustle. They were used, as were the prime movers M33 and M35, to tow artillery guns.

the hard way by our troops. *Never* use flares for signalling in the front lines.

'I looked for the artillery firing into us but they were in such good defiladed positions that I could not even detect any smoke. I had about given up when I heard the welcome sound of Lt Leroy C Stevens' voice over the radio from Air OP (L-4 Piper Cub, commonly referred to as "Charlie Uncle Baker"), naturally for him, violating normal radio procedure.

'(We used a single call sign strict net control by FDC who would use the same call sign as the slave station. To call another FO unit we had to insert "message for" before their call sign, FDC came back with permission, and the called unit then came back with his call sign.)

'"Hello 2 Peter this is 9 Peter. Looks like it's going to be a warm day," letting me know he had decoded my position and saw the incoming mail we were getting.

'"Hello 9 Peter this is 2 Peter, looks that way from here." letting him know I couldn't do much about it.

'"Can you give me a compass?"

'"I don't know. I'll see what I can do".

'We had been taught to get at least ten yards away from any mass of metal to use a compass but I was not about to get out of my M-4 if I could help it. I made a quick reading from the top of the tank to one of the enemy batteries and did a rough check on the map; it seemed good.

'"Hello 9 Peter this is 2 Peter, try 2545, four howitzers. You want the caliber?" I knew Lt Stevens was one of the best, and would know which hill to look behind from that information.

'"Yeah, sure" he came back with a little surprise in his voice. "150's" (FDC had the good sense to overlook our procedure.)

'In a minute or two an "I got 'em" came over the air, then "Gi'me a round of smoke on (coordinates). Four gun battery, 150's."

'(It should be noted at this point that "Give me a round of smoke" is translated to "Fire mission". It was used by most of all the FO's, who lasted long enough, as a loosely coded organization identifier. The reason was to maintain the recognition and respect the 58th Armored FA Battalion felt they had earned but was not getting from the US Army. We were only attached to divisions, often not long enough for them to remember, and the Corps and Armies CG's who knew us well enough to put us in the hot spots were too busy with other more pressing problems. The enemy kept track of certain organizations more closely than others. The 58th had the dubious honor of having "Berlin Sally" broadcast that it had already been wiped out twice. This was recognition and a certain kind of respect. In turn the 58th FO's needled the Jerries that we were still there pounding away at them. Since we were never in a losing situation it was anything but giving "aid and comfort" to the enemy.)

'Lt Stevens' transmission was the beginning of an old fashioned, forward observers dream, all day, fourteen-hour turkey shoot. In a couple of volleys he was in fire for effect and before he finished he had spotted another battery. When he paused I would have another compass reading, number of guns and caliber to transmit up to him and he would have them spotted the next time they fired. In each fire for effect Lt Stevens gave a full description of effect on target much in the manner of a sports-caster, interspersed with excited comments like "It hit the breech," or, "The whole crew on one gun wiped out," or "Geez! Right down the tube." Very few rounds were wasted on adjustments, and my compass readings from the top of the tank proved to be very accurate.

'Under the original combat CO Lt-Col. Bernhard W McQuade (KIA, D-Day — same day orders received transferring him back to the Pentagon as an armored artillery advisor to Chief of Artillery) the 58th never relinquished control of its L-4's to anyone so after the first two hours, "2 Peter this is 9 Peter, my relief is here, just keep feeding him the same information." I gave him a Roger.

'Lt Henry Shaddock was a more quiet and methodical observer and a better than average shooter which got him his battle field commission. The radio talk lessened but the counter battery fire continued to pour out. I had almost forgotten the machine guns and 77 mm firing in from our left flank and with the one radio channel tied up almost continuously it wasn't too practical to try to fire out there.

'Every two hours Lt Stevens and Lt Shaddock with their pilots Lt Charles R Snyder and S/Sgt Thomas K Turner (soon commissioned and later sent back to the States for flight training after over 1000 combat flying hours — and a member of the 58th in Korea) alternated as Air OP and slowly whittled away at the enemy batteries until late in the day when the enemy was down to one or two howitzers per battery and many less batteries, and finally about dark there was no more artillery coming in. All day long the heavy fire from the left kept up causing little more damage to our dozen or so armored vehicles on the hill and minor casualties. It had long become obvious Jerry was firing wildly from the woods and showed no inclination to counter-attack. The location of units from the 30th Infantry Division, if any, had become a problem also. I decided not to fire blindly into those woods when I had a chance as things slowed down during the afternoon based on the situation and the greater danger from incoming artillery. I had a nagging concern about the amount of ammo expended but had considered FDC might ask the 301st Armored FA Battalion for support.

'Once, during the afternoon, FDC gently reminded us to stay with proper *radio* procedure. This was duly "Rogered" by Lt Stevens and promptly forgotten when things got a bit busy again. Sticking to the extra transmissions could have cost us on the ground by allowing the enemy more time to put direction finders on us — and they had them — and wanted very much to verify my position, as I was to learn the next day.

'Lt Stevens was adept at timing his fire to land at the proper moment, as were many of our FO's. When things got slower in the afternoon when he spotted another enemy battery he would ask for "DO NOT LOAD" and wait for the enemy gun crews to leave their slit trenches and then fire. It was very effective in destroying howitzer crews. (Later, in the Siegfried Line, another of our FO's spotted a Jerry infantry company coming out of their pill boxes every morning for reveille formation. He timed them from the time the sergeant blew his whistle until they were in formation at attention for three mornings. Meanwhile, during the day he registered a battery 100 yards to the right of where the formation was held and clocked the time of flight. The fourth morning he had the battery shift left from the registered point 100 yards at "DO NOT LOAD". At the proper second he called for "FIRE FOR EFFECT" and just as the enemy company was lined up the rounds landed on them as planned.)

'The after action report shows sixteen counter battery missions fired by the 58th the first day, but that is probably the result of so many missions piled on top of each other during the morning. My notes show 25 missions fired by Lt Stevens and eighteen by Lt Shaddock, all verified by my observation of direction of incoming mail, caliber of howitzers delivering it, and the radio transmissions. The battalion fired 2623 rounds that day, a large amount by World War II standards, and enough for strict rationing to be imposed the next day. Lt Stevens with S/Sgt Turner flew four missions of two hours each and Lt Shaddock with Lt Snyder completed three missions of the same length. ... THIS DEMONSTRATED CLEARLY THE NEED FOR BATTALIONS TO CONTROL THEIR OWN AIRCRAFT! With the amount of enemy fire being received it was almost certain our small force would have withdrawn from that hill returning to the enemy a commanding position. Unfortunately, this doctrine has seldom been followed (much to my personal danger, dismay and disgust later in Korea as an FO again).

'For some reason — a probable need elsewhere — the tank company with us the night before did not follow us up the hill that day. Our little force remained as was during the night and my crew and I dozed off as best we could in our tank that night. There was still a lot of harrassing fire coming in.

'The second morning on Hill 91 started off quiet. We listened to a one-sided conversation from a tank company commander to his superior on an adjacent channel which fed over into our FDC channel as long as it was quiet. We chuckled a bit as that tank CO adjusted enemy artillery fire on his company by his description of how far he had advanced, proof that he had reached his objective, wanting to pull back because enemy artillery was falling very close to his front and getting closer, and finally stating he was pulling out because it was landing on him. At that transmission the enemy artillery went into "fire for effect". Since it was only down the hill slightly left of the wooded area on our left we could hear the rounds landing quite clearly. It was no longer a joke to my crew and their comments are better left out. The enemy concentration was surprizingly heavy for that era, about 50 rounds of 150 mm, possibly more. Unfortunately, it was not our sector and we could not ask our L-4 for help. Probably the FO with them had to go through Division Air. The tanks did sustain losses.

'About noon we received reinforcements in the form of a depleted tank company. One of our FO's was with them and after a decent interval of quiet I got out and went over to visit. We were sitting between his tank and a three feet high mount of earth relaxing and comparing notes when out of the clear sunshine it started raining 81 mm mortar rounds. After a half dozen had landed and there was no sign of a letup, Lt Michael Runey, the other FO, decided he was better off in his tank and, after thinking it over a couple of rounds longer, so did I, I did the 30 yards to my tank in record time and was up and in without a scratch. I realized I had finally discovered a way to climb up an M-4 without bruising my shin or ankle but I couldn't remember how I did it! Runey was watching to see if I made it and I waved "OK" to him. Suddenly he pulled his head in and 81 landed right on his antenna base. (He told me later his head was ringing for a couple of weeks.) He motioned no antenna and he was going back. I held up the microphone indicating I would call in for him and he nodded "yes".

'"Hello 2 Peter, Over"

'"Hello 2 Peter, Over," FDC replied.

'"Hello 2 Peter, 3 Peter will be over to see you. No big deal, Over."

'"Hello 2 Peter, negative — got both covered. Out".

'When radio messages had to be sent in the clear it was known the Jerries could understand English, had trouble with American English, and, for all practical purposes, could not understand slang. The more outlandish the slang, the greater security.

'Shortly I was to receive one of a couple of

A British CDL (Canal Defence Light) mounted on a Sherman and very similar to the US T10E1 Shop Tractor.

backdoor compliments I was to receive during the war. (The other would be from Sgt Throneburg later and cannot be told during his life.) Over the radio loudspeaker came a rather halting, "Hello 2 Peter this is One Zero Peter, over."

'We looked at each other with a puzzled expression. Our call numbers only went up to 9. Each TO/E FO had two Peeps (¼ ton Jeep) on special authorization from 1st Army but we added an unauthorized "1" to our own call sign to call the standby vehicle, M-4 or Peep. I asked the crew if anyone recognized the voice as the unknown station called again and again. All shook their heads negative but the radio operator-loader did say he didn't know all the possible firing battery provisional FO operators. About the third call it was becoming obvious the operator was being too careful with his pronunciation. I picked up the mike and was about to tell them to blow it out their B-bag but thought better of it. I told the crew I was sure they were trying to DF (direction find) us and it was best we maintained radio silence for a while. Sgt Throneberg suggested we move a little since

the 81's had been too close before so we pulled back about 30 yards to some slight conceal-ment but where we could see as much as ever and had a clear field of fire with the tank gun. No sooner had we done so than everything broke loose again from the wooded area in-cluding the 81's which landed right where we had been. It was apparent Jerry was just trying to verify his original fix on us. It was also fairly apparent he heard the tank move because a lone 88 round cut a tree off next to us about ten feet over our heads. Fifteen feet lower — natural ventilation in our M-4! This startled the driver who jerked the tank enough so that the right half-hatch cover, which I had just gotten perpendicular, came down on my helmet driving me down in the tank and leaving me with a slight headache for a while. I guess I was a bit harsh when I told the driver to cut the engine.

'The enemy fire was hot and heavy for a while but evidently it was his last gasp in that area. Radio silence, self imposed, didn't mat-ter since the same unknown situation existed in the wooded area and the 88 mm never fired again, giving us no reason to call Air OP and give him a compass reading. We sweated a counter-attack for a while after that heavy firing and were prepared to bring fire on the wooded area. None materialized and for the

rest of the day and night we received sporadic small arms fire and little else while we listened to an infantry fight gradually develop in the wooded area.

'The next day we were ordered back for a new assignment. We breathed a sigh of relief but couldn't help wonder what was in store next. We felt pretty good, too. We had been with only a small group of the 3rd Armored Division but we had been the group that held the high ground the battle was named for. Also we had given a fair assist to our Air OP in knocking out almost all the enemy artillery in the area.

'Halfway back down the hill the driver stopped by a medic half-track and told us the bow gunner was very sick. It turned out he had not gotten out of the tank for any normal body waste eliminations for three days. Both Sgt Throneburg and myself were more than miffed at ourselves for not noticing it. Sgt Throneburg was particularly upset with the driver for not telling him.

"We could have fired the seventy-five and given him the empty to use!" was Sgt Throneburg's last comment with a few unprintables thrown in.

'I learned (or should have) that even though they had four campaigns more I shouldn't have taken anything for granted.'

10

The Tiger Tamer: The M26 Pershing

Major General Ernest H Harmon, commander of 2nd Armored Division ('Hell on Wheels'), one of Gen. George S Patton's crack armored divisions, probably spoke for most wartime American tankers when he described the characteristics of his ideal tank as: 'First: gun power; second: battlefield maneuverability; third: as much armor protection as can be had after meeting the first two requirements; still staying within a weight that can be gotten across obstacles with our bridge equipment.'[1] That short paragraph must encapsulate World War II American military thinking on armor and contains the real reasons why they never showed much enthusiasm for very heavy tanks, to match, for example, the Tiger II.

T20 series

Despite this, Gen. Harmon still puts firepower at the top of his list of requirements and, as we have seen, the Sherman did not have the necessary high velocity gun to deal effectively with either the Tiger 1 or the Panther. As soon as Sherman came off the drawing board, work began on designing its successor and it was this development that finally led to the Pershing, despite the fact that, initially anyway, Pershing came into the heavy tank category rather than the medium range of AFVs. The initial tank was designated the M4X and its main characteristics were to be a five-man crew, thicker armor (4 inches on the front) and, on a much lower silhouette than the M4, a 75 mm gun with automatic loading and a powerful engine (the new Ford V-8 Model GAN) which was also much lower in silhouette and thus assisted in bringing down the overall vehicle height. A wooden mockup was built by one of the medium tank producers (Fisher) and then, in September 1942, it was decided to build three pilot models, all with the T20 designation. Reduced to basics, the models were:

T20 76 mm gun and horizontal volute

spring suspension (HVSS) — built and completed by June 1943.
T20E1 75 mm automatic gun and HVSS — project canceled; turret later used in T22E1.
T20E2 3 inch gun and torsion bar suspension — completed but with a 76 mm gun instead of 3 inch and then called **T20E3**.

All three were to be powered by the new engine and weighed of the order of 30 tons.

The T20 and T20E3, which were the only ones to be completed, both had trouble with their transmissions and development work ceased in late 1944. However, much useful information had been gained from the project.

T22 Series

The next step was the development of the T22 series which was taken on by Chrysler in October 1942. It was decided to build two pliot tanks, both completed by June 1943:
T22E1 This mounted a 75 mm automatic gun in a special turret, with an automatic hydraulically-operated loader which had two separate magazines (one for AP, one for HE). The tank commander was able to select remotely from his crew station (left rear of turret) the type of ammunition he wanted. A rate of fire of 20 rpm was achieved during testing but the mechanism was unreliable.
T22E2 This was going to mount a 3 inch gun, but be otherwise similar to the T20E2. However, it was canceled at the design stage.

Trouble with transmission and rear drive, together with the decision that the 75 mm was not a large enough weapon for the future medium tank, led to the project being stopped in February 1944.

T23 Series

The third series to be developed was designated T23. The project was initiated at the

same time as work began on the T22 and the pilot model was in fact the first to be completed of all the three series (completed December 1942). The hull, armament, and general layout was very similar to the T22, but it used the M4 suspension and tracks. Detroit Arsenal built the three pilot models, the **T23**, **T23E1**, and **T23E2**, with a 76 mm, a 75 mm automatic, and a 3-inch gun, respectively. As with the T20 series, the last two projects were canceled before completion. Two T23 pilots were built and were so successful that it was decided to produce 250 more. These were built by the Detroit Arsenal between November 1943 and December 1944. They incorporated certain improvements over the two pilot models, having the improved 76 mm M1A1 gun in the T80 gun mount, an all round vision cupola for the commander, and a rotating hatch for the loader, which incorporated the AA machine gun. The turret was cast, with 3 inches of frontal armor (it had only been $2\frac{1}{2}$ inches on the pilots). The tanks were used in limited numbers for training in America, but were never on general issue and none ever saw combat. Their rejection by the Armored Board was on the grounds that they were too complicated and difficult to maintain, which would have led to considerable retraining problems for maintenance personnel.

Thus, although the T20, T22 and T23 projects did not in themselves lead to the introduction into service of a new medium tank, all three projects did lead to useful modifications being made to the Sherman and in their turn led on to the next two medium tank projects, the T25 and T26 series.

T25 and T26 Series

Advances in metallurgy had, by 1942, enabled the Ordnance Department to build light but more powerful 90 mm guns out of the newly developed, thin, higher physical steel, and it was requested, at the same time as production

Left
The T20E3 pilot model which was completed in July
1943. It had torsion bar suspension and only three return
rollers on each side. The gun is a 76 mm instead of the
3 in gun that was originally going to be mounted in this
particular pilot model. Later, at APG the suspension was
modified with five return rollers instead of three.

Below
The T22E1 pilot under test. Note that a counterweight
has been added to the 75 mm automatic gun, to balance
part of the automatic loading mechanism. Although the
automatic gun gave a better performance than the
hand-loaded one, the 75 mm was considered too
inadequate in firepower and the project work was
suspended in February 1944

Bottom
Next to be produced was the T23 series, this particular
vehicle being the ninth production T23, seen here at
APG. They were rejected by the Armored Board as
being too complicated and the project was dropped in
February 1945.

of the 250 T23 medium tanks was approved,
to modify fifty of these to mount the new
90 mm gun. Forty would merely have the
same armor as the T23, but the remaining ten
would be equipped with heavier armor. The
two models were to be designated the T25 and
T26 respectively. Now, at long last was
emerging in the shape of the proposed T26, a
tank that should have a chance to equal the
firepower and protection of the Tiger.

Two pilot models of the T25 were built at
the Detroit Arsenal (in January and April
1944 respectively) the first T25 pilot was sent
from Chrysler to the Detroit Tank Arsenal for
modification and onward transmission to
Aberdeen Proving Ground in late January
1944. A second pilot was delivered in late
April 1944. Both the P1 and P2 were heavy —
82,310 lbs and 84,210 lbs respectively. They
had HVSS and 23-inch wide tracks, mounted
a 90 mm T7 gun and coaxial .30 caliber
machine gun, in a large cast turret, and were
powered by the Ford V-8 Model GAN tank
engine, with electric drive identical to the
T23. In order to reduce weight it was then
decided to drop the electric transmission and
to go back to the hydramatic transmission
with torque converter which had been used on
the T20 series. Testing of the T25 began in
September 1944, but by then the invasion of
Europe had taken place and the cry coming
back from the operational zone was for more
protection as well as a better gun, so the T25
was dropped in favor of the more heavily
armored T26 series.

The T26E1, which was the original T26
but with hydramatic transmission and torque converter, also had slightly wider
tracks (14 inches), and weighed upwards of
86,500 lbs when fully stowed. In trials at Fort
Knox in comparison with the T26 model it
was found that, although the T26 had a better
overall performance on normal terrain, the

Top left
T25 pilot Number 1 on test at APG. The tank has horizontal volute spring suspension with shock absorbers mounted on all three bogies. The 90 mm gun did not have a muzzle brake and was mounted in a larger, heavier turret than the T23.

Top right
The Number 13 T25E1 which had a new turret roof of increased height in order to make space for the rangefinder, torquematic transmission. It weighed 38 tons.

Above left
The T26E1 Number 1 under test at APG. This tank was later modified to mount the 90 mm T15E1 gun and was sent over to ETO for testing.

Above right
The T26E3, standardized as the M26 Pershing tank. Its 90 mm and thick armor (a maximum of 4½-ins on the gunshield) gave it the edge on Tiger 1, but it was still not really up to the standard of the Panther.

electric drive was really too complicated for the average mechanic to repair in the forward area. The T26E1 was then reclassified as the Heavy Tank T26E1 and full production recommended. However, the path that lay ahead for the new tank was not to be a straightforward one. Ordnance recommended that 1500 be built immediately: the Armored Force, while requesting a high priority for the T26E1 still only recommended that 500 be built; Army Ground Forces refused to approve either of these requests, even saying

that it should be redesigned to mount the 76 mm gun! Fortunately, such a ludicrous idea was ignored, but all this squabbling led to vital time being wasted, so it was not until December 1944 that a 'limited procurement' order was approved, the model being designated as the T26E3, as it did by then incorporate certain modifications.

In fact, the Ordnance Department had already begun production a month earlier, so that in early December there were twenty T26E3s ready for testing. Ordnance proposed that they be rushed immediately out to Europe for combat testing, but yet again, the Army Gound Forces were opposed to the idea and said that they must first go to the Armored Force for testing, all of which would have wasted yet another month. In a way it was fortunate that the Germans should chose that moment to step into the act by releasing their totally unexpected offensive in the Ardennes. Positive proof was soon flooding back from the battlefield that the Sherman and the 76 mm gun were both inadequate in combat against the German Tiger and Panther. It is remarkable how often this lesson had to be hammered home before the message finally sank in. However, on 22 December the American General Staff decided that the 'T26 affair' had gone on quite long enough and

ordered their immediate shipment to ETO. Twenty T26E3s arrived in January 1945 and early the following month were issued for operational use. It is hardly surprising that, once they had proved their worth on the battlefield, the Army Ground Forces, realizing at last how good they were, sent in immediate requests for as many of the new tanks as possible! Full production was ordered in January 1945 and in March 1945 it was finally standardised as the Heavy Tank M26 and given the name 'General Pershing' after Gen. 'Black Jack' Pershing of Mexico and World War I fame. After the war, in May 1946, the designation was altered back to the Medium Tank M26.

Wartime production of the Pershing totalled 1436, of which Grand Blanc Arsenal produced 1190 between November 1944 and June 1945, and Detroit Arsenal produced 246 between March and June 1945. (Detroit Arsenal built a further 992 after the end of the war in the last months of 1945).

Of this wartime total, only 310 reached the European theater before VE Day, only 200 were issued to troops and only twenty saw any kind of action. On the other side of the world, twelve Pershings were sent to Okinawa, arriving there in July 1945, but were never used in action before V-J Day. The Pershing would

Front view of the Pershing, giving a dramatic view of its 90 mm gun with its large muzzle brake. Note the driver's and assistant driver's hatches (closed) and the bow machine gun mounting.

have to wait for 'it's day' until the Korean war, so it is all the more remarkable that the combat evidence of such a small sample of AFVs should have had such an effect, as witness this quote from *The Ordnance Department on Beachhead and Battlefront*: 'Before Barnes returned to the United States he asked Gen Campbell[2] by teletype on 5 March 1945 to ship immediately all the Pershings available, as well as all available HVAP ammunition for the 76 mm and 90 mm guns; and to expedite the production of the T15 90 mm gun and ammunition and the shipment of the twenty-five T83 self-propelled guns produced in February. Campbell promised to do "everything humanly possible" to get the Pershings to the theater on the highest priority and was backed up by AGF's Theater Branch after a personal cablegram from General Eisenhower to General Somervell on 8 March. But the tanks would not affect the outcome of the war in Europe.' A sad indictment of the squabbling that took place is also contained in the same volume: 'Gen. Barnes and Col. Colby maintained that the best

American tank of the war, the Pershing, had to be developed in the face of "bitter opposition" by the using arms. Colby believed that if the AGF had given the go-ahead early enough, the Pershing could have been available in quantities for the beachhead landings on D-day; and the record supports his belief.'

The basic reason for this continued opposition lies in the conception of the primary role of the tank. The AGF and Armored Force saw exploitation as being the primary task of armor. In other words tanks were there to exploit a breakthrough and not to engage in slogging matches with enemy tanks. Although this conception was vindicated after El Alamein in North Africa and to an extent in Europe by Patton's Third Army's spectacular advances, there was still the need for American tanks to be able to successfully compete with their German counterparts in tank versus tank engagements. This became all the more important as German forces withdrew into the Fatherland and reached crisis proportions during the Battle of the 'Bulge'.

General Description

The T26E3 General Pershing was a heavily armored, full track-laying, low silhouette combat vehicle with a 90 mm gun mounted in

a fully enclosed power-operated turret which could be traversed through 360 degrees. It was powered by an 8-cylinder V-type, liquid-cooled Ford GAF gasoline tank-engine. It had a very low silhouette, a relatively flat rear deck, and the turret was mounted well forward of the center of the vehicle. A large projection at the rear of the rounded turret acted as a counterweight for the long 90 mm gun with its distinctive muzzle brake. Six dual, independently sprung road wheels supported the AFV on each side. The upper portion of the track was covered by stowage boxes, fenders and sandshields at the ends and sides. The tracks were driven by final drives at the rear of the tank and ran around idler wheels at the front. The sloping V-shaped front added to its low-slung appearance. The straight sides, without sponsons, made the vehicle seem to be suspended between the tracks and, therefore, considerably wider than other tanks when viewed from front or rear. One .30 caliber machine gun was mounted in the bow of the tank; a second .30 caliber was coaxially mounted on the left side of the 90 mm gun. A .50 caliber machine gun was mounted behind the loader's hatch on an AA pintle mounting, and when not in use could be stowed in brackets on the rear of the turret counterweight.

The hull was of all-welded construction of heavy armor plate sides, with a cast armor steel front and rear sections, all welded to an armor steel floor. The cast armor steel turret could be traversed either by hand or hydraulic power. There was no turret basket. The commander had a dome-shaped cupola, set into a circular opening in the top of the turret on the right, with six bullet-proof glass prisms equally spaced around the cupola's lower edge. In the center of the cupola was a round hinged lid with an opening for installing a periscope which could be sealed by a metal plug when the periscope was not in use. A blade vane sight was bolted to the top of the turret in front of the cupola, for use with the commander's periscope. To the left of the commander's cupola was the loader's hatch, with a spring-controlled lid which could be locked from inside. There were three seats in the turret, the gunner's which also had a detachable backrest and a small removable foot rest; the commander's pad type seat, adjustable in height which could be folded back out of the way when not in use; the loader's which was similar, but not adjustable and could be removed completely if necessary.

The tank was supported on each steel track by the six dual road wheels, each with individual torsion bar springs, and four large cylindrical shock absorbers on each side. The

T26E3 Specifications

Crew	five (commander, gunner, loader/radio operator, driver and assistant driver)
Weight combat loaded	92,355 lbs
Length gun forward	28 ft 4½ ins
Width	11 ft 6 ins
Height	9 ft 1 in
Armament main	90 mm M3 in Mount M 67, with all round traverse and elevation from + 20 to − 10 degrees. Firing rate eight rpm; 70 rounds carried.
secondary	Two .30 cal. MG (one coax, one in bow mount) one .50 cal. AA HMG
Armor thickness max/min	4.5 ins (on gunshield)/0.5 ins (rear floor)
Engine	60 degrees V-type 8-cylinder 4-cycle gasoline Ford GAF, producing 500 hp at 2600 rpm.
Max speed	30 mph
Crusing range	100 miles approx
Max trench crossing	8 ft
Vertical wall	3 ft 10 ins
Fording depth	4 ft

power unit, comprising engine, transmission, and differential, was removable as a complete assembly from the engine compartment at the rear of the vehicle. The cooling unit, which comprised two radiators, four fans, and four oil coolers, could also be removed from the engine compartment as a complete assembly.

Both the driving and fighting compartment had forced ventilation and heating. Dual driving controls were provided for the driver and the assistant driver.

The Pershing in Combat

The new tanks, twenty T26E3s, arrived in Antwerp docks in January 1945. It was decided to get them into action as soon as possible and all were assigned to 12th Army Group, Gen. Bradley then allocating them to First Army to be divided equally between the 3rd and 9th Armored Divisions. By mid-February, the tanks had been delivered to the 559th Ordnance Battalion at Aachen, and training was under way. To facilitate their introduction, a special team, known as 'The Zebra Mission' headed by Gen. Barnes and containing experts from the Tank Automotive Command, the AGF New Developments Division and the Aberdeen Proving Ground. In his definitive book on the Pershing, Richard M Hunnicutt, gives the following assignment of the twenty T26E3 tanks:

3rd Armored Division
32nd Armored Regiment, one tank to each D, E, G, H, and I Companies
33rd Armored Regiment, one tank to each D, E, F, H, and I Companies

9th Armored Division
14th Tank Battalion, five tanks to A Company
19th Tank Battalion, one tank to A Company two to B Company and two to C Company

(3rd Armored was still on the 1942 organisation with two armored regiments while 9th Armored had replaced the two armored regiments with three tank battalions, *vide* the 1943 reorganisation).

By 20 February, 3rd Armored crews had finished their course on the new AFVs and the 9th Armored crews began theirs. One of the highspots of the training was the accurate shooting which Mr 'Slim' Price from the Aberdeen Proving Ground demonstrated. As Richard Hunnicutt explains: ' . . . using German helmets as targets and picking them off with single shots from the 90 at a range of 625 yards. Such a performance quickly overcame any objections that veteran tankers might have had to receiving gunnery instruction from a civilian.'

Action at Elsdorf

First Pershings to see action were those assigned to 3rd Armored Division, who, on 25 February, were attacking across the Roer River, and there was both good and bad news for the Zebra Mission who were eagerly following the progress of their protegees. First came the bad news: the Pershing assigned to F Company of 33rd Armored Regiment had been knocked out on 26 February, while overwatching a roadblock. *Fireball*, for that was the tank's name, was in a bad position, silhouetted in the darkness by a nearby fire. A Tiger, concealed behind the corner of a building only about 100 yards away, fired three shots — the first 88 mm projectile entered the turret through the co-axial machine gun port, killing both the gunner and the loader instantly. The second shot hit the muzzle brake and the end of the 90 mm barrel and the resulting shock waves set off the round that was in the chamber. Even though this round finally cleared the end of the tube, it still caused the barrel to swell about halfway down. The third and final shot glanced off the righthand side of the turret and in doing so took away the upper cupola hatch which had been left open. But that was the end of the Tiger's run of luck. Hastily backing, to avoid retaliatory fire, it reversed into a large pile of debris and became so entangled that the crew finally had to abandon it.

It was not long before *Fireball* was avenged, as Sgt Nick Mashlonik of Lancaster, New York told the author: 'At this time (1981) I am the sole living member of my last tank crew. Since I was the oldest tank commander

alive (not in age but in combat experience) in CO E 33rd Armored Regiment, 3rd Armored Division, I was given the opportunity of selecting a crew and attending school at Aachen, Germany, on the new T26 which is now the M26 Gen. Pershing tank. Our week of school was very interesting. Above all we had a really big gun (90 mm) with good mobility. I was assigned as tank commander to the M26 with the following crew: Cpl Carl Gormick — Gunner; T/5 Earnest Cade — Driver; Pfc Ralph Ruiz — Radio Operator and Loader; Pfc Walter Bozenko — Assistant Driver. Up to this time I had lost or been knocked out of seven M4 tanks, but had also knocked out twelve various German tanks and hundreds of other vehicles.

'Our first exposure to the enemy with the new M26 was very fruitful. We were hit hard by the Germans from Elsdorf. The enemy appeared to have much armor as we received a lot of direct fire and this kept us pinned down. Our casualties kept mounting and the Commanding Officer of our Company asked me if I thought I could knock the Tiger out that was almost destroying us. The Company Commander and I did some investigating, by crawling out to a position where we could see from ground level a sight to behold. The German Tiger was slightly dug in and this meant it would be more difficult to destroy. I decided that I could take this Tiger with my 90 mm.

'Our M26 was in defilade position, more or less hidden in a little valley. I detailed my driver Cade and gunner Gormick to accompany me on this mission. I would be gunner and have Gormick load. I instructed both of them that once we had fired three shots — two armor piercing and one HE point detonating — we would immediately back up so as not to expose ourselves too long on the top of the hill.

'Just as we started our tank and moved very slowly forward (creeping) I noticed that the German Tiger was moving out of the position and exposed his belly to us. I immediately put a shell into its belly and knocked it off. The second shot was fired at his track and knocked his right track off. The third shot was fired at the turret with HE point detonating and destroyed the escaping crew.

'At the time three other German armored vehicles were leaving Elsdorf and were on the road driving to my right flank. I waited until all of them were on the road with their rear ends exposed and then I picked off each one with one shell each getting the last one first, then the second one and then the first one — just like shooting ducks. Then I came back to each vehicle with HE point detonating and destroyed the crews as they were dismounting from the burning vehicles. It was our first day in combat with the Pershing and it was both fruitful and exciting.'

It is interesting to note that two of the 'three other German armored vehicles' Sgt Mashlonik mentions were Panzer IVs and they were knocked out at a range of 1200 yards with just one 90 mm round apiece.

Happily, the damage to *Fireball* did not take long to repair, a spare 90 mm gun barrel from an M36 tank destroyer being used to replace the damaged gun tube, while the shot holes were welded up and new parts fitted where necessary. *Fireball*, was back in action on 7 March. Mashlonik's Pershing was, incidentally, part of 'Task Force Lovelady' (mentioned earlier in the Sherman chapter).

Action at Remagen

Although their debut was later than 3rd Armored, the Pershings of 9th Armored really stole the limelight, as they took part in the historic seizure of the Ludendorf Railway Bridge at Remagen in early March 1945. The Pershing platoon of five tanks had in fact been with A Company of 14th Tank Battalion ever since they crossed the Roer River but had not been used to press. The problem was their greater weight and size, which made it difficult for them to cross the various narrow bridges on the maze of waterways in that area. The Corps of Engineers said some harsh words about the way the wide tracks of the M26s damaged their prefabricated bridges and this led to the Pershings often having to wait until all other elements of their column had crossed these obstacles before they were allowed over. Fortunately, by the time they were in a position to make a final thrust towards Remagen, most of these obstacles had been passed and so the platoon was put 'at the sharp end' of the Company A, who were supporting the 27th Armored Infantry Regiment. Platoon commander of the Pershings was 1st Lt John Grimball, of Columbia, South Carolina. He had already lost one of his platoon, struck by heavy HE shells on 1 March and the tank was still being repaired on the morning of 7 March when the point reached the western bank of the Rhine River and looked down in amazement at the still intact Ludendorf Railway Bridge.

Much had been written about the subsequent action that took place, especially from the point of view of the unfortunate German demolition commander, Major Hans Scheller, who was shot on orders of a drumhead court-martial for failing to blow up the bridge, although he did try three times unsuccessfully. It was not until 1967 that his widow was eventually able to clear his name, when a court held in Landshut, Bavaria, decided there was no evidence that he had committed a capital offence under military law.

Throughout the fierce action which ended in the capture of the partially damaged bridge — the first Allied bridgehead across the Rhine — the Pershings gave valuable fire support to the armored infantry. For example, they engaged troublesome German machine gun nests in the bridge towers with their 90 mm, swiftly silencing them. Once the infantry bridgehead had been achieved on the eastern bank, tank support was able to cross the bridge, but this was in the shape of some Shermans and tank destroyers, as it was felt that the extra weight of the Pershings might

closing stages of the campaign in Tunisia. It was to reach its zenith in Normandy, where, for example, Obersturmführer Michael Wittman and his single Tiger tank held up the entire 7th Armored Division on 13 June 1944, knocking out 25 vehicles in that one engagement to add to his already incredible tally of 119 Soviet tanks destroyed on the Russian front!

Unfortunately, thanks to the vacillations of the American military, by the time Pershing finally made its appearance, not only did it have to deal with Tiger, but also with its partner, PzKpfw V, the Panther. If anything, the Panther was an even more formidable opponent, its 75 mm KwK 42 gun having an even better armor penetration than the Tiger's 88. With over 1,300 Tigers and nearly 6000 Panthers produced by the end of the war, their effect on Allied armor was considerable — especially when it usually took at least five Shermans to knock out one Tiger or Pan-

Above
Pershings belonging to the 2nd Armored Division, Ninth US Army, rumble past the burning town hall in Magdeburg.

Right
The 'Super Pershing' as fitted up by 3rd Armored Division. The two cylinders over the gun mount contain coil springs to compensate for the weight of the new T15E1 gun. 80 mm plate from a Panther has been welded to the gun shield and more plate added to the hull front.

Below
One method of increase the tank's firepower was to install 4.5 in multiple rocket launchers on either side of the turret—a total of 44 rockets which could be fired individually or by full automatic fire, the latter method taking only seven seconds for the full salvo. The photograph was taken at APG in December 1945.

bring the perilous structure down before it could be properly repaired. The Pershings did not in fact cross the river until five days later when, on 12 March, they were ferried over on improvized rafts constructed from engineer bridge pontoons. Not only did the 14th Tank Battalion receive a Presidential Citation for the action (along with all the other units which took part) but Lt John Grimball was awarded an immediate Distinguished Service Cross and six of his tank platoon received Silver Stars. Eisenhower recalls the incident as '. . . one of my happy moments of the war'.

How Good was the Pershing?

The Pershing was designed to meet the threat posed, first and foremost, by the arrival on the battlefield of the PzKpfw VI, known more simply as Tiger I. Although used in small numbers in Russia in the late summer of 1942, the Tiger really made its debut in North Africa, where its deadly 88 mm KwK 36 gun added a new dimension to tank warfare in the

ther! In addition, one should perhaps consider such heavy weights as the Tiger II, the Königstiger, 68 tons of super-heavy tank, mounting a long barrelled and even more deadly 88 mm gun. The King Tiger could eliminate all of its opponents with ease, so it is fortunate that the Germans were only able to produce 489 of these battle winners, which did not enter combat service until June 1944. There was a scheme afoot to upgun and uparmor the Pershing to put it on a par with the Königstiger, by installing a new 90 mm gun of even higher muzzle velocity and adding cutup armor plate (80 mm thickness) to the gun shield, front hull, etc. Only one of these 'Super Pershings' was produced, and as it never had the chance to slug it out with a Tiger II before the war ended, the question as to which would have won is unanswered.

Richard Hunnicutt has carried out a very detailed and completely impartial comparison of the three tanks — Pershing, Tiger I, and Panther and reaches the conclusion that, while probably marginally better all round than the Tiger I, the Pershing still did not compare with Panther. As we have seen, in the limited number of engagements in which they met one another, Pershing was sometimes able to knock out both of the German tanks, while on other occasions it was itself knocked out by them. What is inescapable and must always be remembered, is that the Germans produced their heavy tanks a good three years before the Americans, so the story might have been very different had the AGF and Armor Board not been so inflexible. Nevertheless, it is fair to say that the Pershing was undoubtedly the best all round fighting tank produced by the United States during World War II.

Top
Production pilot model of the T26E2 at APG in July 1945. This AFV mountd the 105 mm howitzer which was lighter than the 90 mm, so the maximum thickness of the armor was increased—in front on the gun shield to 8 ins and the turret sides from 3 to 5 ins. Production began in July 1945 and some 185 vehicles had been completed by the end of the war.

Above
Another way of adding to the Pershing's firepower was by installing the T121 mount which incorporated two .30-cal. or .50-cal. which could be aimed and fired from inside the tank. The drawback, of course, was, the additional height. Mount was tested April 1946.

Left
T26E5 model seen here at APG in July 1945. This model equated to the M4A3E2 'Jumbo' assault tank, having much thicker turret and front hull armor. The 5 inch 'duckbill' extensions had to be added to the tracks to lower the ground pressure due to the extra weight (up from 92,355 lbs for the T26E3 to 102, 300 lbs for the T26E5). By the end of the war 27 of these assault tanks were produced but they were only used for test purposes.

11

'Seek, Strike and Destroy!': The Tank Destroyers

How to stop the *Blitzkrieg*?

One of the understandable reactions in the United States to the lightning successes of the German *Blitzkrieg* in Europe, was to look urgently for a more effective method of stopping tanks. The spectacular way in which German armor was able to carve through French and British opposition was undoubtedly having a very bad effect on the morale of American doughboys and there was an urgent need for new and effective ways of stopping armor in its tracks. As the official Armor-Cavalry history put it: 'A paramount reaction in the United States to the German blitzkrieg in Europe, which appeared to be irresistible in 1940, was the demand for some means of stopping German armor. The German successes were adversely affecting morale of combat troops, and there was an urgent need for new, effective weapons to calm their fears and prove the vulnerability of the tank.'

At the time, it was not considered that the best weapon to use against a tank was another tank. Instead, the War Department came to the conclusion that the answer was to use masses of fast moving, high velocity anti-tank guns. Lt Gen. Hugh A Drum, commanding General of the First Army and the Eastern Defense Command, was one of the prime instigators of the idea of having hard-hitting, aggressive, highly mobile and powerful units, whose primary task would be to find and destroy enemy armor, and his ideas were reinforced by the success of Deutsches Afrika Korps anti-tank guns in the Western Desert. The tactics envisaged were not to commit too many anti-tank guns to static defensive positions, but rather to hold most of them as a mobile reserve, ready to seek out and destroy enemy armored thrusts. This conviction, that the anti-tank gun was the proper adversary of the tank, led directly to the setting up of a separate Tank Destroyer Command and, unfortunately, to hindering the program to produce a more powerful tank to replace the M4.

The name 'Tank Destroyer' (TD) was deliberately chosen to emphasize the aggressive role of the new anti-tank units. Although they stemmed from the divisional artillery anti-tank gun units which they mostly absorbed, they did not replace the normal infantry anti-tank guns in anti-tank companies which began the war armed with 37 mm towed guns and later received the more powerful 57 mm towed guns. The first units of the new force were also armed with towed guns. A TD Center was initially established on 1 December 1941 at Fort Meade, Maryland, but in February 1942 it moved to a new camp in Texas, Camp Hood. The growth of the new force was rapid, many of the new units being made up of National Guard personnel. By late 1942 the strength of the TD Force was nearly 100,000 with 80 active units and a further 64 more planned. The basic unit was the 800-strong TD Battalion, with three Gun Companies each of twelve. TDs, a Reconnaissance company, and a Headquarters company. Peak figures were reached in early 1943, when 106 TD battalions were active — only thirteen less than the total number of tank battalions! From then on the size of the force started to decline. This was due principally to two factors. First, the expected enemy massed armored formations were never used against the Americans in 1943, the bulk of German armor being needed on the Russian Front. Thus the requirement for TD units did not fully materialize. Secondly, heavy casualties were suffered by the active divisions in combat and these led to serious manpower shortages, resulting in TD personnel having to be used as replacements. By the end of March 1945 only 68 TD battalions remained. This does not mean that those TD units which were employed in action were not effective. They lived up to their stirring motto: 'Seek, Strike, and Destroy!' and proved themselves courageous and capable fighters. As the official history explains, they also had a very morale boosting effect on the battle:

'even the psychological influence of tank destroyers upon friendly troops was very effective.'

Tank Destroyers almost became an Arm in their own right, successfully resisting all the attempts of the established Arms to absorb them. However, the writing was on the wall for the TD Force. Battlefield experience against enemy armor showed conclusively that neither a lightly armored TD, with an open turret, nor a towed anti-tank gun, was really as effective as the better protected and better armed tank, which was more versatile anyway and thus more cost effective. Consequently, despite its superlative war record, the TD Force ceased to exist after the war, its units being inactivated, disbanded or redesignated, many eventually becoming tank units.

TD Battalion Organisation

The 'teeth' of the TD Battalion were its three Gun Companies of tank destroyers, each divided into three Gun Platoons of four TDs (two sections of two guns) and a Security Section of two M20 armored utility cars (M8 Greyhounds without turrets, but with a ring mounted .50 cal. machine gun above the hull). The M20s and their crews provided the gun platoons with additional recon and mobile outposts for the guns, as well as performing their primary task of protecting gun sections against marauding enemy infantry. Crews would dismount the .50s to supplement their rifles and the bazooka, which every vehicle carried, so they has plenty of firepower. In addition to its Gun Platoons, a Gun Company contained a Command Post (CP) and a Company Maintenance Section, making up the total Company strength of some five officers and 130 enlisted men. The Reconnaissance Company comprised a CP, Maintenance Section, Pioneer Platoon and three Reconnaissance Platoons, the last named being normally attached to Gun Companies. Recon platoons contained two M8 armored cars and five Jeeps, while the Pioneers had a cars and five Jeeps, while the Pioneers had a powerful truck mounted compressor and four 1½ ton trucks, their job being to help TDs dig fire positions and to create or demolish obstacles. To command and control the fighting elements of the battalion was the Battalion CP, and located close by would be the Battalion medical detachment and Motor Maintenance Platoon (to deal with breakdowns outside the scope of the company maintenance sections). The remainder of the battalion was in rear echelon — HQ Section of HQ Company, the Battalion supply and personnel sections and the Transportation Platoon, with the supply sections and field kitchens of the other companies attached. Their job was to keep the fighting echelon supplied with all its daily needs, quite a task when the battalion was operating on a wide front. The rear echelon normally located itself near the HQ of the formation to which the TD battalion was assigned.

Choice of Weapon

What would be the ideal weapon for the TD Force? The choice was clearly between the towed anti-tank gun or the self-propelled anti-tank gun. A decision was made on this knotty problem in November 1943, when it was decided to go for a compromise solution with half the battalions towed and half SP. Here we are going to look at the self-pro-

pelled TDs only, of which there were three basic varieties: the M10 mounting a 3-inch gun, known as the *Wolverine*, the M18 *Hellcat* with a 76 mm, and the M36 with a 90 mm gun.

The M10 *Wolverine*

The first tank hull to be chosen as a platform for a tank destroyer was the M3 Grant. It was in late 1941 that a 3-inch gun was first mounted on a standard M3 chassis from which the turret and 75 mm gun sponson had been removed. This was known as the T24.

Below
In order to meet the pressing need for tank destroyers, Ford Motor Company was tasked to build just over 1000 based upon the medium tank M4A3 rather than the M4A1, but otherwise identical to the M10. Here, three M10A1s, straight from Ford's, pose for the press.

Bottom
The British upgunned some of their M10s and M10A1s by installing the 17-pdr Mk V gun. The resulting TD was known as *Achilles*. As the 17-pdr gun tube was of smaller diameter than the 3-inch a special casting was welded over the gun shield to reduce the size of the hole. An additional counterweight was added on the end of the barrel just behind the muzzle brake. The photograph shows the *Achilles* IIC (converted from the M10A1). The M10 conversion was known as the *Achilles* IC.

143

Trials soon showed, however, that the resulting AFV was too high and too complicated for mass production, so in March 1942 the project was canceled. It was rapidly followed by the T40, which mounted a 3-inch anti-aircraft gun in a low angle mounting, again on the same M3 Grant chassis. Although the TD Force felt that it lacked speed and mobility this adaptation was considered adequate and 50 guns were ordered. It was standardized as the GMC M9, but only 28 of the required 3-inch gun barrels could be found, so the project foundered and was finally canceled in August 1942. It was overtaken by the T35, in which a 3-inch gun was mounted on the Sherman M4A2 chassis, work on this model commencing in April 1942. Later, the T35 was replaced by an improved model, the T35E1, which had a much lower silhouette and an angled hull to deflect enemy shot (in line with requests made by the Tank Destroyer Board) together with thinner armor— to improve its mobility — and a five-sided, welded, open-topped turret. Standardized in June 1942, it was designated as the GMC M10. Demand was such that, in order to keep up with orders, the M4A3 chassis had to be used also, the resulting TD being known as the M10A1. In all, 4993 M10s and 1713 M10A1s were produced, 1648 of them being supplied to the British Army, who, from late 1944, began converting them, by replacing the 3-inch gun with their more powerful 17-pdr. The resulting TD was much more potent and was known as the '17-pdr *Achilles*', the Mk 1C being from the M10 and the Mk 11C from the M10A1.

The M10 was an armored, full-track-laying vehicle with the engine located in the rear of the hull. Its armament was the 3-inch gun M7, mounted in an open top turret of welded armorplate, which was on top of an all-welded hull. A .50-cal. AA machine gun was mounted at the rear of the turret opening. The consistant use of sloping surfaces on both hull and turret greatly reduced the vulnerability of the TD to damage by gunfire. The turret did not have a turret basket, and the gun had a gunshield that moved vertically with the barrel and formed the front part of

M10 Specifications

Crew	five (commander, driver, and three gun crew)
Combat weight	65,200 lbs
Length (gun forward)	22 ft 5 in (23 ft 10 in for *Achilles* with 17-pdr)
Width	10 ft
Height	9 ft 6 in (over AA machine gun)
Armament main	One 3-in Gun M7 (one 17-pdr Mk V on *Achilles*)
secondary	One .30-cal. AA Browning machine gun (also 2-in mortar on *Achilles*
Armor thickness max/min	2.25 in/0.5 in
Engine	Twin GMC 6–71 diesels (M10); Ford GAA V-8 petrol (M10A1)
Max speed	30 mph
Radius of action	approx 200 miles
Trench	7 ft 6 in
Vertical wall	2 ft
Fording depth	3 ft

the turret. Fifty-four rounds of AP and HE ammunition were carried for the 3-inch gun. A telescope M51 was used for direct laying of the gun onto targets.

The M10 in Combat

'For our mission the M10 was too heavy and slow', Hobart Lutz of Hopkinsville, Kentucky who served on these TDs, told the author, '...we needed to move much more rapidly than we were able and some terrain could not take the weight of it and we had to do some digging out. The gun had been a 3-in anti-aircraft weapon with the normal 42-inch recoil shortened tremendously (to about 19 in I think). This brought some problems, as the vehicle would rock up every time we fired and some time would elapse before we were able to get another round off. They tried to offset this by placing two 500 lb weights on the back of the turret and this worked to some extent but then you had more weight to haul around. Another bad problem we had with the M10 (not really the vehicle's fault) was that we had both gas and diesel fueled tank destroyers in the same company and this led to refueling problems at times. However, even with the short recoil and other drawbacks I liked the weapon. To the best of my memory the projectile had very good penetration up to 1500 yards. It was also very accurate. The biggest problem was definitely its mobility and some German tanks could outrun us in a firefight and that made me mad.'

Master Sergeant Theodore V Brush of Mays Landing, New Jersey, was another TD soldier. He fought with the 3-in towed guns, However, he did train on the M10s as he recalls; 'I was a platoon sergeant at the time when 605 TD Bn trained on M10s and were in fact school troops at Fort Hood, Texas, the Tank Destroyer Center for a period of one and a half years. In March 1944, the battalion was changed to towed. ... We were equipped with M10 with 3-in guns, twelve per company, 36 to a battalion ... we trained on moving targets at distances 800–1200 yards. We had no range finder, only a guess of the commander's judgement. At the beginning of our training with the 3-in guns, we fixed .30 cal. MG firing tracer on the gun barrels for use against moving targets up to 1000 yards. A man would bump off one round each time until he hit the target (usually a buttoned up light tank with added armor). ... One of the problems I remember with the M10 was traversing the turret was extremely hard if the TD wasn't sitting level. You couldn't always get the perfect firing position. Firing HVAPC was a shock the first time. One thought that the barrel would hit the back of the turret, although I must admit that there was little noise, just the rocking of the TD. ... The M10 was hell on roads as we had both steel and rubber treads. In Germany, the steel tracks were awesome on the cobblestones, the vehicle slid all over the place. The M10 with its open turret was absolutely the coldest riding vehicle in the Army's inventory. They also created dust problems on muddy terrains, at least they did in Texas. And of course they were noisy. To be riding four hours continuously in an M10 was like doing ten hours pick and shovel work. It was absolutely nerve-shattering and I never did get used to them.'

The M10s first saw action in North Africa in March 1943, near Maknassy in Tunisia. They continued in service throughout the rest of the war being widely used in North West Europe and Italy. They also served in the Pacific theater and were very effective at knocking out Japanese fortified positions. About 3600 M10s saw combat.

776th TD Battalion was one of the units to see its first action at Maknassy. They had started life as an anti-tank artillery battalion, then, on 21 December 1941, received orders that they would be activated as a tank destroyer battalion. Initially, they retained their towed 3-inch guns, but in November 1942, the M10s arrived and the battalion was re-equipped. Late December saw them en route for Fort Dix, New Jersey prior to service overseas. They sailed from New York on 14 January 1943, arriving off Casablanca, French Morocco eleven days later and disembarking that evening, as their privately published history recalls: 'Refresher courses were conducted in the hills bordering Casablanca, giving us the first opportunity to fire the 3-inch gun with excellent results and range firing with all other organic weapons was conducted. ... On 22 February 1943 the unit was ordered to move to Phillipville, Algeria and then to Tunisia — the territory where heated battles were then in progress. ... The journey towards actual combat had begun.'

The TDs were assigned to Lt Gen. George S Patton's II Corps and moved, by stages, to Maknassy, to reinforce other armored elements of the 1st Armored Division who were preventing the Germans from breaking out of the mountains north of that area. Their informal history tells the story of that first action.

'Company C under the command of Capt Daniel M Carter was detached from the Battalion on 23 March to reinforce elements on the southern flank of the defense line. As the company moved into position near the village of Maknassy, they were repeatedly dive bombed by the German Luftwaffe resulting in two casualties and a jeep knocked out. Later, while supporting an infantry attack to

enemy positions to the east in order to furnish the battalion command with possible enemy moves and new positions. No Axis tanks would move into the open for destroyer to tank engagements and the Battalion employed for the first time a new use for the TD, the role of indirect firing from dug-in, selected positions. Enemy retaliation caused duels to rage on through the day and night. German aircraft continually ranged over the positions, repeatedly bombing and strafing in an effort to reduce our holding strength.

'March 27th, in the sector defended by Company C, the Germans made their awaited move. Infantry, mortars, artillery, air attacks and five Mark IV tanks were used in an effort to break through. Salvo after salvo was exchanged as Company C punched back furiously in a battle that continued throughout the afternoon. The line held with heavy losses inflicted to the enemy both in material and personnel. Two destroyers were lost in action by Company C with Sgt Robert F Jones being killed in action and T/4 Lloyd Holland destroyer driver missing. . . . Acts of gallantry that afternoon were many. Sgt Robert F Jones, with one destroyer of which he was in command, destroyed three enemy tanks and neutralized four 88 mm pieces before his destroyer was hit by enemy fire resulting in his death.[1] 1st Lt John C Welch, platoon commander, under fire against a veteran enemy, rallied his platoon to accelerated efforts to throw the enemy back. The successful evacuation by 1st Lt William C Weir Company C, Capt Hermon L Monroe, Bn Surgeon, S Sgt Guerney C Caddy and Pfc Henry G Wobbema in moving through heavy enemy artillery and machine gun fire to reach burning vehicles and destroyers and rescue the casualties.'

776th held the enemy that day and went on to fight many more actions in North Africa, Italy and Europe, taking part in 550 days of actual combat in five major campaigns and winning no less than three Presidential Citations and seven unit commendations.

secure high ground east of Maknassy, one destroyer was knocked out by direct fire from an 88 mm anti-tank gun, resulting in the death of Pfc Nils Eidsness.

'The remainder of the Battalion on 25 March, moved to the right flank of the line, were rejoined by Company C, detaching Company A and one platoon of the Recon Company to remain on the left of the defensive position to ward off any attack in that sector. Patrols from the Recon Company and the firing companies continually probed the

Left
An M35 Prime Mover belonging to the Seventh US Army, towing a 240 mm gun along a French road in early 1945. The vehicle was a conversion from the M10A1, without a turret and with an air compressor and cables for towing 155 mm and 240 mm artillery guns. A total of 209 was converted between January and June 1944. Note the special bad weather hood over the driver's hatch, complete with windscreen wiper.

Below
Armored Utility Vehicle T41, which was a modified M18, less turret and with revised layout internally. It was meant for use as a gun tower for the 3-in M6 towed anti-tank gun, as a troop carrier (it could hold seven men as well as its two-man crew) and as a recce vehicle. It was standardized in June 1944 as the M39 and ordered under 'limited procurement'. It was armed with a ring mounted .50-cal. machine gun and weighed 35,000 lb.

Bottom
A late production M10 (with the new type of counterweights) fitted with deep wading gear is seen here during the fighting on Leyte in the Philippines. While members of the crew service their vehicle, the commander observes a Japanese barge burning off Ormoc beach.

The M18 *Hellcat*

The *Hellcat*, as it was popularly called, was designed from the outset as a tank destroyer and not merely adapted from an existing chassis as the M10 had been. It was on 2 December 1941 that the War Department G-3 recommended the development of a very fast lightly armored cross-country tracked vehicle with a low silhouette, armed with a 37 mm gun and using the already proven Christie suspension. The powerpack would be two Buick engines. Two pilots were made, the first being completed by mid-1942 and designated the GMC T49. In April 1942, following a conference between Gen. Moore of the AGF Requirements Division and Gen. Barnes of Ordnance, a 57 mm gun was substituted, and the second pilot was completed with this weapon as its main armament. Further development brought about the substitution of the more powerful 76 mm gun for the 57 mm, the adoption of the Wright radial-engine as fitted to the M3 tank series instead of the two Buick engines, and torsion bar rather than Christie suspension. The resulting AFV was known as the T70. The Ordnance history explains: '... it was faster than any track laying vehicle ever before produced; on level ground it could do better than 50 mph. So promising was the design and so great was the demand for an effective anti-tank weapon, that the Army Service Forces in January 1943 ordered 1000 T70s to be manufactured without extensive service tests.' In fact, testing did take place while early production was in progress and some slight modifications were made — such as a simplified shape for the hull front, a new turret complete with a bustle (as a counterweight, as well as providing stowage space). The AFV was standardised in

147

February 1944 as the M18 GMC and in all, 2507 *Hellcats* were built.

The hull was of all-welded construction. Driver and co-driver sat at the front of the hull, side by side, with the driver on the left. Each had a two-piece hatch cover. The turret was in the centre of the hull, the engine at the rear. The transmission was at the front in between the driver and co-driver, with the gearshift lever on top so that both could use it to select the gears (three forward and one reverse). Suspension was torsion bar type, comprising five road wheels each with a shock absorber. Drive sprocket was at the front, idler at the rear and there were four return rollers. The turret had an open roof, powered traverse through 360 degrees, with elevation from -10 to $+19\frac{1}{2}$ degrees. A ringmount for the .50 HAA machine gun was fitted at the left rear side of the turret. Forty-five rounds were carried for the 76 mm gun which was the same as fitted to later marks of Sherman.

An excellent photograph of the GMC M18 *Hellcat*. It was one of the finest TDs of the war and had a splendid cross country performance and turn of speed (40–50 mph). The 76 mm gun is the same as on the Sherman and had a maximum range of 16,100 yards using APCBC/HE-T. Battle weight was 40,000 lb.

The *Hellcat* in Combat

The M18 was undoubtedly well liked by crews who knocked out many enemy AFVs with minimum loss to themselves, thanks to its low silhouette, good cross country performance and considerable speed. It was widely used by tank destroyer units in Italy and North West Europe. Howard Lutz again:

'The Hellcat overcame many of the problems of the M10. It was lighter and far more mobile. Speed was much better. The 76 mm was a good gun although it did not carry the impact power at a distance as the 3-inch did. But we were able to sustain more rapid fire than we could with the M10. Also, I think the suspension system of the Hellcat was much better. It still didn't move as fast as I wanted

M18 Specifications

Crew	five (commander, driver and three gun crew)
Combat weight	40,000 lb
Length (gun forward)	21 ft 10 in
Width	9 ft 9 in
Height	8 ft 5 in (to top of AA mount)
Armament main	One 76 mm gun M1A1, M1A1C or M1A2, with 45 rounds stowed
secondary	One .50-cal. AA Browning machine gun
Armor thickness max/min	1 in/.25 in
Engine	Continental R-975 air-cooled, petrol (340 hp) or C4 air-cooled (400 hp)
Max speed	50–55 mph
Radius of action	150 miles
Trench	6 ft 2 in
Vertical wall	3 ft
Fording depth	4 ft

it to, but I guess you can blame that on the impatience of youth. When in a firefight I wanted to be able to outmaneuver my opponent. With the M18 we were certainly able to do this much better than with the M10. We liked to pop over a hill with only our gun snouts exposed and knock off several rounds (or until we were under fire); then slide back out of sight and pop up elsewhere to knock off a few more. At times we would put a platoon or a company on holding action in front of the advance if we could not find the terrain in our favor. Even then we were always moving as a moving target is much harder to hit than one sitting still. With the M18 many times we were able to outflank the enemy.

'We did not like a frontal attack on a lot of German tanks due to the heavy armor they carried up front, but their suspension and track systems made a good target as well as their motor carriage. Much less armor there and of course they were practically blind in an attack from this direction as they had to turn their vehicles to face or slow down or even stop to turn their turret in our direction and by that time we were off to another site.'

Theodore Brush also thought highly of the *Hellcat*. 'The M18 was a tanker's dream. Electric turret with a 76 mm gun with a muzzle brake. The engines were radial aircraft engines and the best thing we liked about them was the automatic transmission. They were real quiet and very fast.'

704th Tank Destroyer Battalion was equipped with M18s and fought through North West Europe, from D plus 36 to VE Day. Here are a few extracts from their battalion history: 'Moving on to Avranches, 'A' Company had its first opportunity to carry out its primary mission. Several well camouflaged German tanks opened fire and knocked out five half-tracks. Lt Addison from the 2nd Platoon of A Company roared past the column with two guns to flush the Jerries out. Sgt Joe Shedevy, tank commander, spotted the enemy tanks first. T/5 Bleemel Beck, driver, whipped the tank round into a firing position. Pfc Manuel Alvise shoved home a 76 mm APC, the breechblock snapped shut, Cpl Clinton Threet laid the crosshairs on the center of the swastika and the first round fired at an enemy tank by an M18 of the Battalion tore to its mark. Before the Hellcat had stopped rocking another round was in the chamber and Threet was traversing the tube with swift coolness to another tank partly hidden behind a hedgerow. The Jerry, already laid, fired and missed which cost him his life for the second round from Shedvey's gun left the Kraut tank burning. Two other tanks in the vicinity saw the action and panic stricken, tried to escape and exposed their

A 105 mm howitzer was fitted to the M18 in late 1944, but it never got beyond the pilot model stage as the project was still under test when the war ended. The AFV was identical to the M18, except for the gun and sights, and was designated the HMC T88 (105 mm).

positions. Four more rounds were expended and two more enemy tanks were stopped in their tracks, a holocaust of flame. The battle was won and confidence in men and machines was secure. Lt Addison, instantly killed in this battle, was the first officer of the battalion killed in action. ...

'The period 20 September to 7 October 1944, marked a tank battle that again knocked the German 11th Panzer Division back on its heels. The Battalion had contacted the 11th Panzer earlier in Normandy, but never had it shown itself in full strength as it did around Arracourt. The German High Command threw the 11th Panzer into battle in a desperate attempt to stop the famed Fourth Armored "Patton's Butchers". The Fourth sustained losses, but when the 11th Panzer put its tail between its legs and ran, it left three fourths of its strength battered, useless, steel-walled coffins on the battlefield. Tank battles raged in the dead of the night and in the thick blinding fog of early dawn. The green white tracers of the German AP crossed in the night sky the fiery trails of the American shot. There would be a sudden spatter of sparks, a blinding flash, and a pillar of flame would mark the pyre of another enemy tank. C Company in moving down into the Arracourt area ran into trouble around St Genevive and in the vicinity of Chateau Salins. The 3rd Platoon on Recon Company lost Lt Barfus and Pfc Solomos through bazooka fire in some Jerry-held woods near St Genevive. S/Sgt Proto, Pfc Brower and Pfc Defano held off the Krauts until C Company brought up their tanks. They knocked out an AT gun, killed 19 Jerries and captured 26. C Company moved into Arracourt

thinking of a rest, but was sent out on a routine mission near Reichicourt. The 3rd Platoon under command of Lt Leiper came face to face with what seemed to be all the armor of the German army. Guns instantly flamed into action and Cpl Stewart, gunner for Sgt Stasis, knocked out two Kraut tanks before his tank was hit and put out of action. Cpl Eidenschink of Sgt Ferraro's crew accounted for three more before his tank was hit. Cpl Eaton of Sgt Krewsky's section destroyed four more German tanks in fast, furious firing before he too was knocked out of action. Sgt Megurk, with Cpl Sorrentio firing, liberated the crews of two other enemy tanks with neat AP hits. At the same time more enemy tanks moving to assist their apparently "outnumbered" cohorts lumbered across the front of the gun positions of 1st Platoon. That was their last mistake for Pfc Amodio, gunner for Sgt Hartman, nailed five of them before they could even swing their turrets to bear on him. Cpl Ewamtako of Sgt Donovan's crew clouted three more into oblivion. When the smoke cleared the count showed that the eight gun crews had knocked out nineteen German tanks with the loss of three destroyers, only one man killed and five wounded. Truly a record to be proud of. B Company had accounted for six, while the second platoon off B Company working with the 25th Cavalry destroyed five more near Marsal.'

The M36

Last of the trio of TDs was the M36 and it was undoubtedly the most powerfully armed of the three self-propelled destroyers. It owed its increased firepower to a decision made in October 1942, to see if there was a possibility of adapting the 90 mm anti-aircraft gun for use in the anti-tank role, in order to deal with the appearance of heavier armor on the battlefield. In early 1943 tests took place to mount a 90 mm in to an M10 in place of the 3-in gun. The gun went in satisfactorily, but it was even longer and heavier than the 3-inch, so the problems that had been found with the M10 were worse still when fitted with this new gun. Test firings proved successful but clearly a new turret had to be designed. Chevrolet started work in March 1943 on a wooden mock-up, which was completed and the project was then transferred to Ford, who built two pilot vehicles, based on the M10A1

chassis. They were completed in September and testing proved very satisfactory, so the vehicle was given the designation of the 90 GMC T71, and 500 were ordered. However, only 300 M10A1s hulls could be made available for completion (*i.e.* hulls based on the M4A3 medium tank chassis), so the numbers had to be made up by converting M10A1s which had to be returned from the field. Standardized in July 1944 as the GMC M36, the demand for this new hard-hitting TD grew and grew after D Day, when the battles in Normandy showed that the 90 mm was the best US weapon to deal with heavy enemy armor. In order to meet orders for 90 mm TDs various expedients had to be adopted — using standard hulls of M4A3 medium tanks (known as the M36B1) and using M10 hulls rather than M10A1s (known as M36B2). A total of 2324 of all three models was produced during the war.

The new turret arrangement on the M36

Top right
Pilot model of the GMC T71, which mounted a 90 mm gun and had a ring mount for the .50-cal. machine gun over the left rear of the turret. Work started on the mockup in early March 1943; then two soft steel pilot models, based on the M10A1 chassis were completed. Tested at APG, the new TD proved very satisfactory and a 'limited procurement' order of 500 was made, which incorporated some amendments (*e.g.* pedestal instead of ring mount for the .50-cal.), under the designation of T71.

Top left
'Bombing up' a *Hellcat* before assaulting Sarre Union, France, on 2 December 1944. Crewmen remove the 76 mm rounds from their protective cases before loading them into the vehicle's ammunition racks.

Above
An M18 *Hellcat* crosses the Moselle River via a treadway bridge on 15 March 1945. The TD belonged to the 4th Armored Division, Third US Army.

M36 Specifications

Crew	five (commander, driver, and three guncrew)
Combat weight	63,000 lbs
Length (gun forward)	24 ft 6 in
Width	10 ft
Height	10 ft 9 in (over AA machine gun)
Armament main	One 90 mm gun M3 with 47 rounds stowed
secondary	One .50-cal. AA Browning machine gun
Armor thickness max/min	4.25 in/.5 in
Engine	Ford GAA, 8-cylinder, liquid-cooled, petrol
Max speed	26–30 mph
Radius of action	approx 150 miles
Trench	7 ft 6 in
Vertical wall	2 ft
Fording depth	3 ft

Right
Three M36s make their debut in France in August 1944, where they were immediately committed into action. As will be seen in this photograph, the crew of the M36 was five men.

Below
The trouble with the M36 (and all other TDs) was that it was continually being used as a tank, a role for which it had never been designed. Its thin armor and open top did not lend itself to tank versus tank engagements. One of the various improvements made was the installation of a folding armored top for the turret, seen here on the M36B2.

was very similar to that in the Sherman. The gunner sat on the right of the gun, with a telescope M76D for direct laying, plus elevation and traverse controls. The turret could be traversed by both hydraulic and manual operation. The TD commander was located behind the gunner and the loader on the left of the gun. The turret was stil open-topped, but a 3-in gun-shield covered the turret front and the sides of the turret were 1.25 in thick (compared with 2.25 in frontal armor on the M10, with sides only 1 in thick). There was inevitably a large bustle at the rear of the turret to balance the heavy gun, which was also used for ammunition stowage, eleven ready rounds being carried there.

The M36 in Combat

The first of the new TDs arrived in Europe in August 1944 and were immediately committed into action. One of the units to get them was the 771st TD Battalion who had previously been given the distinction of being chosen to train all TD troops in the Replacement System in the ETO. They went over to France in mid-September and, after re-equipping, saw a great deal of action. For example, as their privately published history tells, they were awarded a Presidential Unit Citation for an action around the town of Immendorf in Germany on 16 November 1944. Here is an extract from the citation:

'After the destroyers had moved up and barely occupied their positions, two approaching enemy tanks were sighted and quickly destroyed. When the attack proceeded the following day, the Company moved into Apweiler, so that the exposed flank of the assault units could be covered. During the night, reconnaissance revealed that the enemy was massing tanks to the north. To meet the threat, a reinforcing platoon was brought up and suitable positions were occupied. At break of dawn, the enemy tanks attacked. Fire was withheld until the attackers were within 500 yards of the position: then, in the course of five minutes of accurate and well timed fire, seven enemy tanks were destroyed and the balance forced to withdraw. Two other armored attacks were repulsed the same day, causing the destruction of five additional tanks. During the night, the Company reorganized to prepare for the attacks on Gereonsweiler which started at eleven hundred hours the next day. Only a few minutes later, it was reported that the assault elements were receiving withering fire from several enemy tanks which were skillfully emplaced in a draw so that any TD attempting to engage them would come under their fire at a range of 2500 yards. Fully realizing that the enemy tanks with their 88 mm guns had a tremendous advantage, the first platoon moved out. Three TDs were lost, but their daring action successfully forced the enemy to withdraw and eliminated a serious threat to the assault units. At the same time, the other two platoons moved out, despite the disadvantage, to engage four other Tiger tanks. By brilliant maneuvering and firing, the destroyers succeeded in closing the range, destroying two and forcing the others to retreat. The audacity and brilliant tactical skill displayed by the members of Company C, 771st Tank Destroyer Battalion, are worthy of emulation and reflect the highest traditions of the Army.'

12

The Amphibians: Landing Vehicles Tracked (Armored)

The purist may well raise an eyebrow at the inclusion in this book of a chapter about amphibians, arguing that they were not really tanks. However, the main characteristics of a tank are firepower, protection, and mobility, and the LVT(A)s certainly had all of these. Their mobility was such that they could get to places where other tanks could not go without such awkward aids as the canvas screens of the Sherman DDs. The *Alligators*, as they were appropriately called, got the job done and without them the US Marines would have faced even greater problems in their amphibious assaults on enemy-held beaches during their highly successful 'island hopping' campaigns in the Pacific theater.

The LVTs owe much of their design to the prewar work of Donald Roebling, Jr. (grandson of the builder of the Brooklyn Bridge), who in the mid 1930s had designed a lightweight, tracked amphibian for rescue work in the Florida Everglades — hence the name 'Alligator'. A photograph of this remarkable vehicle appeared in an issue of *Life* magazine in 1937 and was seen by Maj. Gen. Louis McCarty, then commanding the FMF. By 1940, Roebling had redesigned the tractor to

suit Marine specifications and early the following year the commander of the Atlantic Fleet, Admiral Ernest J King, was persuaded to take a ride in one at Culebra, Puerto Rico. The aluminum vehicle broke a track on a reef and the impatient admiral had to wade ashore! However, by mid 1941 Roebling had the first steel-welded *Alligator* ready and a first order for 200 vehicles, designated the LVT1, had been placed. By August 1941, the first USMC tractor battalions were forming to operate the first of over 18,000 LVTs to be built before the end of the war, including 3118 LVT (Armored).

The LVT1 was supplemented by the LVT2, but both these amphibians were made of mild steel only, so cannot truly be classed as AFVs. They were used for carrying cargo and troops from ship to shore and as such were most useful. However, it was soon realized that there was an urgent requirement for another form of amphibian, capable of giving close, direct fire support to the landing troops — in other words, a waterborne tank. The simplest way of doing this was to construct an LVT2 using armor plate 0.25 to 0.5-inches thick instead of mild steel, then

adding decking plates over the cargo spaces and putting a fully armored turret on top equipped with a tank gun. The first of these, designated the LVT(A)1, had the M3 light tank turret, complete with 37 mm M6 gun and coaxial .30-cal. machine gun. In addition, two manholes in the rear of the turret were equipped with scarf mounts on each of which was a .30-cal. machine gun with all round traverse. A fourth .30-cal. in a ball and socket mount was located in the front of the hull and finally, a .50-cal. AA machine gun was mounted on top of the turret. The addition of the armor and turret put about three tons onto the weight of a normal LVT 2.

At the same time as the LVT(A)1 was building, the LVT(A)2 was also constructed. This was really the same as the LVT(A)1 but without the 37 mm turret or decking, so that it could be used as a cargo carrying vehicle — the only cargo carrier with the 'A' designation. It was thus very similar to the LVT2, but with 0·5-inch armor plate in the most vulnerable areas and 0·25 inch plate everywhere else. Weight without cargo was 27,600 lbs and it could carry up to 7600 lbs of freight, but its normal load was reduced to 4100 lbs.

Further Developments

In all some 500 plus LVT(A)1s and 450 LVT(A)2s were built by Roebling and FMC. However, by far the largest production of LVT(A)s was of the next model, the LVT(A)4, of which nearly 1900 were constructed. The LVT(A)4 mounted the turret of the GMC M8 armed with a 75 mm howitzer as its main weapon. The extra machine guns on the rear decking were done away with (to keep the weight down). LVT(A)4 was certainly the most successful and widely used of the LVT(A)s but it did have the problem of not being fitted with power traverse. This

The LVT(Flame), which had the nickname *Sea Serpent*, was a British adaptation of an LVT 4 on which two Wasp flame-throwers had been fitted, plus one Browning machine gun in a rear protected mounting (no top).

omission was rectified, in the LVT(A)5 which was designed in 1945, and so did not enter service in time to take part in combat. Another conversion, the LVT(A)4 with a M24 Chaffee turret, was also produced in 1945 but never got further than the experimental stage. Other weapon systems tried on the LVT(A) were rocket launchers and flame-throwers.

Basic Organisation

USMC Armored Amphibian battalions were composed of four line companies, each of eighteen LVT(A)s, plus three more in battalion HQ. On landing they normally covered four beaches, i.e.: two assault battalions of two separate infantry regiments. Supporting vehicles were twelve LVT cargo carriers, 24 jeeps, twenty 2½ ton trucks, five machine shops, etc. Later the US Army had similar battalions and designated them amphibious tanks.

A Japanese LVT. These were similar in size to US LVTs, but slightly longer and thinner. They had propellors for water movement and tracks for use on land. The one in this photograph was captured in Tokyo Bay during the surrender at the end of the war. The photograph shows it parked, with others, along a road just south of Tokosuka, in August 1945. USMC via Lt Gen Louis Metzger.

Right
USMC crew members of this LVT-1 peer through the tangled jungle trees in Bougainville, Northern Solomons, having pushed the Japanese back into the island's interior. The pintle mounted Brownings, etc, provided firepower but, of course, this was not an armored vehicle, being made of mild steel and designed only for carrying cargo and troops from ship to shore.

Types of LVT(A)

Model	Combat Weight	Crew	Length	Width	Height	Armament	Engine	Performance
LVT(A)1	32,800 lb	six	26 ft 1 in	10 ft 10 in	8 ft 5 in	One 37 mm; three .30 cal. (one coax, two rear on Scarf rings) and one .50 cal. AA machine guns	Continental W-670-9A 250 hp radial petrol.	**Max speed (land)** 25 mph. **(water)** 6.5 mph. **Range (land)** 125 miles **(water)** 75 miles
LVT(A)2	27,600 lb (less cargo) 35,200 lb max	four	26 ft 1 in	10 ft 10 in	8 ft 3 in	One .50 cal. and one .30 cal. machine guns	Continental W-670-9A 250 hp radial petrol.	**Max speed (land)** 20 mph. **(water)** 7.5 mph. **Range (land)** 150 miles **(water)** 50 miles.
LVT(A)4	39,460 lb	six	26 ft 1 in	10 ft 10 in	10 ft 5 in	One 75 mm howitzer; one .50 cal AA machine gun	Continental W-670-9A 250 hp radial petrol.	**Max speed (land)** 20 mph. **(water)** 7.5 mph. **Range (land)** 150 miles **(water)** 75 miles

LVT(A)5   as for LVT(A)4 but with power traverse.

Major (later Lt-Gen.) Louis Metzger, CO of 1st Armored Amphibian Battalion, photographed on the deck of an LVT(A)1 which had been hit by Japanese artillery fire during the landing on Guam in 1944. He is holding part of a 37 mm shell case which had been hit by the direct enemy fire. The LVT(A)1 had a 37 mm M3 gun as its main armament, plus a .50-cal. AA machine gun and two .30-cal. in Scarf mounts on the rear decking. USMC via Lt Col. L Metzger

The LVT(A) in Combat

'My battalion, 1st Armored Amphibian Battalion, was equipped with the LVT(A)1', writes Lt-Gen. Louis B Metzger, USMC (Ret) of La Jolla, California. 'We were the first organization of its kind in the Marine Corps and were used during operations in both the Marshall Islands and Guam. Basically, in both operations we led the assault with one company of eighteen in a line as the first wave on each numbered beach. Once targets on the beach could be identified, the crews opened fire (no easy task because of the smoke and debris from naval gunfire and air strikes and the very low vantage point provided when the vehicles were waterborne). We really didn't expect to hit any specific target, but the idea was to keep the enemies' heads down from the time the prelanding fire was lifted until the troops could be lodged ashore. When the configuration of the beach dictated it, we echeloned back the flank platoons and had them proceed ashore far enough to take positions of hull defilade, while maintaining both

37 mm and machine gun fire. The infantry were then to pass us and we supported their advance until the tanks were ashore. In the Guam operation, because of the reef, our vehicles proceeded back to the edge of the reef and acted both as anchors for the LCMs landing the tanks, and as guides for the tanks transversing the reef. This was an unusual mission, but large holes had been blown in the reef by NGF (naval gunfire) and bombs, and where an LVT would merely swim into one of these, a land tank might have problems.

'In the Guam operation, the assault was against the middle portion of the island where the harbour and all the military installations were, and as the attack swung north to uncover the areas where the B-29 airfields were to be located, very little military action took place in the southern end of the island. To secure this area, my battalion sent platoon and company patrols along the coast. Remaining waterborne, but landing to clear certain areas. I can't really say this was an effective mission, but one we were assigned. We also, in all our operations, defended the landing beaches against enemy attempts to land forces in our logistic support areas (i.e. the beaches): and, as a "ho hum" task we were detailed to protect the Island Command Post.

'We were assigned twelve LVTs to our battalion and they were quite useful. First of all, they were the vehicles which carried our palletized machine shops, spare parts, etc. By

palletized I mean our maintenance equipment was designed to fit into one of these vehicles for transportation. On the beach the maintenance shops were pulled out and set up to operate (in those days we were not bothered by echelons of maintenance, we did everything ourselves). The LVT2s were also employed during the assault for logistic support of the battalion. Although in the early phases we were to be refueled by Navy ships, it was always comforting to have extra fuel and ammunitions, as well as a representation of corpsmen to handle casualties. Departure and landing only on call (radio). I suppose in theory they should have been despatched by the regular control system exercised in the Navy, but in those days I was so ignorant of doctrine that I just had them float off the beach and radioed when I wanted them. . . .

'During the Guam operation there was one engagement of particular interest. On request of higher headquarters, my executive officer ordered a platoon (five LVT(A)1s) to attack some Japanese 75 mm guns located in caves on Orote Peninsula. It was an ill match and the Japanese 75 mm gunners scored several hits and near misses on these little vehicles trying to blast them with flat trajectory 37 mm guns. A US destroyer seeing what was happening came to the rescue at near top speed. End of battle, except for the dead and wounded. Thirty-six years later, I still regret this engagement.'

Tank versus Tank Engagements

There were very few significant engagements between LVT(A)s and enemy tanks. One of these took place on the airfield on Peleliu in September 1944. Fortunately, the author was able to contact an eyewitness, Brig.-Gen. Bob Denig, who at the time was attached to the 3rd Armored Amphibian Battalion, armed with 75 mm howitzers, as an observer prior to taking over command at the end of the operation (in fact he was switched to command the 6th Tank Battalion Okinawa — see the Sherman chapter). Here is how he explained the operation in a letter home, written on 25 September 1944, quoted verbatim.

'We are allowed to write where we now are and what we have been doing since "D" Day. This is D+10 day and the division is still working on the Nips on the Northern end of the island. But getting back to D Day — I will try to let you know what I have been doing.

"D" Day the 15th (September) came along in fine shape. It was a nice clear day with enough clouds to tend to keep it a little cool. My ship launched its LVTA's, LVT's and the assault waves therein and they shoved off for the

Advancing through a grass-hutted village on the island of Leyte, Central Philippines, a Sherman clears the way, while the infantry shelter behind an LVT 4, which, with the engine now in the front, was able to incorporate a large ramp door at the rear of the hull, which made loading and unloading much easier. Note also the heavy machine guns behind armored screens at the front. Armor could be 'bolted-on' while from early 1944 the cab was armored.

assembly point. All the LST's then withdrew from the launching area so that the LVT's would have room along with the LCVP and Ducks. The Navy put down quite a bombardment and the first wave hit the beach at 8.30. The first wave was armored tractors. I watched the approach to the beach from the ship until the LVTs entered the area 1000 yards from the beach. There was so much dust and smoke I couldn't see anything. Up to that point I never saw a Nip shell hit the water. My LST had an LCT on deck so we went quite a way out from the beach and finally managed to launch it. We didn't get back to the beach area until about 3 pm. My LST had been designated as an Amtrack repair vessel so we hove to about 1200 yards from the beach. As soon as we took our station we began to receive aboard damaged Amtrack and I spoke to the crews of some of them. They said that as soon as the Armored jobs crossed the reef the Nips opened fire and hit quite a number of them. Then they worked over the Amtracks and Ducks getting quite a number of them. They further said that things on the beach were quite a mess. So many Amtracks had been damaged or lost that they were having trouble getting men and supplies ashore. I could see from the ship that the various beaches were under continuous mortar fire and larger explosions, from what I guessed were field pieces, were kicking up

dust. Every once in a while an Amtrack or Duck would go up in blaze. We repaired Amtracks all night but the facilities were limited.

'The next day (D+1) they were still having trouble getting stuff ashore. Lt-Col. Narren of the 8th Amtracks (personnel carriers) came aboard the ship about 9 am and said that it was hot as hell on the beach and that the Nips had worked the areas over all night with mortar and artillery fire. He said all you could do was sit in a hole (he was an observer) and there was nothing to see except the explosions from the Nip fire, so he got off the beach. He also said that the Armored Bn had lost quite a few tanks and that the Bn was scattered all over the place. He advised me in not going ashore but wait until (D+2) and return to the beach with him. So I stayed aboard all day and helped the skipper, of the ship, in getting the repair facilities functioning more smoothly. On (D+2) Narren and myself went ashore in an LVT and I immediately looked up the CP of the Armored Battalion. Both the Bn Comdr and the Exec got through okay and were sitting on the tail end of an Amtrack with a tarp rigged over it. They had the armored tractor run up to a portion of the beach that had a coral cliff running up about 12 feet. At high tide the tractor just floated and at low tide the fringing reef dried for about 200 yds out. It made a nice place to hang out as the tractor was in a small cove. The exec Major Parker who used to be at Hdq, as security officer or something, had his tractor badly damaged and just after he abandoned it a mortar shell went into the open turret, so no more tractor. I spent the night on the back end of the tractor with Boyer (the CO) and Parker. The next day I went over to Division and saw Major Magee, he used to be

my JO on the St L. I also said hello to some other agents but everyone was quite busy trying to get the attack rolling. We still only had a small beach head that was under mortar fire but one regiment had cut the island in two and they were working on the Nips in both directions. From Div Hdq I went to the CP of the Tank Bn and saw Jeb Stuart. He was quite happy as the tanks were really doing a fine bit of work. All companies were really pushing the fight and the infantry was giving them close support. In addition on D day at about 4 pm the Nips launched a tank attack across the northern end of the Airport. The infantry had no anti tank weapons and there was no spot for them to get under the ground, so the infantry withdrew nearly to the beach. Jeb Stuart had portions of A&B Tank Companies in that area so they immediately engaged the Nip tanks and blew 13 of them apart. One round was all that was necessary so the tank Commanders reported. It is thought that only one Nip tank during the short engagement, which was accompanied with a lot of dust etc, got away. The Nips hit the barrel of one of the 75 guns and dented it and one of our tanks got off a wild shot and damaged the track of another of our tanks. That was the sum total of our damage. Since then the tanks have been in continuous battle and the Nips haven't been able to penetrate their armor. Mortar fire just bounces off but every once in a while a mortar shell damages the tube of a 75 mm gun. Mines have damaged the track and suspension system in a number of tanks so the sum total of tanks brought along has decreased. But they have plenty to finish the job. No one yet has been killed in a tank which proves to my mind their worth. In addition numerous strong points have been wiped out by them.

'As far as these tanks are concerned (Armored Amphibian) the lack of armor and the open turret has been their downfall. A mortar burst nearby ruins their pontoons and keeps them from going out into the ocean again. They have used a few as gun boats to shell the beach. Some regts tried to use them as tanks. I personally don't think that they are worth the effort. Regular land tanks are the ticket. Possibly a Company of these to be used out in the water and away from effective mortar fire would be of value. But a whole Battalion of 75 Armored jobs cluttering up the landscape is a waste of space aboard ship.

'Major Milne who was at Jacques Farm with me is an observer, from the 29th Regt with the Tank Bn. He landed on D day with Stuart, and had been dodging mortar fire for 3 days when I saw him. He said that he wanted a bath and some chow. So after getting all of the foregoing dope from Stuart,

Milne and I went down to the Hdq of the tractors and bummed a ride out to my LST, getting aboard about 4 pm. The Captain of the ship was glad to see us and had the doctor set us up to a Rye high-ball on the Navy. We had a good meal and then decided to spend the night aboard ship.

'On (D+4) Milne & myself returned to the beach and I spent the night on the tail end of the Command Amtrack. We had an Air alert so we just sat on the end of the Amtrack as the beach area where we were tied up is solid coral in for about 100 yds inland. Although they have had a few air alerts I don't think that any Nip planes have put in their appearance, at least I have heard no bombs fall.

'On (D+6) the Armored Bn moved to a beach area on the southern end of the island where we have been ever since. Major Milne left on this day to rejoin the 29th. The area where we are now situated is still full of bombs sunk in the ground along the beach, but for some reason the Nips never armed them as we have found boxes of fuzes and detonators in a Jap bivouac area near our CP. Since this date (D+6) I have been hanging around the Armored Bn (CP). The 1st Tank Bn has more or less come to rest as most of the fighting is along a razor back ridge that goes along the tail of the island from the airport Northward. The Nips as per usual are dug into caves which I understand are quite elaborate. The day before yesterday I wandered over to the division and saw a captured mortar that was taken in the hill mass. The tube is about 6 feet long and must be about 155 mm in diameter. That must be one of the mortars that worked over the beaches for the first three days. On the way back from Division I ran into Major George Hanna who used to be one of my JOs on the St L. He had a 155 gun Bn of Corps troops. They are just up the road from here, so after lunch I am going to take a spin up and see how he is making out. The blast and noise from his gun nearly throws me out of bed at night.

'The night before last the Nips tried to reinforce the island. Their barges were seen and a platoon of Armored Amtracks took to the water. They claim that they sunk two of the barges. The Navy got the remainder, ten in all were destroyed but of course they don't show how many troops got shore. One prisoner was captured by the Armored Amtracks yesterday noon. They went out to investigate some of the barges that were still afloat. That is how they found out that the Nips were coming and not going. Lt-Col. Boyer is now called Commodore after his fleet engagement.

'So far things for me have been going fine. It is hot as hell during the day but there is a

Waterborne LVT(A)4s which were part of the 1st Armored Amphibian Battalion, are pictured here heading for the beach on Okinawa on D Day, 1 April 1945. Note the sandbags and extra armor for the sides and front of the gun mount. The gun is, of course, the 75 mm howitzer from the M8 GMC. USMC via Lt Col. L Metzger.

nice breeze at night. The Infantry on the lines has been having a great deal of trouble with the sun and heat prostration. No one knows when the Nips will be removed from the Island. They are really dug in in the hills. Each cave and emplacement must be destroyed in turn. No one realized that they would be so strongly dug in to the North but they should have suspected it after Saipan, etc.

'Up to this writing no one that I know has been injured or killed. I don't think that the casualties have been excessive when you consider how the Nips were dug in to the island. As usual the Naval Gun fire didn't do what they claim it will do.'

Getting the Job Done with Un-artillery

In the assault on Okinawa, Gen. Louis B Metzger was still commanding 1st Armored Amphibian Battalion, but by then they had been re-equipped with LVT(A)4s mounting 75 mm howitzers. Their previous battle experience had taught them how easy it was for a .30-caliber bullet to 'whistle through 20-gauge metal' and, despite the new turrets, the rest of the LVT(A) was still only 20 gauge metal. Consequently, they took steps to add more protection. 'Pin-on' armor was added to the bow and sides of the vehicle's hull. The area just below the turret was reinforced with sandbags, and an armor plate was used on top of the turret to protect the crewman's heads. Even suits of aircrew anti-flak armor were issued in sufficient quantity to equip all crews. These extra defences would guard against enemy small arms and mortar fire, but could do little to prevent damage from larger caliber direct-fire weapons and mines.

In an article in the Marine Corps' *Gazette* of November 1978, Gen. Metzger explained

how his battalion was reorganized with the new equipment: 'It was a relatively simple task to organize each of the four line amphibian companies into three firing batteries, one from each five vehicle platoon. It was imperative that normal organization be maintained, because the primary beach assault role could not be degraded. Fire Direction Centers (FDC) were developed from each of the company command vehicles. Then each platoon headquarters was trained to a level so that it could function as a substitute FDC if the company HQ suffered heavy casualties during the beach assault, not a remote possibility. The result was 12 firing batteries consisting of 5 or 6 tubes each (six if the three command vehicles from Co. HQ were added to the batteries), with five primary FDCs and 12 alternate FDCs.'

Gen. Metzger goes on to explain the rigorous training that his battalion put in during the build-up to Okinawa operation. This included an indirect fire demonstration attended by the Divisional Commanding General, at which the shooting was so good that the division commander became suspicious 'that what he was seeing was a canned demonstration rather than a realistic test of the ability of the armored amphibians to fire indirect fire. Everything was too perfect. He pointed to a single bush some 150 yds in front of the tower (a viewing platform about 20 ft high which could hold 7 or 8 men plus the necessary communication equipment for the

LVT(A)4s belonging to the 3rd Armored Amphibian Battalion, attached to 1st Marine Division, on Okinawa, about D plus 3. Weighing about 40,000 lb, the LVT(A)4 had a crew of six, carried 100 rounds for its 75 mm howitzer and had a land radius of action of some 150 miles (100 miles in the water). USMC via Lt Col. L Metzger.

'Given the alternatives of no artillery support until late on D Day or allowing the armored amphibians to shoot indirect fire didn't seem to be a difficult choice. They shot. On 1 April 1945, the division landed on Okinawa on the left of the assault, led by the armored amphibians. By the time the infantry had pushed far enough inland to call for indirect artillery fire, the LVTs were in position and registered. They maintained their on-call indirect fire until the artillery was ashore and ready to assume the mission.

'On several occasions, the unique character of armored amphibians allowed them to provide fire support, which otherwise might not be available. On Motobu Peninsula during the battle for Mount Yaetake, an infantry unit found the enemy between it and the supporting artillery. Because of the mountainous terrain, the artillery was masked and could not fire in support, nor could it displace forward, because bridges had been destroyed. Naval gunfire was not available, because the waters surrounding Motobu Peninsula had been mined. No problems for the armored amphibians. They simply swam to the required position, climbed ashore, registered and commenced fire missions. Later in the assault on the Naha-Shuri-Yonaburu line, the availability of 105 mm ammunition became limited. No wonder. The volume of fire was tremendous. Fortunately, 75 mm howitzer ammunition was plentiful, and so it was used in profusion to pound the enemy.

'When the last great battle of WWII ended, the armored amphibian battalion had proved its worth. In addition to the assault, beach defences and water borne flank assault direct-fire missions, it had fired over 19,000 rounds of indirect fire — not bad for unartillery.'

forward observers, and reached by a single ladder, wide enough for just one man at a time), and said "Hit that". The artillery FO called the shift to the fire direction center. Nothing happened. The silence was deafening, the wait interminable. Finally, the radio crackled. Up from the FDC boomed the words: "Below safe elevation". At that point, the arty regt CO exercised his expertise and issued the order: "Safe to fire". Within seconds the three howitzers — one from each platoon — which were being used to register, coughed at the edge of the jungle behind the observation tower. The report "On the way", came through. Howitzer shells travel at a much slower speed than gun shells, yet these could be heard approaching all too rapidly. To the major the approaching shells had the sound of doom. He had heard enough "incoming" to know all was not well. The first shell landed just 100 yards in front of the tower, and the other two were still in the air. The major practically pushed the general down the ladder. The remainder of the Marines simply jumped off the tower. About this time the second shell impacted 75 yards in front of the tower, and the third, not long after, 50 yards. All three were in direct line between the tower and the target. There were no casualties. There wasn't much to be said and little was. The division GG did congratulate the major on a good shoot, but was heard to grumble that he didn't want the armored amphibians shooting too close to his men. It was a bad day.

Footnotes

Introduction
[1] Quoted in 'The World War I Experience', T K Nenninger, *Armor Magazine*, January/February 1969.
[2] Instead of the familiar side sponsons, the Mark VI had one 6-pdr gun centrally mounted in its nose. It was only produced to mock-up stage and then abandoned in favour of existing models.
[3] 'The Tank Corps Reorganized', T K Nenninger, *Armor Magazine*, March/April 1969.
[4] Bob Grow was, during the period 1939–40, intimately connected with the development of mechanization and went on to command 6th Armored Division ('The Super Sixth') throughout World War II.
[5] Quoted in *Forging the Thunderbolt*, M H Gillie.

[6] Equates to adjutant in the British Army.
[7] Quoted in *Armor-Cavalry*, Part I, of the Army Lineage Series.
[8] *Armour in Conflict*, Ian Hogg.

Chapter 1
[1] *The Ordnance Department: Procurement and Supply*, H C Thomson and L Mayo.
[2] *Tanks Are Mighty Fine Things*, W W Stout
[3] US Army Lineage Series, *Armor-Cavalry*.
[4] *The Ordnance Department: Procurement and Supply*, H C Thomson and L Mayo.
[5] Quoted in 'Armor Development in the Soviet Union and the United States' A J Alexander, from *Roosevelt and Hopkins: An Intimate Study*, R E Sherwood'.
[6] *Ibid*.

Chapter 2
[1] Tables of Organization and Equipment prescribed the standard form of units no matter where they were stationed. They were modified by theater commanders to suit the tactical situation, and amended from time to time in the light of battle experience.
[2] The M4, mounting a 105 mm howitzer, which was used in the close support rôle.
[3] The name 'Peep' was sometimes used to describe the $\frac{1}{4}$-ton truck as it reflected its reconnaissance rôle; however, it was better known as the 'Jeep'.
[4] 'S3' equates to the adjutant in the British Army.

Chapter 4
[1] *The Ordnance Department: Procurement and Supply*, H C Thomson aand L Mayo.
[2] *Battle History of 1st Armored Division*, G F Howe.
[3] Quoted from a short history of the 1st Tank Battalion kindly supplied by HQ USMC.
[4] *Ibid*.

Chapter 5

[1]*The Ordnance Department: Procurement and Supply*, H C Thomson and L Mayo.

Chapter 6

[1]The British developed their own light tank, the Tetrarch (Light Tank Mk VII), for the glider-borne rôle. The Hamilcar glider was specially designed to carry one of these small AFVs (crew two, battle weight 16,800 lbs, armament one 2-pdr gun and one Besa machine-gun). The Hamilcar was later used to carry the Locust during Rhine-crossing. It was designed by General Aircraft Ltd of Feltham, Middlesex, and produced by the Birmingham Railway Carriage and Wagon Co. Ltd. It was towed by Halifax, Lancaster, or Stirling bombers. Its loaded weight was 36,000 lbs and it was 68 ft long with a span of 110 ft.

Chapter 8

[1]The codename of a recent British reconnaissance in force to test the enemy's reaction.
[2]*The Rommel Papers*, B H Liddell-Hart (ed.).
[3]The Cruiser Tank Mk VI Crusader (A15) stemmed from the same line of development as the Covenanter. Fast (27 mph), but lightly armored and mechanically unreliable, it was never a match for the German PzKw III which was its main opponent in the desert.
[4]From *The Pageant of Motoring*.

Chapter 9

[1]Marjorie E Hillenmeyer (*neé* 1st Lt Wood) was a US Army dietician with 24th General Hospital in North Africa and Italy. They first met in Florence where Herb conducted what he entitled 'his most successful compaign!'
[2]*Sherman, a history of the American Medium Tank*, R P Hunnicutt.
[3]Lulworth: Royal Armoured Corps Gunnery School, Lulworth Camp.
[4]The German Panzerfaust 30 went into production in October 1943 at the rate of 20,000 per month. It had a penetration of 5.5-inches at a striking angle of 30 degrees, and its fighting range was 30 meters. A second model, the Panzerfaust 30 Klein used a smaller bomb, and 100,000 were produced per month from about the same time. A new design, the Panzerfaust 60, with a range of 60 meters, entered service in summer 1944, followed by the Panzerfaust 100, with range increased to 100 meters, in November 1944. The final model was the Panzerfaust 150, with a 150-meter range, of which 100,000 were made between January 1945 and the end of the war. All models could deal effectively with *any* tank of the period.
[5]From *Spearhead in the West, a history of the 3rd Armored Division 1941–45*; published here by kind permission of the 3rd Armored Division Association.
[6]The battalion was part of Task Force 68 of CCA 6th Armored Division ('The Super Sixth').

Chapter 10

[1]Quoted in *The Ordnance Department: On Beachhead and Battlefront*, L Mayo.
[2]Maj.-Gen. Gladon M Barnes (Chief, Ordnance R & D Service) and Maj.-Gen. Levin H Campbell Jr (Chief of Ordnance).

Chapter 11

[1]He was the first soldier in the battalion to be awarded the DSC for this action.

Select Bibliography

Published Works

Bradley, Omar N: *A Soldier's Story*; Eyre & Spottiswode; 1951.
Carver, Michael: *El Alamein*. Batsford Ltd; London; 1962.
Chamberlain, Peter and Chris Ellis: *British & American Tanks of WW2*. Profile Publishing Ltd.; Windsor, U.K.; 1972.
H. M. Cole, *The Lorraine Campaign* (part of *History of the United States Army in World War II*). Historical Division, Department of the Army.
Frankel, Nat and Larry Smith: *Patton's Best. An informal history of the 4th Armored Division*. Hawthorn Books Inc; 1978.
Gillie, Mildred Hanson: *Forging the Thunderbolt*. The Military Service Publishing Co; 1947.
Green, Constance McLaughlin, Harry C Thomson and Peter C Roots: *The Ordnance Department: Planning Munitions for War*. Office of Chief and Military History, US Army; 1955.
Hart, B H Liddell: *The Tanks* Vol 2. Cassell; 1959.
Hart, B H Liddell (ed): *The Rommel Papers*.
Hogg, Ian: *Armour in Conflict*. Jane's Publishing Company; London; 1980.
Hofmann, George F: *The Super Sixth, history of 6th Armored Division*. 6th Armored Division Association; 1975.
Houston, Donald E; *Hell on Wheels — The 2nd Armored Division*, Presidio Press; 1977.
Howe, George F: *The Battle History of the 1st Armored Division*. Combat Forces Press; 1954.
Hunnicutt, Richard P: *Sherman, a history of the American medium tank*. Taurus Enterprises; 1978. *Pershing, a history of the medium tank T20 series*. Taurus Enterprises; 1971.
Jones, Ken and Peter Chamberlain: *Classic AFVs Number 2, Lee & Grant*. PSL/Airfix; 1977.
Joslen, Lt-Col. H F: *Orders of Battle WW2 1939–45*. London HMSO; 1960.
Leach, Capt Charles R: *In Tornado's Wake, a history of the 8th Armored Division*. 8th Armored Division Association; 1956.
McMillan, George: *The Old Breed, history of 1st Marine Division in WW2*'; Infantry Journal Press; 1959.
Mittleman, Capt Joseph B: *Eight Stars to Victory, the history of the 9th US Infantry Division*. 9th Infantry Division Association; 1948.
Mayo, Lida: *The Ordnance Department: On Beachhead and Battlefront*. Office of the Chief of Military History, US Army; 1968.
Perrett, Bryan: *The Stuart Light Tank Series* (Vanguard 17), Osprey Publishing; London, 1980.
Ross, G MacLeod: *The Business of Tanks 1939–1945*. Arthur H Stockwell; 1976.
Stout, Wesley W: *Tanks Are Mighty Fine Things*. Chrysler Corporation; 1949.
Stubbs, Mary Lee & Stanley Russel Connor: *Armor-Cavalry* Part I. Office of the Chief of Military History, US Army; 1969.
Thomson, Harry C and Lida Mayo: *The Ordnance Department: Procurement and Supply*. Office of the Chief of Military History, US Army; 1960.
Zaloga, Steve: *Stuart US Light Tanks in action*. Squadron/Signal pubs; 1979.
Various Authors: *AFVs of the World, Volume 4: American AFVs of WW2*. Profile Publishing Ltd; Windsor, U.K.; 1972.
Young, Col. Ford E, *To The Regiment*.
Not Known: *Hellcats, a history of the 12th Armored Division*. The Battery Press; 1978 (reprint).
Not Known: *Spearhead in the West, a history of 3rd Armored Division 1941–45*. The Battery Press; 1980 (reprint).

Privately published Works

Fourth Armored Division Association: *The History of the 4th Armored Division*.
Grow, Maj.-Gen. Robert W: *The Ten Lean Years*.
Haemmel, William G: *Tank Soldiers' Journal*.
Hillenmeyer, Herbert F: *The Little Picture, Tales of WW2, for my children*.
Roberts, A Eaton: *Five Stars to Victory, the exploits of Task Force Lovelady*.
Rubel, Lt.-Col. George Kenneth: *Daredevil Tankers, the story of 740th Tank Battalion*.

Short Histories of the 1st, 2nd, 3rd and 4th Tank Battalions, USMC.
Tankers in Tunisia. Armored Replacement Training Center, 1943.
630th Tank Destroyer Battalion unofficial history.
704th Tank Destroyer Battalion history.
754th Tank Battalion history.
771st Tank Destroyer Battalion history.
776th Tank Destroyer Battalion informal history.

Articles

Alexander, Arthur J: 'Armor Development in the Soviet Union and the United States'; pub September 1976, in E R Sherwood's book *Roosevelt and Hopkins: An Intimate Study*.
Crawford Richard H and Lindsley F Cook: 'The United States Army in World War II — Statistics'. Office of Chief of Military History; 1952.
Gardiner, Col. Henry: 'We fought at Kasserine'; *Armored Cavalry Journal* (March/April 1948).
Leech, James: 'Flying Tanks'. *Pegasus* (Airborne Forces Magazine).
Metzger, Lt.-Gen.Louis: 'Getting the job done with un-artillery'. *Marine Corps Gazette*
Nenninger, Timothy K: series of four articles from *Armor Magazine*: 'The World War I experience' (January/February 1969); 'The Tank Corps Reorganized' (March/April 1969); 'Experimental Mechanised Forces' (May-June 1969); 'A Revised Mechanised Policy' (September/October 1969).
Cannon, Peter: 'The Secret Tanks of Lowther Castle'. *Pageant of Motoring*, (brochure issued at Carlisle Castle during a motor rally in 1976).

United States Military Pamphlets

TM 9-727 Light Tanks M3A1 and M3A3
TM 9-729 Light Tank T24(M24)
TM 9-731A Medium Tanks M4 and M4A1
TM 9-731G 3 inch Gun Motor Carriage M10A1
TM 9-732 Light Tanks M5 and M5A1
TM 9-735 Heavy Tank T26E3
TM 9-750 Medium Tank M3
TM 9-775 Landing Vehicle Tracked Mks I and II.
Mechanised Flame Thrower Operations in World War II.

Index

Page numbers in *italic* refer to illustrations